Because this examination has been undertaken at a time when large-scale immigration no longer refreshes the Scandinavian populace, this book is also an exploration in some depth of the future of ethnicity of any kind in America.

It provides a reflection of how the Scandinavian-American communities and kindred appear to the mother countries and the extent of their continuing interest in their American kin.

A result of the first joint meetings of all the elements of these five cognate communities, this volume is an important and unusual contribution to the content and bibliography of the Bicentennial, not only for the five per cent of the population which derives from Scandinavia, but for anyone who is interested in the diversity of North American society.

THE SCANDINAVIAN PRESENCE IN NORTH AMERICA

THE SCANDINAVIAN PRESENCE
IN NORTH AMERICA

EDITED BY Erik J. Friis

HARPER'S MAGAZINE PRESS

Published in Association with Harper & Row

New York

"Harper's" is the registered trademark of Harper & Row, Publishers, Inc.

FIRST EDITION

Designed by Sidney Feinberg

Library of Congress Cataloging in Publication Data

Seminar on the Scandinavian Presence in America,
    Minneapolis, 1973.
    The Scandinavian Presence in North America.
    Sponsored by the Center for Northwest European
    Studies, University of Minnesota and Scandinavian
    Airlines System.
    1. Scandinavian Americans—Congresses.
2. Finnish Americans—Congresses. I. Friis, Erik J.
II. Minnesota. University. Center for Northwest
European Studies. III. Scandinavian Airlines System.
IV. Title.
E184.S18S45 1973   973'.04'395   75–27362
    ISBN 0–06–122515–0

76 77 78 79 10 9 8 7 6 5 4 3 2 1

Contents

Education and the Scandinavian Presence

Tore Tallroth, Nils Hasselmo, Gene G. Gage, Franklin D. Scott

Communications and the Scandinavian Presence

The Immigrant Newspaper   163

The Presentation of Scandinavia in America Through Books, Periodicals, and Nonliterary Media   179

Scanpresence as Seen from the Mother Countries

Preface

The largest convocation of specialists on Scandinavian-American affairs ever brought together took place in Minneapolis, Minnesota, on May 2–3, 1973. It was sponsored by the Center for Northwest European Studies at the University of Minnesota and by SAS/Scandinavian Airlines. The specialists came together for discussion and further elaboration of the present state of and future prospects for the Scandinavian presence in America, or Scanpresence.

The reasons for calling the Scanpresence Seminar flow from the United States Census of 1970, which indicated that the Scandinavian-American communities in North America are faced with new and different circumstances from those of the past. A glance at the past, taking stock of the present, and planning for the challenges of the future would, it was thought, be useful to all the organizations and groups represented at the meeting.

An attempt was made to attract a balanced representation of the various elements of the Scandinavian-American communities—Danish, Finnish, Icelandic, Norwegian, and Swedish—as well as interested agencies in Scandinavia. The Seminar was also unique in that it brought together representatives of most of the various subgroups within each nationality, such as the churches, fraternities, educational, and regional organizations. Thus it may be said that the Seminar was indeed ecumenical.

The gathering of educators, editors, journalists, ministers, officials of fraternal and other organizations, foreign service officers, and student participants was divided into eight panels, each with a specific area for thought and attention. In the scheme of the Seminar, virtually every participant was assigned an active role on one or more of the panels, and was expected as well to contribute to all aspects of the discussions. Papers had been prepared beforehand, and the entire group was asked to serve as audience for each speaker. The discussions were often spirited, conducive to further debate, and showed cross-fertilization of ideas.

At the end of the two days, the proceedings were informally summarized by Einar Haugen, one of the grand old men of Scandinavian studies in America. In conclusion the participants voted in favor of a resolution supporting the bill, then before the United States Congress, known as the Ethnic Heritage Act.

There was general agreement that the papers and the ensuing discussion threw much light on the entirety of Scandinavian America, its past as well as its present and future, not only as an immigrant group in the context of a larger, all-engulfing society, but also as a group consisting of five very similar, but only slightly interacting national subgroups. The decision to make the papers and the discussion available in printed form was therefore met with great enthusiasm by everyone involved in the Seminar.

To the undersigned it has been a privilege, as well as an unalloyed pleasure, to act as editor of the volume. The advice given me by Mr. S. Ralph Cohen of Scandinavian Airlines and the panel chairmen, who each prepared a draft condensation of the papers given in his section, is hereby gratefully acknowledged.

ERIK J. FRIIS

Introduction

The Bicentennial of the United States will focus attention on the great variety of national and ethnic strains in the American amalgam and what they have contributed to the whole.

In this exercise, the Scandinavians—Danes, Finns, Icelanders, Norwegians, and Swedes—will not be overly modest in speaking their individual pieces. They will have much to tell, for the Scandinavian contributions to America start in Viking times and continue through the later explorations and the colonial settlements into the mass migrations of the nineteenth and twentieth centuries.

However, the Scandinavian-American communities are concerned with more than history. As the Bicentennial approaches, they have been giving serious thought to their future as an identifiable presence in America and to what they can continue to contribute to their adopted country. This is what Scanpresence, the Seminar on the Scandinavian Presence in America, was all about.

This also makes *Scanpresence,* the book, an important and unique contribution to the content and bibliography of the Bicentennial, not only for the five percent of the population that derives from Scandinavia, but for anyone who is interested in the diversity of North American society.

As a book, *Scanpresence* is evidence of the concern that these five ethnic components of America have for their survival. It is an unusually complete picture of the ethnic institutions of some ten million Americans; an assessment of where they stand in the process of American assimilation; a statement of their hopes and fears for the future; and even a prescription for some of the steps they can take to realize the former and lay the latter to rest.

It is as well an exploration in some depth of the future of ethnicity of any kind in America, and, to a lesser extent, a reflection of how these communities and kindred appear to the mother countries in Scandinavia, and the extent of those countries' continuing interest in their kin over here.

In this volume, the editor has very wisely given each participant as much latitude as possible to make his own points in his own accent and style. The record is therefore a fascinating mosaic of the many components of the five Scandinavian communities—churchmen, educators, fraternal societies, historians, students, diplomats, publicists, editors of the immigrant press, and many more.

Given this diversity, much of what each has to say is peculiar to his own case, but like Scandinavians generally, who stick together because geography has stuck them together, they have much in common. In essence, they all face the same situation: to determine whether and how institutions and ideas heavily influenced by and fashioned for the immigrant generations can survive, grow and increase their usefulness into still another century and in the context of a changing American society.

The summary report of the Seminar by Professor Einar Haugen is one of the principal distinctions of this volume, and I would not want either to duplicate or compete with his account of its discussions and recommendations. However, there are certain aspects of the general consensus which should be stressed here.

The first is that the ideas, values, and social attitudes that the Scandinavians brought to America have been beneficial and are worth perpetuating.

A second is that, despite the passage of the generations, even those of the many millions of Scandinavian-Americans who have most easily assimilated into our Anglo-Saxon dominated society are still interested in knowing more about their origins and maintaining some contact with them. In fact, this interest is height-

ened in our day by the particular traumas of other ethnic groups
that they see about them. As Dr. Fishman observes and documents
in his contribution to this volume, ethnicity *is* here to stay.

As a footnote to this point, it should be mentioned that in
conversation about Scanpresence shortly before his death, the late
Chief Justice Earl Warren, himself a descendant of Scandinavians,
asked whether this kind of return to ethnicity meant a relapse
into an outmoded hyphenated Americanism. The fact that the
question did not occur to the Seminar is perhaps the best reply:
it is obvious from all of the attitudes expressed in Scanpresence
that a renewed interest in Scandinavian origins in this country pro-
ceeds from a base of absolute security in the American identity.

If the Scandinavian presence is worth preserving, how does one
go about it? Here the answers may vary according to the community, its comparative acculturation, its own internal resources
and the encouragement or support it has received from philan-
thropy at home or abroad. Yet there was a strong consensus that
the Scandinavian element in America is undergoing substantial
change. As it progresses from an "ethnic" community to a stage
in which its concern is with "heritage," sentimental attachment is
being replaced by a deeper and more sophisticated interest in
Scandinavian culture and its relevance to Americans. As new
generations arise, Kierkegaard and the ombudsman begin to mean
more than lutefisk and frikadeller.

By the same token, it is broadly evident that, to paraphrase a
famous bread baker, one does not have to be Scandinavian to be
interested in Scandinavia. Some of the strongest elements of the
Scandinavian presence in America are the growing number of
people, citizens as well as scholars, who want to know more about
matters Scandinavian because they are relevant to the American
condition and the American future. This has become evident in
such institutions as the Society for the Advancement of Scandinavian Study, whose scope has become increasingly inter-discipli-
nary, or the Scandinavian Seminar, whose students are predominantly Americans of other origins.

As Professor Haugen points out, no one element of the Scandinavian spectrum commands the resources it needs to meet its own problems fully, while each has something which can be of assistance to the others. This applies equally to the fraternal organizations and to the academics, to the immigrant press and the historical societies, and to the churches, even though they have to a large extent submerged their national identities in a broader Lutheranism.

All of this adds up to one further conclusion which I believe is implied in the general consensus—that Scanpresence is not a one-time phenomenon, significant and complete in itself. Rather it should be regarded as a first step toward the objective of all of its constituents—to assure a strong, relevant and constructive Scandinavian presence in America through generations to come.

Some of the ideas brought forward in the Seminar have already become part of the action plans of individual organizations. The dialogue between the academic and fraternal elements that was initiated by Scanpresence is being continued. But there remain many areas in which joint consideration and action is required and in which pooling of resources, intellectual and economic, is necessary. There remains a great requirement for better bridges: between the immigrant generations and their descendants; between the various ethnic groups as a whole and the elements within each of them; and between the Americans of Scandinavian background and the Americans interested in Scandinavia. In this area of bridge building, another great need is to build a better connection between modern America and modern Scandinavia, for it is evident in the testimony of Scanpresence that what exists today is to a great extent nostalgia for a lost Atlantis.

Thus, Scanpresence has not been an end but is rather the beginning of a process of reconsideration and action which should extend into the Bicentennial and beyond. It suggests an agenda of quite specific projects and ideas whose practical implementation should be the basis of an equally fascinating and useful Scanpresence II. For this reason, the Scanpresence Committee has taken steps to maintain an organization and identity. Should the opportunity offer, it is prepared as well to extend its representation, in order to assure that there will be an examination of that other side of the coin which was only briefly glimpsed at Minneapolis—the American presence in Scandinavia, or the view from the mother countries of this other Scandinavia abroad.

Scanpresence is the achievement of many people and institutions and to mention any of them would mean neglecting others whose contributions have been equally valuable. All of them, however, would agree with me that particular appreciation is due to the University of Minnesota and SAS/Scandinavian Airlines, who made Scanpresence possible in the first place. This joining of forces between a great university and a great international airline is something rather special which symbolizes the union of intellectual and practical resources essential to the continued healthy Scandinavian presence in America.

MARION J. NELSON

Minneapolis, Minnesota

THE SCANDINAVIAN PRESENCE
IN NORTH AMERICA

Panel   Rudolph Vecoli (Chairman), S. Ralph Cohen, Joshua
Fishman, Franklin D. Scott

Avant Propos: The Statistical Background

S. Ralph Cohen

In preparing for a symposium graced by so many doctors and professors of divinity, I thought it might be appropriate to use a biblical text, and after an assiduous search I settled on Daniel V, verses 25 through 28. The reader will immediately recall that these verses have to do with the handwriting on the wall at Belshazzar's feast—*Mene, mene, tekel, upharsin.*

The handwriting on our wall comes from the 1970 United States Census. These 1970 statistics are being gradually unriddled and released by the Census Bureau, and it has become apparent that those of us who are interested, for one reason or another, in the preservation of the Scandinavian presence in America are faced with a new set of circumstances. One way or another, we are approaching a critical point—if not a watershed, at least a point where our accustomed roads may have to take a turning.

We have for many years assumed a Scandinavian-American ethnic population in the United States and Canada totaling as many as ten million and extending now into the fifth and sixth generations since the start of mass immigration from the Nordic countries.

In a very real sense, however, the nucleus and main components of this Scandinavian ethnic base in North America are the so-called first and second generations. These are the generations of those born in Scandinavia and the children they begat here. They are the "ethnics" by the United States Census definition. They are also the people by whom distinctively Scandinavian-American institutions have been created and molded and for

3

whom they largely exist. And these institutions are the channels through which we are able to communicate with them, and through which they work to pass on their heritage to succeeding generations.

Like all statistics, the census figures lend themselves to interpretation and analysis from a variety of points of view.

For those of us who have been impressed by the extent of Scandinavian immigration to America—by the transplantation of a quarter of the populations of Sweden and Norway to this new world—it may come as a shock to realize that immigration to the United States has now come virtually to an end. During the entire decade of the 1960s, only 46,032 Danes, Norwegians, Swedes, and Finns emigrated to this country. In 1969 and 1970, in fact, there were far fewer than 1,000 immigrants to the United States from any one of these countries.

Parallel but not strictly comparable figures for Canada indicate that immigration from all the countries concerned is now and has for some years been less than 1,000 per annum.

I should note, with regret and respect, that the movement of population from Iceland has apparently not been significant enough to give that country figures of its own in the United States Census statistics so far available; but we do know that Icelanders have a greater weight in the general Canadian mix than here in the United States.

Nevertheless, as regards both Canada and the United States, we are reasonably certain that immigration during the last decade has been for the most part what might be called immigration at the top. Today's immigrant does not come to break the prairie or get a job on the railroad; he comes here as a professional, the possessor of skills or crafts, or as a salesman and prospective business executive. As such, he assimilates quickly and almost painlessly; and he is less likely than the immigrant of preceding generations to have any strong feeling of ethnic community.

Taken all in all, then, there is little likelihood that the essential Scandinavian immigration will be increased and the Scandinavian

stock in North America replenished. Barring some disaster or
upheaval in Scandinavia, we have come to the effective end of
the era of immigration.

We might look next at what has happened to the first, or Scan-
dinavian-born, generation. In 1940, its numbers stood at almost
one million. By 1960, this figure had dwindled to little more than
500,000. If we can extrapolate this rate of change to 1970 and
beyond, the first-generation Scandinavian population of the
United States now probably stands at something like 300,000;
and, in actuarial computation at least, it may come close to practically zero in the next ten to fifteen years.

The second generation component, which was 920,000 in 1940,
grew to 1,770,000 in 1960 and is close to 2,000,000 today; but in
view of what has happened to the first generation, and since the second is itself aging, it would seem likely that this number has not
significantly increased and will gradually diminish.

Again, we must comment separately on Canada because its census and statistics run a somewhat different course and operate with
rather different sets of definitions. We know that the total number of
Canadians of Scandinavian derivation was approximately 300,000
in 1941 and suspect that it stands today at about 400,000.

Whatever the gaps and disparities, we believe that it is safe to
assume that the total Scandinavian "ethnic" population of North
America—that is, first and second generations in the United States
Census definition—has peaked and must decline.

It is further logical to postulate that with each succeeding generation the Scandinavian-American, or the Scandinavian-Canadian,
becomes more and more American or Canadian.

The problem we are about to examine, therefore, is whether
he or she will at the same time become less and less Scandinavian.

Obviously, we can long continue to talk about the millions of
Scandinavians in North America. But what will that actually
mean? What will be the real degree of their awareness of their
own connection with Scandinavia? How willing and able will they
be to relate to countries increasingly remote? Will they be interested

in and apt to support ethnic institutions fashioned by and for earlier generations? Will the general respect of North Americans for their compatriots of Scandinavian descent and for the countries whence they came wane or wax? And what, if anything, should those of us who are concerned with these matters do about them?

We would certainly not pretend that this is an entirely new problem; that thoughtful people in all of the communities involved have not already applied themselves to it; or that some at least have found effective and satisfying answers. But it was the conviction of the core group that recommended Scanpresence that the time had come for all parties concerned to look at it together, on an ecumenical basis, so that we could have the greatest and fullest possible exchange of information and advice while the basic institutions of the Scandinavian communities in America are still alive and comparatively well.

To consider these matters, it may be well to look at our Scandinavian situation in the context of the America in which we live. Lest we allow a natural pride to mislead us, we may want to bear in mind that of the whole of the so-called "ethnic" population of the United States of all origins, first- and second-generation Scandinavian-Americans constitute at most five percent. And of the 203,000,000 Americans registered in the 1970 census, these first- and second-generation Scandinavian-Americans together constitute less than one percent. If we stretch our definition of Scandinavian-American into succeeding generations, these probably constitute at best around five percent of the total American population.

In the Canadian context, the Scandinavians, by the wider definition, represent only about two percent of the population.

This does not mean that Scandinavians need feel humble, but it may be well to bear in mind that they constitute only a few pieces in the intricate mosaic which is America, and not necessarily the largest ones.

It may be helpful as well to look at the distribution of the

"ethnic" Scandinavian-Americans on this continent. Forty-four percent of the first and second generations live in some twenty-five
metropolitan and urban areas, all concentrated in seventeen of
the fifty states. Except for Florida, California, and the District of
Columbia, all of these states are in the northerly parts of the
country.

In only two cases—Chicago and Minneapolis, with New York
a possible third—do any of these cities contain more than five
percent of the total Scandinavian-American ethnic population, or
total more than 100,000 all told.

Only nine cities have concentrations of more than 20,000 ethnic
Scandinavian-Americans of all national origins (although Detroit
is close to being the tenth); and only ten cities have as many as
10,000 of any one of the various national groups.

The largest single national "ethnic" concentrations are: 66,538
Swedes in Chicago; 40,335 Norwegians in Minneapolis and the
39,552 in New York; and as for Danes, 18,197 in and around Los
Angeles and 17,070 in Chicago.

The distribution of the Finnish ethnic community shows a
somewhat different pattern, with 70 percent concentrated in the six
states of Michigan, Minnesota, California, New York, Massachusetts, and Washington, with the largest concentration of about
50,000 in Michigan.

Chicago and Minneapolis are still the Scandinavian capitals of
America; but the only one of the twenty-five centers of concen-
tration where the ethnic content is actually rising is the Tampa-St.
Petersburg retirement area.

It may also be worth noting that only ten cities have as much as
one percent of the total Scandinavian ethnic population; and that
55 percent of this total population is scattered among communities
and areas in which there are fewer than 10,000 of all nationalities
involved.

In Canada, the Scandinavian ethnic population—in the broader
Canadian definition which includes all generations—is to be found

in ten provinces and in the Yukon and Northwest Territories. The bulk are in British Columbia, Alberta, Saskatchewan, Manitoba, Ontario, and Quebec, for the most part in rural areas.

One can read many implications from all these figures. Since I am professionally concerned with communications, I am struck by how scattered the Scandinavian populations of North America really are; by what small islands they constitute in this vast sea of peoples; how fractionized they are as between Danes, Norwegians, Swedes, Finns, and Icelanders, and, thus, by the difficulty and cost of serving and preserving such a scattered constituency.

The biblical text which I chose is not of itself an optimistic one. *Mene,* according to the King James Version, means "God hath numbered thy Kingdom, and finished." *Tekel* means "Thou art weighed in the balances and art found wanting." And *Peres,* the root for *Upharsin,* means "Thy kingdom is divided and given to the Medes and the Persians."

I would not want to equate the census with divinity, nor do I for a moment think that Scandinavian America is finished. But we have come to a time when its future must be weighed in the balance; and it may well be that this divided community may lose its identity in a highly mobile, urbanized, computerized, conglomerated, and homogenized society.

It is the case that social change is heating up. New life styles are being created in which many of the old distinctions between a people and the traditional elements that helped to preserve them are rapidly disappearing. The generation gap occurs more quickly and yawns more widely than ever before. Intermarriage has become a problem for virtually all established religious or ethnic groups.

There is also a sort of international homogenization in process, for what happens in America is only a reaction to or a precursor of what has occurred or will happen elsewhere. This Holiday Inn is not much different from Holiday Inns in a score of other countries. Che Guevara is not Latin-American or Cuban, but international; and while it may be heresy, he may mean more to many

young Americans, Scandinavian-Americans or Scandinavians, than
Leif Erikson.

Again, in the peculiarly Scandinavian-American context, the
passage of generations has also meant relaxing the bonds of kinship. Aunts, uncles, and grandparents have passed away; brothers
and sisters have become cousins; and first cousins have become
second cousins twice and thrice removed.

Moreover, we are all aware of the fact that the Scandinavian
who has "made it" in America can change very much, in social
and political attitudes, from the Scandinavian who stayed at home.

This does not necessarily mean that the auguries are all bad.
Most American ethnic communities have now experienced the
cycle of reaction and reattraction, in which the first generation
born in America tends to shy away, with more or less violence,
from the values of the immigrant elder, while succeeding generations become more relaxed and curious about their backgrounds.
The same tendencies may be more muted in the Scandinavian
case, because they have not been assisted by an Israel, an Ulster
or a *Godfather,* but nevertheless they do exist.

It is also possible that new generations may be more sympathetic to modern Scandinavia than their elders, for Scandinavia
has many attributes that are currently of great interest to younger
Americans, Scandinavian by origin or not.

In a computerized and depersonalized society, youth of all
origins are going through a crisis of identity. They want something
to tie on to and by which to differentiate themselves from the
mass. And in American eyes, the Scandinavian identification is an
eminently worthy one.

But whether the future is bright or bleak, and whether these
interpretations and comments are entirely valid, the fact is that
we are going through a period of critical evaluation of almost
every phase of American society—political, industrial, commercial, educational, and cultural. The figures before us underline the
need to re-evaluate Scandinavian-American institutions before
they, too, have become obsolete.

It is recorded that Daniel and Shadrach and Meshach and Abednego were given "knowledge and skill in all learning and wisdom." One hopes that Scanpresence will mobilize enough of these qualities to suggest whether Scandinavia in America can be preserved and strengthened—or if it must be lost among the Medes and the Persians.

Introduction of the Keynote Speaker

RUDOLPH VECOLI: Mr. Cohen has given us much food for thought, some of it rather dark thought. But some students at the University of Minnesota have developed statistics which give a more positive view and I'd like to cite a couple of them. In 1944 and 1945, there were eight companies manufacturing lutefisk in Minnesota, each with an annual production of more than 150,000 pounds. While the number of companies has decreased, those which still exist produce a total of approximately 3,000,000 pounds of lutefisk per year. And yet another statistic is somewhat inspiriting: exports of aquavit to the United States have increased from 6,870 cases in 1967 to 8,557 cases in 1972, an increase of 25 percent!

To be serious, Joshua Fishman, who opens the Seminar, is a distinguished scholar who has addressed himself in his writings to the problems of ethnicity and of cultural and linguistic maintenance in a more thorough and analytical fashion than anyone else I know. We are indeed proud to have him here to speak to us about the third century of non-English language maintenance and non-Anglo ethnic maintenance in the United States.

Professor Joshua Fishman was born in Philadelphia and attended the University of Pennsylvania; received his doctorate from Columbia University; and has also received an honorary doctorate from Yeshiva University. He has held many academic and research appointments, among which have been Professor of Human Relations and Psychology at the University of Pennsylvania, and he is currently Distinguished Professor of the Social

Sciences of the Graduate School of Yeshiva University. He has come a long way to be with us for this Seminar, since he is on leave this year as Visiting Professor and Director of the Language Behavioral Section of the Hebrew University in Jerusalem.

Professor Fishman is the author of numerous books and articles, all of which address themselves to the issues with which we are concerned, and most particularly of *Language Loyalty in the United States—The Maintenance and Perpetuation of Non-English Mother Tongues by American Ethnic and Religious Groups,* which appeared in 1966. This volume, I believe, is one of the most important studies of American culture and history to have appeared in the last decade and has indeed foreshadowed and informed much of the discussion in recent years about ethnicity and ethnic groups.

The Future of Ethnicity in America

JOSHUA A. FISHMAN

The American bicentennial celebration will undoubtedly provide us with many opportunities for stock-taking, culturally, socially, educationally, and economically. Such opportunities should be welcome, for they are needed in every society and particularly in such as ours, marked as it is more by change and haste than by stability and reflection. Indeed, such national stock-taking should also provide us with opportunities for gaining better perspectives on ourselves, as individuals, as citizens, and as professionals engaged, at least part time, in the process of building a better America. For those of us who are in or near our fifties—and nowadays that seems to be the case for almost everyone who is not below thirty—the fact that we are "suddenly" roughly a quarter the age of our country will come as something of a shock. It's not that we didn't know that America was a young country, but we always felt it was "older than that." And it's not that we didn't know that we were getting older, but we always thought we were "younger than that." We really don't know how to explain it, but in the last few years a great injustice has taken place, namely, most of us have suddenly become a great deal older and the country as a whole has become a great deal younger, whereas, in all justice, it should have been the other way round.

Among topics that should gain from "bicentennial perspective" are non-English language maintenance, non-Anglo ethnic maintenance, and, indeed, the teaching of English to speakers of other languages, all of which are every bit as old on American shores as the republic itself, if not a good bit older. Of course, 200 years is a rather brief perspective for social historians, but as the man said: "That's all we've got." However, since the pattern of the American past is rather clear in connection with these topics, and since we have all of time and all of space—reaching far beyond the time and space of the United States—to give us additional perspective on the American experience, our task may not be an unreasonable one after all. I propose, therefore, to dive in, using language maintenance as my initial vantage point and ethnic maintenance as my basic concern. My goal throughout is to clarify what has happened, what is happening, and, if possible, to speculate gingerly as to what will happen on the language maintenance and ethnic maintenance fronts during the approaching third century of the American adventure.

The Basic Pattern

The predominant pattern of non-English language maintenance during the first two centuries of American national life, and certainly during its one century of post Civil War industrialization, has been: (a) rapid and widespread adoption of English as a second language by the immigrant first generation, and (b) widespread transmission of this second language to the young as their mother tongue. Although there are exceptions to the above general pattern—and they must be commented upon separately, because only a clinical awareness of exceptions brings about a rich awareness of the real essentials in any pattern—nonetheless it *is* the general pattern, notwithstanding the fact that the largest immigration in modern world history was an immigration substantially non-Anglo in language, culture, and religion.

This basic pattern was neither inevitable nor miraculous, neither a foregone conclusion nor manifest destiny. It is certainly not the only pattern that obtains between immigrants and hosts. Immigrants do not always adopt the languages of their hosts. For example, Anglo and New-Canadians coming to Quebec until recently have not even learned French as a second language, let alone passed it on as a first language to their children; nor have immigrant Amharas learned Galla; nor have immigrant Tamils learned Hindi; nor have the immigrant French in Alsace-Lorraine or in Luxembourg learned local German; nor have immigrant Russians learned the languages of the various Soviet republics and autonomous regions to which they have migrated. Indeed, as several of the above examples imply, it is not at all unheard of for hosts to adopt the language of a major immigrant group, either as an L_2 alone, or subsequently also as an L_1. Furthermore, where immigrants have adopted the languages of their hosts as second languages it is by no means inevitable for these L_2s to then become the L_1s of the second generation (e.g., this tends not to happen among the overseas Chinese, among ultra-orthodox Jews whether in Israel or in the Diaspora, among the most recent generations of immigrant Dutch-speakers in Brussels, nor among most newly urbanized populations in Africa). Indeed, as we study immigrants-hosts interaction throughout the world we find ample evidence for two patterns that are quite rare in the annals of American history, namely, (a) where both immigrants and hosts increasingly shift to a third language which is the regional *lingua franca,* and (b) where populations live side by side for generations—one being historically the immigrant group and the other being historically the host group—without any widespread bilingualism developing on either side, and with meager intergroup communication being channeled via bilingual middlemen. Finally, it is not even the case that immigrants speaking narrow languages (in regional or world perspective) necessarily shift to the languages of hosts speaking wider languages (in the same perspective), otherwise the Roman and Greek cities of the ancient Mediterranean world, and the German cities of nineteenth-century Eastern and Southeastern Europe, would not have been engulfed by hitherto rural vernaculars as readily as they were.

From the above examples alone it is obvious that the clearly predominant outcome in the American case is not a result of immigration per se, nor of differential language status per se. Indeed, an outcome as nationwide as the one we are dealing with (and yet as unprecedented on the world scene) must have been supported by many different social processes. Yet it seems to me that one cluster of processes is predominant over all: interaction-based social mobility.

The Basic Process

America! America! America! How many have blessed you! After living abroad for three years, and in a comparatively rapidly developing country at that, I see even more clearly than before the extent to which America represented (and still represents) the promise of a better life: a more comfortable life, a freer life, a safer life. Notwithstanding the initial years of sweat shops, discrimination, intermittent depressions, and dawn-to-dusk, seven-days-a-week labor, the industrialized green-backing of America "paid off" quickly. Within their own lifetimes illiterate rural-based immigrants could become "self-made men" and proud suppliers of labor-saving conveniences for their womenfolk, good educations for their children, and small inheritances for their grandchildren. However, the fountainhead of all these benefits was the Anglo-controlled economy, the Anglo-controlled government, the Anglo-controlled school, and the Anglo-dominated institutions and style of life. Those who could achieve mobility without interacting either with the Anglo institutions or with the highly diversified urban immigrant populations (drawn to a *lingua franca* that facilitated communication and mobility within the ranks of the Anglo power elite) escaped the full brunt of language shift somewhat longer. However, these were largely rural and agricultural settlers coming en masse to good public land that could be worked without major investment for equipment and irrigation. The new city dwellers—and the brunt of our immigrants came to and stayed in the cities—neither had nor sought an opportunity. Their mobility derived from interacting intensively with immigrants from other backgrounds, rather than from interacting exclusively with their "own kind" and with the Anglo authorities. There were few sections in the country in which one non-Anglo group alone clearly predominated and controlled the means of production. Breadwinners (and even teen-agers were breadwinners until a mere fifty years ago) eagerly brought English into their own homes and families, because it was through English that their own status as providers flowed. With it they sought to open doors for their dear ones as well, even at the risk of cultural dislocation. It was this readiness to make virtually any accommodation needed in order to improve one's lot in life that prompted the view that many immigrants were "Americans" even before they arrived on these shores.

However, there were two major exceptions to the story of "rapid success at any price" which interactive social mobility made possible for so many. One, those who slowly moved ahead economically from a rural base and with far less interaction, has already been mentioned. The other consisted of those who did not move ahead economically (certainly not relative to the mobility of their neighbors), and, therefore, who not only became the rural and the urban poor of a fantastically rich society, but who also anglified little if at all. The latter, not caught up by either industrialization or interactions, were usually ignored by their betters, as if the American dream did not pertain to them and as if the dream was fully confirmed regardless of what happened to these unfortunates. They did not vanish merely because they were ignored and we will return to them. Indeed, they very forcefully called themselves to our attention and, in doing so, changed the future of non-English language maintenance and non-Anglo ethnic maintenance for years to come.

Had we been dealing with diversified indigenous rural populations drawn to the cities the process would have been the same. The rootlessness and powerlessness of our immigrants merely hastened it. Traditional family practices, role relationships, ethnic beliefs and observances (even those intertwined with religion, as most were) gave way under the dislocating impact of supra-ethnic and non-ethnic and anti-ethnic industrial efficiency, rationality, monetary commensurability, and blatant materialism as an end in itself. De-ethnicization was not, by and large, a plot of America's Anglo populations. They too were swept up by the same processes whose gatekeepers they were, to such an extent that Old World English ethnicity and Old World Scotch-Irish ethnicity weathered the storm not a whit better than did traditional German, Jewish, Italian, Polish, French, or Spanish ethnicity. The difference, of course, was in the language. Anglo-ethnics did not have to undergo language shift in order to acquire their share of the American dream; the non-Anglo ethnics did. Nevertheless, the resulting de-ethnicization was finally about the same, and all lost at least part of their souls in order to gain some part of this world.

In contrast to interactive social mobility the importance of other factors is weak indeed. Interactive social mobility is encompassed by such empirical indices as educational requirement for employment, ethnic diversity in district of residence, ethnic diversity in place of employment, interactive requirement of employment, and so on. In comparison to the foregoing the total size of the immigrant group, the particular culture and language of origin of the immigrant group and their developmental stage vis-à-vis Anglo/English culture and language, the original motives of immigration (political, religious, or economic), and the absence or presence of successive waves of newcomers, all these and many more made little long-range difference. Indeed, more recent newcomers have often made the transition much more rapidly than did old-timers of similar backgrounds. Not only have they been helped by their *landslayt* who preceded them here, but the latter often went out of their way to show the newcomers that they (the old-timers) were no longer country bumpkins and that they too owned, used, and appreciated all the finer things or better ways of modern life.

By the time we come to imposition of racist immigration controls in the early twenties, the process described above was already so well established as to make these controls superfluous vis-à-vis the immigrant masses that had already arrived. By the time of the Black and Brown protests of the sixties, and their further disruption of old ethnic urban neighborhoods throughout the United States, non-Anglo ethnic maintenance and non-English language maintenance among ethnic participants in interactive social mobility was at low ebb quantitatively and qualitatively. The mother tongues of such groups were no longer functional mother tongues and were not even second tongues used by any but a small and shrinking proportion of the second and third generations. The ethnic characteristics of these groups had departed substantially from their original moorings, and had become increasingly disjointed pastiches of original and American elements, often lacking either rationale or respect among their own people.

And yet, after twenty, fifty, a hundred, or even two hundred years of Americanization, non-Anglo ethnicity remained an ingredient in American life of the early 1960s. Just as non-English language maintenance never died, so non-Anglo ethnic maintenance never disappeared. Of course, both were commonly dependent upon transfusions from abroad. Even two hundred years is a brief period (the life span of no more than three or four men) and few social phenomena disappear completely that quickly. Whatever the explanation, and we will have to look for a satisfying explanation later, ethnic maintenance and language maintenance were both there, often battered and bruised, when the fitful mid-sixties arrived and gave them both a new lease on life.

The New Ethnicity

We have all lived through it so recently that we really have no perspective or objectivity about it. It is as if it were a massive projective technique, interpretable only on the basis of the emotional, intellectual, and group biases of the beholder. However, all of a sudden there "it" was: ethnic hairdos, and ethnic dress,

and ethnic foods, and ethnic music, and ethnic soul, and ethnic
courses, and ethnic studies and even a bill for an Ethnic Heritage
Act (see Congressional Record, vol. 118, no. 168: Tuesday, Oct.
17, 1972). Where did this all come from, and why? The first
question is far easier to answer than the second.

The "new ethnicity" (called by others the "new tribalism" and
the "new apartheid") had one major source and three minor
auxiliary sources. All in all, it derived from the groups that had
experienced least interaction-based social mobility and for whom
a variety of standard American English had rarely become even
their L_2. From these origins it spread to other non-Anglo groups
who had, by and large, adopted a variety of standard American
English as their L_1 and who normally had to struggle to maintain
even a metaphorical grasp of their erstwhile ethnic mother
tongues. It is clear testimony to the emotional urgency of the
Black protest (and, in part, also the Mexican-American, Puerto
Rican, American-Indian protests) that it so widely triggered
corresponding reactions among Jewish-Americans, Italo-Ameri-
cans, Polish-Americans, Franco-Americans, and others. It brought
about a massive redefinition of the WASP category, to such an
extent that few wanted to be included in the "soulless" group
devoted to material comfort, middle-class values, environmental
pollutants, and Vietnamization with which it was variously identified. The Black protest was initially against exclusion, rejection,
exploitation, and discrimination. However, like all other ethnic
mass movements it eventually took a positive turn and also became a movement for Black (and, more generally, ethnic) personality, for Black pride, Black roots, Black dignity, and for Black
culture with as much historical depth and substantive content as
possible.

The same phenomenon repeated itself, with greater or lesser
contrast to the Black protest, depending on local circumstances,
in the cases of all other major and several other minor ethnic
groups in the country. The full dimensions and impact of this
phenomenon (to call it a "whirlwind" or "tidal wave" would be

to imply a passing and destructive phenomenon) can not yet be gauged. It still engulfs some of us and surrounds all of us. However, two new and major ingredients have been added to the American ethnic scene since and as a result of its onset.

Ideological Ethnicity

One need not study ethnic and linguistic diversity long as a worldwide phenomenon to realize the frequency with which it is not merely politicized but ideologized in many parts of the world. Ethnic differences are not merely instruments exploited by politicians at election time. They are not merely the bases upon which in-group leaderships and enterprises and organizations are built for the attainment of short-range goals. They are also related to ideologies, to *Weltanschauungen,* to philosophies of life-and-death. Until the ethnic explosion of the mid-sixties the U.S. was remarkably free (not entirely free but still remarkably free) of ideologized ethnicity. Whatever weak ideologies did exist were either intellectual/rational, and therefore lacking in mass gut appeal (here I would classify Horace Kallen's philosophy of cultural pluralism to which I personally subscribe wholeheartedly), or they were apologetic and therefore lacking in righteous anger (here I would classify all of the attempts to "prove" that it is "not bad" to be bi-cultural or to know two languages, etc.). They were pseudo-ideologies rather than real ideologies because they were afraid to be vehemently against anything "American." "America" was the sacred cow of ethnic groups and movements. Ethnics wanted to be loved by America as completely as they themselves loved it. To be critical might be mistaken for being anti-patriotic, ungrateful, disloyal.

In the "new ethnicity," as a movement primarily of second, third, and fourth generation Americans, this fear of criticizing America is completely gone. Indeed, the "new ethnicity" is so "at home" with America that it relishes a good scrap rather than back away from criticizing those American traits and values that it finds wanting. One's ethnicity, no matter how far back its genuine roots may lie, is viewed as a supreme value, a supreme beauty, a supreme tenderness, a supreme authenticity, because . . . well, because all ethnicity is authentically beautiful and tender. It claims that if America is any good at all, any better at all than the purported "bad guys" elsewhere, then it should value ethnicity, protect ethnicity, develop ethnicity, foster ethnicity, particularly ethnicity X that has contributed so much to the poetry, music, wit, wisdom, humor, and gentleness of life in this world and the next. And indeed it asks, "What is America without ethnicity?" What has Anglo-conformity produced, it insinuates, other than Coca-Cola, and Rice Krispies, and color TV, and oil-scarred beaches, and despoiled forests, and genocidal attacks on Vietnamese villages, and napalm, and police brutality, and get rich quick with the devil taking the hindmost? If there is any soul left in America, it is in the Waspishly neglected and subverted medley of forgotten ethnicities. These ethnicities must be revived, restored, reborn, regrouped. They alone can provide the pure air and the pure hearts which America has so tragically lost in its wild stampede after the superficialities rather than the essences of life. The rejection and degradation of ethnicity led to the decline and fall of America. The revival and re-enthronement of ethnicity will lead to America's rise and glory! What we note here is a re-evaluation of self and others on a massive scale. What we have here is revivalistic, messianic, and powerfully moving. Ethnicity has never been that before in America, particularly not for the American-born young.

As a devotee and practitioner of a particular non-Anglo ethnicity, and as a speaker and partisan of a particular non-English language, I nevertheless find the "new ethnicity" overly simple and overly brash. Others may find it downright wrong. But it is not the purpose of ideology to be right, let alone to be subtle. Its purpose is to mobilize and motivate, to clarify (even by distorting) and to activate (even by over-dramatizing). The Blacks and Chicanos and Indians and Ricans (Nuyoricans and Puerto Ricans) have contributed an ideological tenor to ethnic life and labor in the United States. This ideological tenor has influenced other groups as well, and it has even found acceptance among segments of the Anglo power structure. It is a new element to be reckoned with. It will not easily or quickly go away. Ideologies are exceptionally self-sustaining (even when they are not successful), much more so than are traditional behavior systems, once they have reached the massive, white-heat stage. We have witnessed a decade of tragic disappointment with America, particularly among many of our young. In many cases ethnicity has been associated with this conscious disappointment and has transmuted itself and the disappointment in the process. More than ever before, therefore, ethnicity is here to stay, as an ideologized, and, therefore, as a long-term, social-issue-related, part of the American scene. Never before did ethnicity have anything to fight for but itself. Now it is fighting for justice, honesty, decency and beauty, for itself and for all of America!

Publicly Subsidized Pluralism

Another novel aspect of non-English language maintenance and non-Anglo ethnic maintenance efforts in the sixties was the extent to which they aimed at public support. The "new ethnics" have viewed themselves not only as tearing down American Anglo-conformity but as building up a new society that would diversify, enrich, and ennoble American life. As such they expected that the courses, programs, pageants, publications, organizations, and communities that they demanded and fostered be supported from the public till, since they were intended to serve the general good. It is not surprising, perhaps, that in the age of the welfare state such demands should have been made. It is, however, somewhat surprising to note the intimate identification with America that such demands imply. They amount to a demand that the much maligned "system" pay for its own compulsory modification; but they also amount to an attempt to remain within the system, rather than entirely outside of it. Finally, most surprising of all, is the extent to which the demands have been met.

Only a decade ago nearly the entire world of American non-English language maintenance and non-Anglo ethnic mainte-nance was dependent on meager resources raised within the group for its financial wherewithal. This amounted to a double penalty, for the ethnics were primarily those already a notch or two below the economic level of their de-ethnicized peers. The hope for public subsidy never disappeared, and, indeed, was restated again by an impartial observer just before the "new ethnicity" appeared on the scene. However, it was definitely the fury of the Black protest (and, secondarily, that of its Brown and Red counter-parts) that broke through the traditional Anglo silence and foot dragging on this score. The stance taken could not be morally denied, once its major premise (that the U.S. is a multi-ethnic society and that each of its strands, functioning for the cultural enrichment of the whole, deserves the recognition and support of the whole) was granted. However, it was not entirely the rationality or morality of the case that ultimately won the day, but the com-bined political, economic, and even physical pressures.[1]

The combination has paid off most dramatically in the recent burgeoning of ethnic studies, a field that I consider simultaneously the greatest asset as well as the greatest debit of the "new eth-nicity." It is a debit because it easily shades into ethnic "interest" of a merely intellectual sort, rather than remaining fully in the area of ethnic maintenance per se. You don't have to be Black (Jewish, Scandinavian) to take Black (Jewish, Scandinavian) studies. However, it is without doubt an asset as an institutional-ized avenue of keeping ethnicity young, relevant, and in inter-

1. There is a tendency to overemphasize the role of force in the attain-ment of ethnic goals in the United States. There is also a tendency to fear overly that the "new ethnicity" will lead to and prolong inter-ethnic hostility in the United States. I believe there is enough opportunity in our social and economic system to obviate both of these dangers. However, if I am wrong on either count the result will be a strengthening rather than a weakening of ethnicity.

action with the best of general American culture. While it is true that ethnic-studies-at-general-expense have flowered far too quickly and too widely to make it likely or even possible for that growth to be characterized by "proper qualitative standards," it is also true that the pursuit of "proper standards" can be an interminable delaying factor. No such subjective delaying tactics were permitted to hold back the growth of American academic expansion in other areas, particularly during the early sixties when federal, state, and local governments were willing and able to pay the bill. "Standards" ultimately caught up with supply and demand, and this will probably be the case also in connection with many of those ethnic studies programs that began not quite at the level at which their critics would like to see them. Indeed, "standards" have always come after rather than before growth in the history of American education and in the history of every other aspect of American life. Thus, it appears to me, that the real question that we must examine is not the one of instant standards (neither sociology nor any other discipline produced satisfactory answers for several years after its appearance in American universities) but, rather, since standards always take time to evolve, whether the "new ethnicity" forces can keep the pressure on to a sufficient degree so that their courses and programs will continue to be maintained until their qualitative standard is improved. This query, in turn, brings us full circle, for it again prompts the question: is ethnicity necessary? Perhaps it will just vanish after a while from the American scene, and the programs so massively pushed through can be quietly shelved and Anglo-conformity quietly returned to as in the good old days.

Question: Is Ethnicity Necessary?

Just as language shift does occur, so does ethnicity shift. Throughout human history populations have been re-ethnicized into different cultural systems from those that their ancestors once participated in. Beginning with nineteenth century Europe this

process of re-ethnification reached many millions of hitherto ethnically unmobilized city (and later rural) denizens via mass nationalist movements. For those made conscious of and fiercely
loyal to their ethnicity via such movements, no further rapid deethnization and re-ethnization was possible (without catastrophic
defeats and dislocations). Finns no longer became Swedified;
Czechs no longer became Germanized; Poles no longer became
Russianized; Ukrainians no longer became Polonized. Only the
passage of a generation or more of post-nationalistic calm and
concentration on other issues would again make ethnic shift and
language shift possible for their progeny. However, most of those
countless millions who crossed the Atlantic, the Rio Grande, or
the Caribbean Sea into what was or became the continental United
States had not yet been ethnically mobilized one way or the other.
Their ethnicity was largely of the little tradition variety, i.e., it was
neither fierce nor conscious, although it was extremely integrated
and satisfying for all that.[2]

The confrontation with the American dream was the major
mobilizing experience for our immigrants and their children. This
confrontation not only de-ethnicized them to a large extent, by
piercing and crumbling the folk-ethnicities that most immigrants
had brought with them, but it bid mightily to re-ethnicize them
in the image of the "Standard American," a product of the un-
hyphenated culture that the American dream was rapidly fash-
ioning. Once so re-ethnicized and mobilized it would be difficult,
if at all possible, for the original ethnicities, or reasonable fac-
similes thereof, to be reconstituted. "Americanism" was well on
the way to becoming the secular unifying religion of our theologi-
cally diverse and permissive society.

However, like most messianic dreams of the past hundred
years the American dream had two faults built into it: (a) it did

2. Even among Germans and Jews, the two immigrant groups coming
with the proportionally largest urban and intellectual contingents, conscious
and integrated nationalist (rather than localist) commitment was rather
restricted and ephemeral.

not pay off as widely or as all-inclusively as promised (thus leaving and ignoring huge pockets of dissatisfied non-partici-pants), and (b) it did not recognize the "local color" needs that modernization (for all its massification and mechanization) elicits rather than eradicates. As a result of these two chinks in the armor of Americanization, non-Anglo ethnicity was not crushed among those who never had a chance to fully savor the creature comforts and patriotic poetry of Americanism, and did not fully die out among many, many of those who had the benefit of both. Eth-nicity remains and, indeed, it even becomes modern "everyman's" personal link with socially patterned unique intimacy and intimate uniqueness. As such it is always available to soothe, to comfort, to provide tenderness and rootedness, even when it is not needed as a launching pad for social action. As such it is a great depriva-tion to those who have lost it and who do not know where or how to recover it.

As a result of both the inner need for ethnicity, as well as the disappointment generated by the outer "non-ethnic" American world, non-Anglo ethnic maintenance remained, transformed and weakened to be sure, far beyond the staying power of non-English language maintenance. It remained in the very structural warp-and-woof of daily American life, with its ethnic humor, clubs, politics, foods, and celebrations—among the Scandinavian-Americans, among the German-Americans, among the Irish-Americans, among the old Sephardic and German-Jewish families —i.e., among those whose Americanization and social mobility was greatest. Non-Anglo ethnicity was always a quiet, hidden, lost continent, a veritable Atlantis. American life, for millions of Americans, was always bicultural. Below the public surface, with its *cultura franca* and *lingua franca* of general American life, there was the private depth, the color and individuality of non-Anglo ethnicity.

What has happened in the past ten years is that this invisible continent has come into view and that many Americans have come to feel, believe, and say that this is as it should be. Will it sink from view again, perhaps to be fully and finally disintegrated? Perhaps, but probably not. It will probably settle a bit and be less noticeable than it was from 1968 to 1972, and, indeed, it has already begun to do so. However, mobilized ethnicities that have developed their own ideological systems (as has the "new ethnicity" in the United States) disappear very slowly, if at all. Remember also that they have become part and parcel of the generational self-definition of many of our young people. For them it is related to a view of the world, to a view of themselves, to a view of what America is all about and must yet become. Ethnicity has become a base for tackling social problems and, as such, it will be infinitely more capable of self-regeneration and innovation than in former days. It no longer tries to be a pale copy of "long ago" in "the old country." It is a happily evolving, open-ended, creative process with both American and old-country nuances, but with a resultant force and flavor of its own.[3] It still fosters intimacy, but it also seeks relevance and quality, a trinity that is hard to beat!

My prediction, therefore, as we approach the third century of American life, is that non-Anglo ethnic maintenance will continue to bear fruit, and that for some of its adherents it will include and will foster various degrees of non-English language maintenance as well. Indeed, I am convinced that there will be all degrees and all combinations of both non-Anglo ethnic maintenance and non-English language maintenance. Both will be conducted somewhat more quietly, perhaps, than they have been of late (provided our overall political and social scenes also quiet down and ease up with respect to the reward systems under their control) but basically they will both be sufficiently multifaceted to appeal not only to Blacks, Chicanos, Indians, and "Ricans," but also to the fancy Protestants, fancy Catholics, and fancy Jews. In sum, my prediction is that when your and my great-grandchildren celebrate the 300th anniversary of the United States they

3. Note, e.g., the "Scandinavian," "Slavic," and Jewish ethnicities that exist in the U.S.A. without any concurrent "old country" equivalents at all.

will still find non-Anglo ethnic maintenance and non-English language maintenance with us. They will find them changed. They will find them enriched. They will find them creative. They will find them stimulating. They will find them self-critical and critical of others. They will find them wonderful. They will find them part and parcel of America, just as they have always been. And they will find America richer because of them, more exciting because of them, and more mature because of them!

Commentary

FRANKLIN D. SCOTT: Professor Fishman's analysis is judicious, relevant, filled with insights. Nevertheless, the prisms in our eyes, while looking at the same phenomena, catch different flashes of light and color, note different emphases. To some extent these differences are doubtless matters of terminology; still they may be worth pondering.

Dr. Fishman has neatly analyzed and illustrated the fascinating blend we have in the American people—a complex of adaptations to the new world and retentions of the old. As he so rightly states, two hundred years is but a brief moment in historic time and we cannot therefore know what the ultimate result of this blend will be. It will certainly be several generations before we attain the old ideal of a "composite nationality for the American people." Americanization (whatever that may mean) is a slow and halting process. It is the complexity of this process that I wish to emphasize.

As to language, we might easily have had a regional patchwork quilt. Even small Switzerland has nourished four separate languages and yet maintained its national identity. In the United States there are only scattered pockets where anything but English is the first language. The reasons for this are important historically and currently. "Interaction-based social mobility" is surely a factor, but there are other factors that deserve to be recognized. Again, Switzerland has had manifold forms of social interaction for centuries yet has retained her four tongues. What would have happened in America if the Dutch or Swedes had held political dominance over a long period? Would their languages have been able to withstand the challenge of the diverse tongues of successive waves of immigrants? Was English more viable, perhaps, because of its increasing strength as a global language, and the accompanying fact that some immigrants knew at least a little English before they arrived?

Another factor may have been of even greater significance: the vast majority of immigrants came to the United States and Canada deliberately, of their own volition. The hundreds of thousands and the millions were converts to the American dream before they left the old world; they reached out for "the riches and the perfection that lay beyond the sunset." Language was to them incidental; the English language was just a part of the new life that they were not only ready but eager to accept. The naturalness of their mother tongue and its associations with religion and nation held large numbers of the first generation to its use in home and church, but such influences had a diminishing effect on their children.

Also of importance is that maintenance or non-maintenance of language and customs depended not alone on the immigrants themselves. Especially in times of national crisis the larger community exerts powerful pressures toward conformity. The Scandinavians suffered these pressures during World War I when the use of non-English languages in churches and newspapers was viewed with suspicion. The abandonment of the mother tongues was due to come anyway with the shift of generations, but wartime pressures speeded the change. During World War II suspicion was much less unreasonable (except for the attitude toward the Japanese), partly because the use of other languages had greatly diminished, partly because the process of Americanization had built up stronger American loyalties. Dr. Fishman, I suspect, would call both these tendencies deethnization; the little prism in my eye gets instead a primarily positive reflection: while the language shift must be admitted as loss, the building of a stronger sense of belonging to the new community must be reckoned as gain.

Ethnicity, or national origin, is an inheritance, something indissoluble, impossible to renounce. In migration, unto the second and the third generations and farther, ethnic inheritance influences a person's earliest and most intimate social relations, his sense of belonging, his identity. In some the concept of ethnic affinity may be subconscious, unrecognized until a special circumstance, such as a casual trip to the ancestral country, brings it to the surface. A common experience is for the supposedly Americanized grandson or great-granddaughter to feel a need to trace his/her ancestry, to satisfy a yearning to know where he came from, to discover the roots of his identity. Questionnaires cannot hope to discover the extent or the depth of this urge to establish contact with one's past; here is something we cannot measure with the computer. But it is a real and lasting urge, and its fulfillment may enrich one's life.

Therefore, I would like to raise certain questions and to provide additional items for consideration.

1. First, I cannot quite accept the statement that "most of those countless millions who crossed the Atlantic, the Rio Grande, (etc.) . . . had not been ethnically mobilized one way or the other." The Germans who flocked to America in the late nineteenth century veritably personified nationality in migration. The Irish used the United States as a base for nationalistic agitation. For our present purposes the most relevant example is of the Swedes and Norwegians, migrating vigorously during just those decades when the conflict over the Union was hottest. They were bitterly conscious of national status, and this bitterness complicated their relationships (in church and school and politics) for decades, and on to this day.

When to this politically conscious nationalism we add the deep love of the northern mountains and the forests, of the scenes and friendships of childhood, it seems irrefutable that the Scandinavians came to their new home still retaining warm affinities with the land and the people they left behind, imbued with a strong sense of nationhood. Ethnicity itself migrated, and in the process it was frequently strengthened.

2. I wish to emphasize the point that Dr. Fishman makes that the persistence of ethnicity in our Anglo-dominated society is largely owing to the diversity, the almost limitless multiplicity of ethnic groups. In countries where only two or three groups attempt to coexist confrontation is invited—witness Northern Ireland, the Middle East, Uganda, Vietnam. But in the United States no single group has been strong enough to challenge the dominant element, and for the most part has not wanted to. Since there has been no threat, tolerance of ethnicity has been the rule, and it is only in the last decade that we have seen serious protest by the Negroes, the Indians, the Chicanos—and they have not yet combined their efforts.

3. Ethnicity alone is not enough. Meaningful maintenance requires a group and a community of interest. A fisherman of Lofoten and a lawyer from Oslo would probably have very little in common, whereas a university man from Oslo and a university man from Copenhagen might quickly establish bonds of mutual interest. In America the same factors are at work. The rough speech and manners of a Swedish-American railway worker may actually repel his fellow Swedish-American reared in the cultural circles of Hollywood or Cambridge. For either language maintenance or ethnic maintenance there must be factors of personality and education and interest that nourish a group relationship. Only the *combination* of ethnicity and class creates a firm foundation for intimacy and perpetuation of bonds. This combination is what Milton Gordon refers to as "ethclass."

4. The ethnic base in America is broadening, partly on account of the factors just mentioned. Persons with common interests, even if their ethnic inheritance is not pure, may be effective supporters of ethnic maintenance. In the colleges and universities, to cite just one illustration, courses in the Scandinavian languages and cultures have been burgeoning. And who are the students who

come to learn the Nordic languages and cultures? According to
Gene Gage's recent surveys, a surprisingly small percentage come
from Scandinavian backgrounds.

5. Now, two questions. First, what do we mean by language
maintenance and ethnic maintenance?

Even in their own countries people do not maintain their
languages intact from century to century and generation to generation. Language is a living, changing thing. Immigrants brought
with them, for the most part, the peasant dialects of their provinces. Is it this we wish to preserve? Clearly not. And in language
classes it is the current speech of each country that is taught. Is
this really language maintenance? The language that must be
taught is a *new* language, and it can be learned just as well by
a student of any ethnic background.

Second, what do we understand about the term ethnic maintenance? Or the Scandinavian presence in America? Is it bicultural-
ism, implying equal concern for the inherited culture and for the
adopted one? Such is difficult to maintain—how, for instance,
could a man get his work done if he observed all the religious
and political holidays of two cultural traditions? There are, of
course, a few talented persons who are thoroughly bilingual and
bicultural, but they are rare. Ethnic maintenance cannot depend
on them.

Do we mean, then, by ethnic maintenance merely the preservation of a few isolated folk customs such as Midsummer, or
the recently sanctified Saint Lucia's Day? Certainly such things are
not in themselves sufficient to signify ethnic maintenance.

For me, the most meaningful term and idea is "the dual
heritage." Like an inheritance from one's parents it may be
small or great, it may be quickly squandered, or it may be cultivated and expanded. One portion of it may be forgotten, another
portion treasured. The maintenance of a dual heritage might mean
for one person the continuance of the religious traditions of his
forefathers but abandonment of other facets of the former culture,
while in his professional life he adopted the practices of his new

land. For another it could mean sustaining business and personal contacts with the home of his ancestors, and for still another the preservation of the literature or the art of the old country along with the cultivation of similar interests in the new. But he need not become de-ethnicized; he need not renounce a love of the midnight sun or of salmon fishing in clear streams just because he has also come to love the Rocky Mountains or the waving fields of grain. People who enjoy the full completeness of the dual heritage are few, but those who possess it in some degree are many, and they are significant for the development of mutual understanding.

My last question underlies the whole idea of Scanpresence. What is the content of this ethnic maintenance or Scandinavian presence? Scandinavians in America have already modified the heritage they brought in their immigrant chests. They have adapted and borrowed from their new neighbors, and they have reinterpreted their own past. Are we now talking about preservation of these borrowings and reinterpretations, or are we thinking of some "pure" nineteenth-century old-country background, or is it in our minds that ethnic maintenance means keeping in touch with the Denmark, the Finland, the Iceland, the Norway, the Sweden of today? Or does the Scandinavian presence in America involve the blending of all these traditions and associations?

Discussion

JOSHUA A. FISHMAN: Professor Scott has brought out many important issues. He has pinpointed them and highlighted and refined them. It is his certainty that it is not the local dialects or the peasant dialects or any particular regional customs that are of concern. Perhaps he is right, but perhaps not. It may be that many local variants have become more important here than they were in the old country. Perhaps the articulation of local and national is part of the dual heritage. But it might be well to stress that this dual heritage is also one of infinite variety and that in a voluntaristic society, where ethnicity is a voluntaristic enterprise, it is as much a voluntary pursuit as is contributing to the Red Cross or any other activity responding entirely to the process of mutual consultation and influence. It is a cloth of many colors and many strands and, therefore, probably not merely as problematic as presented, but infinitely more problematic, and infinitely more problematic than it would be in the very home countries from which national groups derive the ethnicity to which they voluntarily subscribe.

There is a great exodus from ethnicity all over the world and, in fact, the very same ethnicities that purportedly are being preserved and developed in the United States are, at the same time, being abandoned in Scandinavia and in other parts of the world. That is part of the problem, and going back to Scandinavia, hearing standard Norwegian, or some variety of Norwegian, or standard Swedish does not at all motivate ethnicity on the part of the American who experiences it, because it is not the same experience for the Norwegian or the Swede with whom he is in contact.

Some of the very things that are unacceptable "at home" or "in the old country" might be quite acceptable in the United States. Some of the things that have relatively little prominence in the old country may acquire great prominence here. The whole problematical context is different. It may be just as it is with the Jews and the Ukrainians and the Armenians, with the overseas Chinese and the overseas Indians and the French Canadians with their feeling that the real ethnicity has gone to pot in the old country, and that we out here are the only ones who are doing it right, who are taking it seriously, and who are facing the challenge of doing so, not only in terms of self-preservation, but in terms of interaction with the best of mankind. All of that is what we are faced with here, and if it turns out that the peasant or the rural has a particular attraction for us here and now, that is to be expected in terms of our need here for ethnicity of a kind that is no longer necessary in the old country.

Therefore, we must realize that just as the Americanization possibility is sometimes greater for certain populations abroad than

it is for some of our native-born ethnics, just so the ethnicity possibilities are sometimes greater for some native-born Americans
than they are for actual immigrants. In both cases—in all cases—we
are embarked on something extremely difficult; and you will not,
I believe, be able to decide what language maintenance "really"
is and what ethnic maintenance "really" is, because, to use another
Old Testament parallel, "I am what I am." Ethnic maintenance is
what it happens to be for any particular group at any particular
time. And that's what language maintenance is. It is a whole
orchestration of different voluntaristic decisions. Each decision will
have to compete with the other. There are going to be a great
number of partially satisfying and partially dissatisfying solutions,
all of which have the potential of growth and creativity exactly
because of the kind of challenge and the kind of problem that they
face as a result of being "here" and not "there."

JOHN CHRISTIANSON: Professor Fishman's statement about standard Norwegian is particularly appropriate in talking about the
new ethnicity. I have the impression, at least, that standard Norwegian is whatever the person the Norwegian is talking to chooses
as his standard. This important element of choice has been
touched upon, but needs to be emphasized with regard to the new
ethnicity, for it seems to me that choice is one of its important
characteristics.

It is an eclectic kind of ethnicity—you might even call it
plastic. Professor Scott regards ethnicity as an inheritance and
went on to discuss the element of choice. There is a paradox here.
The old folk ethnicity of a preliterate or barely literate and more
or less culturally isolated community is not the kind of thing we
are talking about today. The new ethnics do not get their values
from that kind of folk community. They get their values from an
increasingly wide range of media. If they want to know how a
peasant dresses, they don't go and look at their neighbor who
happens to be a peasant, because they can't find any peasants.
They look in *Vogue* and see the costumes that are being featured

for the "rich peasant look"; and that very phrase has been used in *Vogue* recently. They look at movies, they look at pictures, they read books, they take Scandinavian or attend ethnic studies classes and they put their ethnic values together in this eclectic way. This media orientation of the new ethnicity, this voluntary factor or this resolution of the problem of alienation that Professor Fishman pinpointed so exactly, is another aspect of the same thing and it needs to be emphasized.

It seems to me that this is one of the reasons why the specific ethnic background—mixed, pure, or whatever—is more or less irrelevant to the actual choice. If a person is interested in folk dancing, he might join a Danish folk-dancing group, deck himself out in a Danish folk costume, and become a new ethnic of one kind or another. If he is interested in Scandinavian studies, he may go to a university or college and learn to speak one of the Scandinavian languages fluently, then perhaps go on to live in Scandinavia temporarily or permanently. But in either case, his own ethnic background is more or less irrelevant. The element of choice, choice through a wide range of media, is an important element of the new ethnicity which really forms the framework of much of our activities.

BJØRN JENSEN: What concerns us is how the points raised by Professor Fishman apply to Scandinavia. And that's why we should bring in, at the earliest possible moment, this consideration: that of all of the European immigrant groups, and all immigrant groups generally coming to the United States, Scandinavians—perhaps, but only perhaps next to the Irish—are closest to the white Anglo-Saxon community.

GENE G. GAGE: Both Mr. Cohen and Professor Fishman have noted that Scandinavians are adept at forming organizations and that these are formed solely because of the ethnic presence in America. There are a couple of pertinent exceptions. Two of perhaps the strongest and most comprehensive Scandinavian organizations—The American-Scandinavian Foundation and the Society for the Advancement of Scandinavian Study—have been founded by boards of trustees who have been about 80 percent Anglo or non-Scandinavian. This interest in Scandinavia on the part of non-Scandinavians goes back a long way: easily into the middle of the last century.

Another point that will no doubt arise is that of conflicting movements and pressures in American society. For example, ethnicity seems to have a connection, both implicit and explicit, with the family. And if we have an Atlantis of ethnicity rising from the sea, it is a very small one compared to the Women's Liberation movement. I don't know which will be the more powerful, but they're certainly not compatible.

We should make some definitions right away if we can. There are so many special things about Scandinavia and the Scandinavian presence in America that it boggles the mind. Nothing has been mentioned so far about Scandinavian studies. You may think that these are obviously offered for Scandinavians, but that's not the truth at all. I happen to be in the statistics business and I can prove that the overwhelming majority of young Americans studying in Scandinavia are not Scandinavian by background at all.

S. RALPH COHEN: My interest is directed to the question of existing ethnic organizations and where they go from here. Certainly, we should consider the much broader area of American interest in Scandinavia without ethnic connection. I have had the experience of talking to Scandinavian clubs and study classes in New York colleges: in one case, the whole group seemed to be of Jewish or Italian background; in the other, the three Scandinavians were outnumbered by five Puerto Ricans.

In thinking about ethnicity, one has the feeling that we are dealing with situations in which individuals are complex in themselves and, particularly in this country, rendered even more so by circumstances. Professor Vecoli has referred to himself at various times as an Italian, a Midwesterner, and a Yankee. I am sure he is all of these things and probably more. Professor Fishman and I come from similar backgrounds, yet I suspect that there may be cultural differences between us. Most of us in this country have a quality, perhaps unique to Americans; we are polyhistors. We can all be Irish on St. Patrick's Day.

Both Mr. Gage and Professor Fishman have pointed out something new and explosive in the situation we are now considering—an interest in ethnicity that comes from a broader spectrum of the population and from the generation of protest. This is both a challenge and an opportunity. The fact is that the new interest in ethnicity is in large part a radical expression. The matter before us is whether the Scandinavian-American establishment as we know it today will be willing and able to accept this new interest and adjust to it; and, if so, how one goes about ensuring this adjustment.

MARION J. NELSON: Bjørn Jensen has asked how we are to handle the closeness of the Scandinavian group to the WASPs. After all, we are white, we are Protestant and almost Anglo-Saxon. We considered this very seriously in our planning and at one point, actually thought of making it the subject of the Seminar: where do the Scandinavians stand in the new lining-up of ethnicities in America? Should we be on the side of the WASPs or on the side of the Spaniards, the Italians, the Greeks, and the Slavs? I could still, after this Seminar, conceive a conference devoted precisely to the question, because if we consider ourselves one unified body, there may come a time when we will have to choose where we do fall. If we accept the new individuality we have been discussing, and voluntary ethnicity as authentic ethnicity, then we might never have to face it.

CARLTON C. QUALEY: In some quarters "ethnicity" has become a term of controversy which obscures constructive action. A black has called it "the new tribalism." Someone else has termed it "the new apartheid." And *The New York Times* has said it is a red herring.

However, I quarrel with investing the idea with any serious ideology: so much of current ethnicity is self-serving in the sense that it has been adopted by groups with problems of their own that they seek to project on the general community for solution. Thus the sense of ethnicity and the whole movement so evangelistically treated by Professor Fishman may not be very helpful in solving the problems set forth for this Seminar. It may be a matter of terminology and a rather subjective thing, but I don't think it is particularly helpful.

TORE TALLROTH: Professor Fishman indicated that the increased awareness of ethnicity began to develop around 1965. This may be true in the United States. The world trend, on which he touched lightly, shows an increased wave of nationalism in many countries. It has had political and other effects as well; for example, one can observe that the Belgian language problem is more acute and difficult than it was ten or fifteen years ago. And someone has said that we might become involved in local wars. I sincerely hope they would be very local, but people will find themselves taking shelter in their national identity because they are afraid we cannot solve the urgent problems of living together on a broader scale. An increased interest in national origin may be a good thing, but there is the inherent danger that people who may feel themselves excluded from the organized ways to influence politics will take this flight into national identity instead.

C. PETER STRONG: There is another interesting feature which, just in passing, might be considered. It seems to me that we have had a generation that feels powerless and almost disinherited and that has turned its back on its own ethnic identity; this is the counterculture. It has probably come and gone, but there could be a new promised land such as we saw in the mid-1960s.

Håkan Berggren: We have been forbidden to be too historical. Nevertheless, if we were to have a conference on the American presence in Scandinavia, what topics would be considered? There would be Sweden as a marketplace, a test tube for American products, and a number of other things. We would also want to consider the origins of the Swedish welfare state. How did the original concept of welfare come about in Sweden? It was the influence of America, of the hundreds of thousands of interesting suggestions that flooded back from liberal groups in the 1880s.

From what I have seen and heard in various colleges and universities here in the United States of what students are concerning themselves with, I believe that in defining the kind of presence we want to maintain and the sort of institutions needed to maintain it, we will have to touch strongly on professional and intellectual, rather than purely nationalistic interests.

Joshua A. Fishman: I would like to point out that we are involved in a human experience that is not merely historical, but which is constant, and that we must not treat it as being unprecedented or unreasonable.

De-ethnicization movements such as Women's Liberation are strong in the world, but they have been strong for a long time, and the fact that we are still discussing our own topic indicates the limits of that strength. It is certainly no stronger than such movements as urbanization or industrialization. I submit that Women's Liberation will not be around a hundred years from now, whereas ethnicity will be. This is because Women's Liberation has nothing to do with special identity, but only with social role. It will fractionate into various other social problems which will come up after it peaks, as I think it already has done in its extreme manifestations. There are even so many ethnic subdivisions within Women's Liberation, among the Puerto Ricans, in the Orthodox Church, and in most ethnic groups—all dealing in terms of the participation within the ethnic community as redefined by different groups of women.

Of course all of these crises are opportunities for ideologized movements to move in on them and make of them what they can. That has always been the American experience: ethnicity is constantly being reinterpreted. The de-ethnicized ethnic society is about a hundred years old in the United States and is still with us: the case of the Scandinavian society on whose board most members are non-Scandinavians is paralleled among Germans, Greeks, and many other distinguished groups. And that is one of the ways of reinterpreting ethnicity and of movements like Women's Liberation within it.

There is another way, which we have not touched upon, and that is traditionalization—returning to tradition, finding and preserving the pure tradition—and that is going on, too.

If we feel more comfortable with an even less precise term than ethnicity, if we even find ourselves somewhat disturbed by it and embarrassed when it is called a new tribalism, or multiple apartheid or self-serving, do not fear: you can go home without deciding on a thing, without understanding a thing and ethnicity just won't be there.

Settle down and be comfortable with it. Ethnics and minorities are not destined to be the uniquely non-self-serving groups in society. Republicans are not non-self-serving, or so we're told. Not even the March of Dimes is. Nobody is. No social formation is non-self-serving, and minorities must not enter into a mutual destruction pact, nor resort to self-destruction, in order to assert their dignity.

There is, of course, a danger of isolation, ghettoization or extreme politicization. But I submit that there is less danger of this among ethnic groups in American life now than there was previously. We are even past the peak with respect to those that have been ideologized.

Everyone, or almost everyone, assumes a dual heritage and if it is non-isolating and non-encapsulating, there is nothing to fear. One can enjoy his in the most constructive, enriching, gratifying, and stimulating way he can think of; for never before or anywhere else has ethnicity had such limitless horizons.

THE INSTITUTIONAL ANATOMY OF
SCANPRESENCE

The Church and Scandinavian Ethnicity

Panel: RALPH J. JALKANEN (Chairman), CONRAD BERGENDOFF, DAVID W. PREUS, ENOK MORTENSEN, WESLEY M. WESTERBERG, PETER A. MUNCH, DOUGLAS J. OLILLA, JR. (Guest Informant), DUANE R. LINDBERG (Student Representative)

Introduction

RALPH J. JALKANEN: If anyone is to speak for tradition, it must be the religionist. For is not religion, by its nature and from time immemorial, one of the most traditional concerns in any society?

Here, we wish to explore not only the traditional aspects of religion in our heritage, but also the messianic or futurist aspects unique to the Judeo-Christian tradition. Within it, for the first time, history was not regarded as cyclical, but as a process begun at a given point in time with a purposeful pursuit of a goal in the future. Hence, whatever we say about history and heritage must be interpreted in the light of Pollock's "Image of the Future," wherein all of man's actions and aspirations are oriented toward the future, resulting in the historical paradox in which man is said "to imagine the past and remember the future."

Religion is normally defined as divisive and it often is, especially when situated in the midst of a competitive society and culture, because it emphasizes belonging to in-groups that exercise hostility, or at least indifference, toward out-groups. Nevertheless, in its stance of ethnic inclusiveness, religion may be regarded as binding, nurturing, and healing.

For our purposes religion may be defined as that vehicle by which man expresses his supra-empirical concern, limited to how this is expressed through the church. Of course one is free to make the judgment with Lukmann that religion is invisible and therefore is manifested in multifarious ways in the life of man. Here, however, we are considering that religious concern which is exemplified through the denominations and their congregations in America.

Consider: Christianity manifests itself in visible form in church, denomination, sect, or cult. A church is the universal sphere, the ecclesia, exemplified in the Roman Catholic Church, the Church of Finland, or the Church of Sweden. Typically, it is monolithic, societal and inclusive. There is no church or ecclesia in America. In America we speak about denominations and it is to this group we address ourselves. The third group, the sect, is informal, exclusive and limited in its membership and goals.

In America, the sect often becomes a denomination, as in the case of the Methodists, which began as a sect and ended up as one of America's largest denominations. Thus, we have a continuum from church to denomination to sect to cult (which consists of a group of persons with a similar passionate interest and commitment, but no formal organization). Consequently our discussion is limited to the denominations and possibly some sectarian elements.

The Augustana Church in America and in Sweden

CONRAD BERGENDOFF: The Augustana Church offers a unique example of the creative ability of a large body of immigrants to build an influential social and religious organization within the new environment. It also provides a pattern of how such an organization finally adapts to the new society of which it becomes a part.

How large a segment of the Swedish immigration does the Augustana body represent? It is difficult to be precise because of the vague periphery of the body, that is, membership statistics may give a central focus but the edges extend into an enlarging penumbra. It makes a difference, too, what year or period is taken as representative of the whole era.

The first organization of the Lutheran congregations dates from 1850 at the very start of the real immigration of the Swedish population. In 1860, at the organization of the Synod, 20 percent of the Swedish nationals were identified with the new body. A decade later the percentage had fallen to 16.8. Nor was the Synod able to gather in the growing emigration of the eighties and nineties. From 1881 to 1900 the incoming waves numbered over 500,000—the Synod grew from 70,000 to around 200,000. A number of factors convince me that the height of the Synod's activity among Swedish immigrants was reached around 1910. A few years later World War I put an end to the influx, and the groups that came after 1920 proved largely alien to the church. In 1910 at the fiftieth anniversary the venerable Eric Norelius, our best historian of the early years, estimated the membership, in a loose sense, at some 300,000. There were then over a million people of Swedish stock in the United States. This means that the Synod had won only about a third of the entire number. Even when we recall that in practically every one of the more than 1,000 communities where Augustana had congregations the church included more than the confirmed and baptized (family relationships increased the reach of the membership), I doubt that the Lutheran Church can count more than half of the immigrants in its sphere of activity. Nevertheless, it would still be true that the Synod stands out as the largest single organization of the Swedish immigration, and for a hundred years it helped fashion the ideas and ideals of the newcomers to American life.

Of even greater interest is the character of the institutions they brought into being. At first the preservation of the worship they knew from the homeland was primary. Much has been made of the antagonism of these immigrants to the Church of Sweden. A careful study will reveal that such hostility as existed was directed toward the ministry. It did not extend to the liturgy, to the sacraments, to the practice of confirmation, or to the devotional literature, especially the "Psalm book." The achievement of the Synod was to create a worshiping community in the new land, and when educational and publishing agencies were required, to build schools, colleges, a seminary, and to publish a religious literature —in short, to reproduce in a foreign land a culture that was the heritage of these people. Because that culture was so intimately related to religion in the homeland, the ideals envisioned in this land included literature, music, and art as well as doctrine, ethics, and social behavior. A little-recognized factor is a more or less conscious criticism of the religious life of the new homeland.

I do not think we have sufficiently understood how little was borrowed in those early days from the "Yankee" environment. The lines of communication went back to Sweden as the new church structured its life and program although not so much to the ecclesiastical establishment—in 1895 and even in 1910 the appearance of a Swedish bishop in America awakened curiosity, even opposition. But all the cultural and religious roots were in Sweden, and models were found in tradition. Through children's and old people's homes, hospitals, and even mutual insurance societies, this community sought to assure the material welfare of its members.

There were those in Sweden and in America who thought a Swedish colony could preserve itself here. They were mistaken. The leaders had no such goal. They wanted to preserve the most precious of their possessions, their religious faith. But they knew they must recognize others of the same faith. The very year that saw the separation of Swedes and Norwegians in the original Synod witnessed the drawing together of Augustana with fellow Lutherans in the older Eastern states. Joining the General Council signaled the way of the future. For from its inception in 1867 the Council prized the membership of Augustana, and in this fellowship the Augustana Synod began to learn to speak, worship, sing, study, and work in the language of the new land. When the General Council merged with two other bodies in 1917 to form the United Lutheran Church, Augustana was not ready to give up its customs. But close relations continued until in 1961 it did lose its identity along with Finnish and Danish synods in a comprehensive merger resulting in the Lutheran Church in America.

At the time it ceased to exist as a church body, the Augustana Church had grown to a half million members, served by 1,400 pastors in almost as many congregations. In the past half century its Swedish character had been modified by intermarriage, by a home mission policy that embraced a community rather than a cultural group, and by educational institutions that gradually led the way to integration with American society. Now a part of a three-million-member church body, Augustana people may well ask, what of future relationships with modern Sweden?

The Augustana Book Concern, the leading publisher of Swedish literature in America and of all the religious books of Augustana, belongs to the past. The Augustana Seminary, for a century the training center of the ministry of the Synod, is now a part of the Chicago Lutheran School of Theology. The Swedish-America which some of us remember from our childhood has vanished; another generation will have no idea of the nature of its existence.

Yet, when an old tree dies, new shoots may spring up from the roots. We are in a fourth and fifth generation. And some of these are asking about the places in Sweden whence their ancestors came. An increasing number are searching the church records of Sweden, and establishing contacts with Swedish cousins or second cousins. Since the visit of Archbishop Söderblom in 1923 new contacts have been developed with the clergy and universities. Augustana men have been active as translators and interpreters of Swedish theologians, notably Billing, Aulén, Hygren, contributing to the American theological stream in universities and journals. Dean Wald of Augustana pioneered in summer schools in Sweden and in bringing Swedish students to the campus. Gustavus Adolphus has won fame for its Nobel commemoration. The Augustana Library and Historical Society have long lists of publications and have been persistent in the collection of archives, cooperating in film reproduction with the Royal Library of Sweden. Augustana churchmen have worked closely with Swedish leaders in the Lutheran World Federation and the World Council of Churches with results that carry over into the new Lutheran Church in America.

In a sense the Augustana Church has not ceased to exist. It lives on in the conscious or subconscious memory of multitudes who still think of Sweden as somehow associated with the sources and the goals of their lives. If I were to estimate in what respects the Augustana element has influenced the larger church of which it is now a part, I would list: (a) a strong liturgical interest, (b) a social consciousness that insists on the relevance of the Gospel to current issues, (c) a doctrine of the ministry that stresses higher education of pastors but at the same time allows an active role for the laity, and (d) a pervasive ecumenical endeavor. Issues of an earlier pietism linger, but these often give way to a rising secularism, still (e) an evangelistic strain points in the direction of an emphasis on distinctive Christian faith and life.

Norwegian Lutheranism in America

DAVID W. PREUS: Norwegian influence in the life of the American Lutheran Church is still markedly present, but increasingly unidentified as Norwegian. The greatest indication of ethnic awareness is the frequent use of ethnic jokes at conferences and conventions. Humorous asides about Norwegians, Germans, or Danes are frequent.

Norwegian-language use is virtually at an end. The Norwegian Memorial Church in Minneapolis is still a Norwegian-language church. It is the only ALC church to my knowledge where Norwegian is the primary language. There are a handful of churches that maintain a monthly or annual Norwegian service. As a part of the sesquicentennial observance in 1975, we intend to hold festival Norwegian-language services in sixteen different locations in the United States. Preachers are still available who can handle the language.

The elements of church life that continue to reflect a Norwegian heritage are both formal and informal. *The Service Book and Hymnal* provides the main link, but the new "Red Hymnbook" really signaled the end of the immigrant era for the Norwegians. The primary service now used is Germanic and Swedish in background. The old Norwegian service is used only on commemorative occasions and then requires a special printing because of its unfamiliarity. The "Red Hymnal" includes a handful of Norwegian hymns but a substantial additional number of German, Danish, Swedish, and English hymns that were used in the Norwegian Church.

There is widespread American awareness of the American Lutheran Church located in Oslo, Norway, and there is considerable official traffic back and forth between officials of the Norwegian Church and the American Lutheran Church. Within the last several months, Bishop Lønning of Norway visited extensively in the United States and Dr. Schiotz is currently visiting in Norway. Seminary teacher exchanges occur occasionally.

The close identification of the American Lutheran Church with its colleges has resulted in a mutual affirming of our ethnic heritage. St. Olaf College and Luther College with their strong historical associations, libraries, and museums are centers of Norwegian consciousness. They both reflect their churches' historic background and also feed a continuing ethnic consciousness into the life of the church. Their musical organizations use a good deal of Norwegian material. Their athletic teams are known as "Norsemen" and "Vikings." Their radio stations have continued to provide Norwegian services and a good deal of news from the Norwegian Church. The same is true in a lesser degree of Augsburg, Concordia, Augustana, Waldorf, and Pacific Lutheran University.

Many formerly Norwegian Lutheran congregations continue an "Inner Mission" type of piety that has direct ethnic roots. The memory of this rootage is rapidly fading, however, and while the particular emphases are retained, they are not identified as Norwegian in background. I refer to many churches where special

evangelistic services are held, where special meetings for edifica-
tion, prayer, and support of missions are ongoing activities. The
Lutheran Evangelistic Movement, a collection of Scandinavian-
background people who band together for these purposes, gives
the most formal structure to this pattern. As with the old "Inner
Mission" activity, it becomes something of a church-within-a-
church movement. This type of activity continues to be influential
in a much wider range of congregations than those who have some
formal tie to an original "evangelistic" movement.

Many congregations, especially in rural areas, still have
enough population stability to think of themselves as "Norwegian"
churches. The number diminishes each year, however, and with
population mobility and intermarriage and absence of new immigration, the consciousness will gradually end. I do expect, however, an ongoing awareness of the contribution of "Norwegian"
Lutheranism to "American" Lutheranism. Our people think of
themselves now as American Lutherans who are heirs of Norwegian, German, and Danish church history.

The great majority of churches founded by Norwegian Lutheran immigrants are no longer viewed by the surrounding population as "Norwegian" churches. When the Norwegian Lutheran
Church in America changed its name to the Evangelical Lutheran
Church, the process of re-identification was well on its way. After
ten years of life in a mixed ethnic background church named the
American Lutheran Church, and with the mixed ethnic background of most congregations, there is little community identification of churches as "Norwegian."

There will continue to be a Norwegian influence in the
American Lutheran Church. It will be recognized, however, only
as one of several "heritages" that are recognizable in our history.

On the Danish Churches in America

ENOK MORTENSEN: Among the hundreds of Lutheran churches
built by Danish-Americans, only one or two, to my knowledge,

still use the adjective "Danish." But there are other evidences of Danish origin, such as the use of Danish place-names—one congregation, for example, being named after the Danish flag—and a considerable number of churches called St. Ansgar's in memory of the Apostle of the North. Architecturally, few church buildings in the beginning deviated from the norm of the typical Protestant structures found all over America. In some instances, however, particularly in Canada, attempts have been made to copy half-forgotten village churches of Denmark with their white walls, red roofs, and painted gables. It is noteworthy that while the early churches were built mostly in a plain and simple style like so many midwestern churches, it is only in the later years that attempts were made to copy the Danish village churches. The majority of these churches had an altar painting and an incredible number featured a replica of a statue of Christ. Yet another reminder of Danish origins was, and still is, the model of a ship suspended from the ceiling above the nave.

Today, except for an occasional service in the Danish language at Easter and Christmas, very few congregations have retained the Danish language. Even before the mergers of 1961, that is, the establishment of the American Lutheran Church and the Lutheran Church in America, both the Lutheran Synods of Danish origin cooperated with other American Lutherans in the publication of *The Service Book and Hymnal*. However, the introduction of the new "Red Hymnal" came to be viewed almost as radical and traumatic a departure from tradition as the loss of the Danish language. The old hymnal, based upon our own heritage in hymnody and published and utilized by the two Danish Synods in America, was indeed a cherished volume. Typically, many people were relatively unconcerned about the intricacies of theological and doctrinal discussions lying behind the new publication. The Danish heritage was to them a particular view of life, best symbolized by their hymnbook with its rich and hallowed treasures. In it, over 150 out of a total of 450 hymns consisted of Danish translations. In contrast, the new *Service Book and Hymnal* with its 602 selec-

tions contains only seventeen hymns of Danish origin. Consequently, some congregations continued to use the old familiar
hymnal, others compromised by including a supplement of some
28 Danish hymns in the new hymnal. Moreover, the supplement
has been reprinted several times, the last edition as recently as
1973.

The new hymnal, along with the merger of the Lutheran
Synods, introduced strange, new liturgical forms to Danish wor-
shipers. In spite of the usual chanting of collects and responses, the
service in the Danish tradition was singularly plain and unorna-
mented, especially in congregations with strong folk church
traditions.

However, the majority of congregations accepted the new
forms, although with a certain reluctance. Yielding to conformity
was involved. Did not the majority of other Lutherans springing
from Northern Europe use the services? Few relished the idea of
being conspicuously different.

But there are congregations which still cling to the old patterns, accepting minor changes in an effort to embrace the new, but
doing so within the familiar forms. For example, the custom of
having a deacon read the opening and closing prayers is retained in
several parishes. Needless to say, there have been occasional con-
flicts in which a zealous young pastor from a different ethnic and
religious background has confronted a congregation with pro-
nounced Danish traditions. One such dramatized his resentment of
the heritage by tearing from the hymnals the supplement containing the Danish hymns.

However difficult to pin down by definition, rituals and forms
have deep roots. Consider here that sector of the Danish-American
church influenced by N. F. S. Grundtvig, or the so-called "happy
Danes." (I don't know why the "holy Danes" couldn't also be
happy, and I think they are.) In any event this group possessed a
view of life with a quality all its own, wary of pomposity, verbosity,
and evangelistic exhibitionism. In its perspective man was clearly

created in the image of God, implying that the totality of his life, not only his soul but his body, was good and acceptable to God. God was present not only in his life in the world of the spirit, but his entire earthly existence was under God's care and judgment, and under his love and grace. The Danish-American folk schools of the so-called "happy Danes," that were an integral part of the Danish-American Lutheran Church, have today all but disappeared. But once having meditated on the concern of God for the totality of man's existence, the enlightenment permeated the whole fabric of the church, and the flavor still lingers. In the year 1972, for example, several congregations observed the centennial of Grundtvig's death. Although few members of the participating congregations would have been able adequately to articulate and define the essence of his great contribution to their life and faith, the subtle influence of his presence did and will continue to color the tapestry of congregational faith and living in many churches of Danish origin.

In the Lutheran mergers of the early 1960s people of varying traditions brought their peculiar gifts of heritage and history, of common confessions and high hopes, to the altar of new churches bonded together by confession. Actual assimilation will require more than organizational unity and will take time. According to my observation, people of different backgrounds attending conferences and conventions tend to gravitate to their own kind, and these affinities will no doubt persist for some time to come.

During the merger proceedings of the LCA, the Danish Special Interest Conference was established with the purpose of "mediating the insights and values of a century of church life in America rooted in the Danish church and culture, and to relate these to the contemporary church." To what degree this has been accomplished is difficult to measure. However, the conference continues to sponsor periodic meetings of a cultural-religious nature, and arranges itineraries for guest speakers from Denmark. The last meeting arranged by the conference in the summer of 1972 drew a large attendance, perhaps encouraged because it coincided with the observance of the centennial of the Danish Lutheran Church in the U.S.A.

The Conference publishes a semimonthly periodical edited by Dr. Johannes Knudtsen, originally published as a Danish paper. An increasing use of the English language is indicated. It is evident that readers and contributors alike, even among younger people, are anxious to keep in touch with people of their own background, and are eager to perpetuate the cultural and spiritual traditions that characterize the Danish Lutheran Church in America.

Ethnicity and the Free Churches

WESLEY M. WESTERBERG: The non-Lutheran or free church groups, while not constituting a large percentage of the Scandinavian population in America, have exerted an ethnic emphasis out of proportion to their size. Some of these groups may in fact offer some of the few remaining religious-ethnic opportunities that remain for Scandinavians in this country.

The free church movement developed from the evangelical revivals of the last century under the stimulus of German Pietism and English Methodism. These impulses came with the immigrants to this country and inspired the formation of groups that were parallel to those springing up in Scandinavia and which were known here as the Swedish and Norwegian-Danish Methodists, the Swedish Baptists, the Evangelical Free Church associations for both Swedish and Norwegian-Danish constituencies, and the Swedish Evangelical Mission Covenant. The Salvation Army and the Pentecostal churches were more recent developments but are included in this survey.

All of these groups have undergone the transitions created in our Scandinavian-American culture by the ebb of immigration, the political pressures of World War I, the decline in the use of the Scandinavian languages in the 1930s, and their virtual disappearance from church life in the 1940s. With some groups the rate of change was slower than in others, but the pattern, with some exceptions, is essentially the same.

The first immigrant church of any kind in the last century was, strangely enough, the Methodist. Olof and Jonas Hedstrom, the one at New York Harbor and the other in Victoria, Illinois, happened to be at the right place at the right time. The Scandinavian Methodist congregations were a home missionary project of American Methodism and, even while they functioned through their own conferences from 1877 to 1943, they were never independent of the parent church. During the first part of this century the language question was always a burning issue because the steady decline in the use of the Scandinavian languages would eventually mean the end of Scandinavian Methodism.

It is understandable, therefore, that these churches, whose peak membership was about 25,000, should attempt to maintain their Scandinavian character as long as possible. Sture Lindmark, in his recent study, *Swedish-America, 1914–1932* (Chicago, 1971), points out that by comparison with Augustana and Covenant churches in Illinois, the transition to English among the Methodist churches proceeded more slowly, and yet the trend was irrevocable. Debates on "merger with the Americans" began in the 1920s and culminated in the early 1940s with the absorption of the Scandinavian conferences. Meanwhile, the Scandinavian languages had already disappeared in the church publications, and the two theological seminaries had merged their assets to start a junior college.

The feared loss of identity was undoubtedly motivated to a great extent by the size of the parent body. Could the impact of what had dwindled in the 1940s to 20,000 Scandinavians be felt in a sea of eight million Methodists? Would those spiritually nurtured in old world Pietism survive in the more secularized environment of the American church?

It is impossible to measure quantitatively the effect of this ripple on the surface of an ocean. Scandinavian piety and church-

liness were recognized, however, in the growing stress on confirmation and the inclusion in the new hymnal of *"Tryggare kan
ingen vara."* The American church also received a college, two
homes for the aged, and a host of loyal churchmen who could
now satisfy their hunger for Scandinavian identity only through
other associations.

The Swedish Baptist churches faced the same language
trends in the thirties and forties but reached a different outcome
by reason of church polity. Although cooperating at some points
with the American Baptists they had reasons to continue their
identity as a national body. These reasons were their theological
differences with the Americans, and the possibilities of expansion
through already existing Baptist congregations of a more conservative theological commitment.

In 1945, therefore, after two decades of difficult language
transition, it was decided that the ministry to the Swedish immigrant and his descendants had been completed. The word "Swedish" was dropped from the name, and the denomination became
known as the Baptist General Conference. Local churches also
Americanized their names, turned their faces toward the whole
of the changing communities, and opened their doors to all nationalities. The Baptist General Conference became an avowedly
American denomination. The last official exchange or contact with
Baptists in Sweden occurred in 1952 and marked the end of an era.

Since 1945, because of church extension under the new emphasis, the number of churches has grown from 283 to 688. Although the leadership of the national body, judging by names, is
overwhelmingly of Swedish extraction, there is no reference at
this moment to anything Swedish except in acknowledgment of a
heritage. Nevertheless, perhaps half a dozen local churches, mainly
in the Northwest, continue to conduct Swedish services or Swedish
Bible classes.

The Evangelical Free Church of America developed out of
two associations, one Swedish and the other Norwegian-Danish.
The change to English, complete by 1934, had the unusual effect

of minimizing the differences between Swedes and Norwegians and so increasing the sentiments for merger of the two groups in 1950. Even though the language question arose as early as 1893 in the discussion, "Should English be used in the churches?" the dominant interest was religious rather than cultural, as can be seen in a statement by one of the leaders of the Norwegian-Danish group in 1921:

We shall soon face the change of language. We are looking for the coming of the Lord, but must prepare for the change of language if the Lord should tarry. Either we cooperate with other groups of like faith and principles [in this case the Swedish Free Church] or we shall be swallowed up by the large denominations and what we have worked so hard to build up will be no more.

Unlike the Scandinavian Methodists and the Swedish Baptists, the Evangelical Free churches had no large American body to absorb them. It was not as simple as giving up a foreign name. "It was necessary for us," writes Roy A. Thompson in *Diamond Jubilee Story* (Minneapolis: Free Church Press, 1959), "to demonstrate the importance of the continued existence of the Evangelical Free Church movement irrespective of nationality." With the merger of the Swedish and Norwegian-Danish sections of the movement in 1950, the "language barrier" ended. "We are henceforth Americans, and Christians, by the grace of God."

Like the Baptists, however, this decisive step led to a significant increase in the number of congregations cooperating with the EFCA, once again through the addition of many churches of similar theological orientation but non-Scandinavian in origin. Since 1950 the number of churches has doubled while the total membership has tripled; but as of now there are still two or three churches, located in Chicago and Brooklyn, that hold services in Swedish and Norwegian. No attempt is made in the national headquarters, however, to preserve the heritage of the past, although membership and leadership are still predominantly Scandinavian.

The Salvation Army and the churches of the Pentecostal movement are now the only segments of the free church movement

that are carrying on a deliberate ministry to Scandinavians, and
both are of non-Scandinavian and more recent origin. Although the
Army's Scandinavian Department was dissolved in 1964 and its
Swedish paper, *Stridsropet,* died in 1963, the former Scandinavian
corps are still the strongest units in the country, and much of the
Army's leadership is Scandinavian. Until a year ago, every former
Scandinavian unit was staffed by a Scandinavian officer; now an
exchange of leadership with non-Scandinavian officers is taking
place, as the shortage of men with language background begins to
take effect.

As examples of Scandinavian activities in the Salvation Army,
the Lake View (Chicago) Corps has a Swedish service every
Saturday night throughout the year and some Swedish adult classes
in their Sunday School; the Jamestown Corps has a ten-week
Swedish school every year; Chicago, Rockford, Jamestown, and
Worcester sponsor weekly Swedish radio programs; New York,
Jamestown, and Lake View (Chicago) Corps issue Swedish
newsletters; and Julotta, Midsummer, and Lucia festivals are observed quite generally.

The motivation behind these activities is not cultural, but
religious. As one of their leaders said: "We found out that we were
reaching people—recent immigrants together with members of the
second and third generations—and these people not only responded but were able to support the programs financially."

An important factor in maintaining the ethnic interest of the
Salvation Army is the frequent contact with Sweden. The identification with Sweden is very strong, and there are regular exchanges
of leaders and musical organizations. In music alone, some of the
foremost composers of songs and band music for units around the
world are Scandinavians. Not being history-minded, the Army does
not speculate on how long the ethnic interest will continue, but it
appears there is no decline at the present time.

Swedish churches identified with the Pentecostal movement
were organized in the United States as The Independent Assem-
blies of God. Although Swedish at its inception, this fellowship has

lost much of its Swedish identity, with only 25 percent of the churches having Swedish origins—the result of a gradual transition that began in the thirties.

The continuance of activities in the Swedish language, however, is noteworthy. The Philadelphia Church in Chicago, frequently referred to as "the Swedish Church," holds an average of ten Swedish services a year plus a one-week Swedish campaign with imported singers and speakers. Frequent contacts with Sweden make it possible to engage all music groups and speakers from Sweden for special services that attract 400 to 600 Scandinavians from all over the Chicago area. These audiences are made up largely of the elderly, but they also include young people who are recent immigrants. Los Angeles, Brooklyn, and communities in Wisconsin and Minnesota are other centers of Scandinavian activity.

The Evangelical Covenant Church of America, more than any other free church group, brought the Swedish church tradition, coupled with the emphasis on individual conversion, across the Atlantic. Like the Methodist societies in England, the mission societies of the last century were reluctant to withdraw from the Lutheran Church either in Sweden or in the United States and thus remained carriers, in a sense, of the church tradition in the guise of dissenters. This characteristic is still present in the "Covenant" today, and we may regard this group of churches as reasonably loyal to their ethnic origins and desirous of maintaining them.

This sensitivity to ethnicity has survived a number of changes noticeable in all of the free church bodies:

1. A gradual switch to English after World War I with a culmination in the thirties.

2. Disappearance of Swedish in the annual reports by 1933 and in all publications by 1955.

3. Removal of "Swedish" from the official name of the denomination in 1937.

But unlike the other groups that merged with parent bodies or abandoned their mission to Scandinavians, there has been no significant watershed. The membership and leadership are still largely of Swedish descent. It was noted by one observer that in many non-urban churches the non-Swede would feel strange, not for religious but for social reasons. Therefore, while the ethnic emphasis began to decline in the twenties and thirties, it has not disappeared, as is evidenced by the following facts:

1. North Park College continues to offer Swedish classes, houses the archives of both the denomination and the Swedish Pioneer Historical Society, makes its facilities available to Swedish societies and events in Chicago.

2. The Seminary curriculum, while drawing inspiration mainly from American and European sources, requires an exposure to denominational history.

3. The theology of Waldenstrom is still an important measuring rod in the church.

4. Contact with the counterpart in Sweden is frequent.

5. Confirmation and infant baptism are maintained, and Julotta is still celebrated in many places.

6. Many Swedish songs and hymns have been translated into English over the years and have recently been published in a special edition for use in the pews.

Resistance to change has been stronger in the Covenant, says Sture Lindmark, than in the former Augustana Synod. Perhaps the Covenant, having no ties to a large body, was less dependent on language for its existence than on a more unconscious ethnicity which determined the spiritual life and structure of the church. While it is less true of the present generation and the younger leadership, there has been a constant reference to Swedish origins and the impulses deriving from them. Karl Olsson, in his history of the movement, *By One Spirit* (Chicago, 1962), states how this gradual transition occurred:

Several events within the church pointed to the new times, but no aggressive or massive measures were taken to invade the American community. The old Swedish image was out of focus; the new American image was still unformed. In the interim the church contented itself with consolidating its position, strengthening its institutional life.

Perhaps the Evangelical Covenant Church will be in the strongest position for a longer time to contribute to the preservation of ethnic values.

One of the great influences of the past in terms of ethnicity was, of course, the newspapers that served the memberships of these church bodies—publications like *Sändebudet* and *Den Kristeliga Talsmand* for the Methodists, *Chicago-Bladet* for the Evangelical Free groups, *Förbundets Veckotidning* for the Evangelical Covenant, *Standaret* for the Baptists, *Stridsropet* for the Salvation Army, and *Sanningens Vittne* for the Pentecostal churches. There is nothing comparable to aid the present generation in identifying itself with Scandinavian culture. There is still the possibility, however, that the colleges maintained by those churches that have not totally severed themselves from the Scandinavian image can transmit the Scandinavian presence to the third and the fourth and the fifth generations.

The Church as Complementary Identity

PETER A. MUNCH: I shall try to give my view of the role of the church as I see it, from outside so to say, from a sociological point of view, but also with reference to the historical situation. In the first place, let me emphasize that we are indeed concerned with ethnicity, which I distinguish from a mere interest in the cultural heritage of Scandinavia. We are concerned with ethnicity in the sense of a matter of identity, individual and social identity. This is a universal human phenomenon, as indeterminate as most other social phenomena because it must be defined by those who live in the community. As Professor Fishman aptly said, mobilized ethnicity does not disappear, it merely transforms. Translated into my language, you could say it adapts, noting that adaptation does not necessarily mean assimilation. Ethnicity is a matter of collective identity, and here we are concerned with what I would call complementary identity rather than with categorical differentiations. In other words, we are concerned with identities that may exist within a larger identity. It is characteristic of all collective identities to seek symbolic expression, and here is where the various collective identities differ from one another. Ethnic groups are simply collective identities that seek their main symbolic expression in the confessed identity with a particular ethnic stock.

When the Scandinavian immigrants came to this country, the church needed the ethnic identity and tied on to it very strongly in order to reinforce its own organization and its own identity. Very soon, however, the church came to a crossroad and was faced with a dilemma: whether to serve as an ethnic catalyst, as a symbolic expression of ethnic identity, or to serve its confessed purpose as a Christian, or Lutheran, or whatever religious or denominational identity. It found itself in a situation where, as sometimes happens in collective identities, the symbolic form in which the identity was expressed became more important than the identity itself. During my studies of Norwegian settlements in Wisconsin, I was told the following story. During the strife about shifting from Norwegian to English in the church—the struggle over Norwegian, as Professor Haugen has called it—an elderly member of the congregation demonstrated his broad-mindedness by saying, "I have nothing against the English language, I use it myself every day. But if we don't teach our children Norwegian, what will they do when they get to heaven?" Well, here is where the symbol of identity, the Norwegian language, has become so bound up with the identity of the church that any change disrupts both the religious and the ethnic identity.

What has happened in more recent years, it seems to me, is that we are experiencing a change in that ethnic identity in this country is now seeking other symbolic expressions. I have seen it clearly in one community with which I became well acquainted some twenty-five years ago. When I made a study of the community, it was still what it had been in the past, a very Norwegian community with about 97 percent of the population of Norwegian stock. Westby, Wisconsin, had separated itself deliberately from the American society because, as I felt it in the community at that time, these Norwegians had built their own community in order to realize their own American dream. This dream was not concerned with refrigerators and wealth; it was the dream that here is a country where you can be yourself. And so by expressing their Norwegian identity, they were indeed expressing their own freedom to be themselves. This kind of complementary identity had also a clear expression in the 15th Wisconsin Regiment under Colonel Heg during the Civil War, with commands in Norwegian and a banner, which is now in the Norwegian-American Museum, with the inscription "Our God and our Country" in Norwegian: *Vor Gud og vort Land.* There is no doubt that the country they were referring to was America. This was the kind of complementary identity within the American society that was possible at that time.

During World War I a change occurred when the larger American society demanded undivided loyalty and forced this kind of complementary identity underground, so to say. Here the church played a role by becoming a kind of refuge for ethnic identity, because denominational differentiation was recognized in the American society as a complementary identity within the general American community. No one was accused of being un-American because he was a Lutheran or a Methodist. There was a harbor in which ethnic identity could come to expression in the various "ethnic" churches and denominations. But then came the dilemma of the church: which role should it play; should it take on this role? There were divided opinions among the church leaders and all the way down to the grassroots, with an increasing dominance of the answer, "No, we will not play this role, at least we will not let this role get in the way of the main purpose of the church." And so the churches have diminished in their role as a symbolic expression of ethnic identity. The church is no longer an ethnic catalyst, or at least not to the extent that it was. The ethnic churches today are more or less lively remnants, but remnants nonetheless, of the former convergence of the religious and ethnic identity.

I don't know how this will develop—it seems that it will go further in the same direction as expressed in the various mergers of Lutheran churches, these mergers being themselves rejections of the symbolic role of ethnic identity. This is an element of the past that is in a process of change. I mentioned Westby which today is still very Norwegian. But the ethnic identity is expressed in a different way. It is no longer the Norwegian language, although that still plays a role in a certain symbolic sense; it is no longer primarily membership in the Lutheran church. New symbols of ethnic identity have come into being. For one thing, Westby is the center of a famous ski meet. Another expression is linguistic, not in the sense of using the Norwegian language in everyday conversation, but by having a "Welcome to Westby" sign in Norwegian outside the town, and by having Norwegian signs on the stores. Thus a grocery store is a *kolonialhandel,* there is even a *bedehus,* there is a *spisestue* as they call a restaurant there, there is a *jernvarehandel,* and so on, and the signs on display in the windows are in identical lettering, which makes me think it is a community project.

This is indeed a new way of expressing ethnic identity. What role the church, or churches, will play in the future in this new kind of ethnic expression, I don't know other than the one area in which the influence of the churches will remain strong. That is in colleges with church origins, and with continuing church affiliations.

Finnish Religious Organizations

DOUGLAS J. OLILLA, JR.: It would seem appropriate to introduce the Finns in America by making several general observations. First of all, the Finns are different from the rest of the Scandinavian-Americans because they came to this country late and they have not yet completely acculturated. The first wave of Finns came here from 1880 to 1900, organizing churches and cultural societies. The second wave began to arrive after 1900, continuing until after

1920. These Finns tended to be oriented towards radicalism, organizing socialist societies of various kinds. Because of this late arrival, ethnicity and ethnic organizations are still an important factor in the life of the Finns. You can still hear the Finnish language on the streets of Hancock, Michigan, and Lake Worth, Florida. Finnish-language worship services are conducted in many parts of the country, while eight Finnish-language newspapers are still published. A few of the first generation are still alive, and many of their children maintain the language and customs.

The second factor concerns the divisiveness of Finnish-Americans. Broadly, the Finns were divided into Whites, or conservatives, and Reds, the radical groups. These two groups have had little or nothing to do with each other, creating among themselves bitterly warring factions. Churchmen divided into the Suomi Synod which was modeled after the Church of Finland. The National Lutheran Church was an orthodox Lutheran people's movement. Five groups of low-church, sectarian-style Lutherans called *Laestadians* or Apostolic Lutherans were organized. There were also other minor sectarian church groups.

The socialists followed the same patterns as the church and engaged in internecine conflict over correct interpretations of Marxian socialism. Utopians developed a communitarian colony in British Columbia, only to have it fail because of capitalistic tendencies among members. The powerful Finnish Socialist Federation was the largest foreign-language group in the American Socialist Party, but died out in the 1950s. The Socialist Federation faced a crisis in 1913 when a majority was radicalized and joined the Industrial Workers of the World. Communists further factioned the Federation, founding their own movement in 1919.

A generous estimate of the radical groups now would include about 25 percent of the Finns in America. The distinctive story even today is the record of the conflict between radicals and churchmen, whose differences were seemingly irreconcilable. Churchmen still write horror stories about the godless radicals, and the socialists, in turn, harbor great suspicions toward the reactionary church and its petit-bourgeois clergy, whom they dubbed "blackfrocks."

Another factor is the continued division and rivalry among the particular Finnish communities in America. It is said that two Finns in a community usually create at least four organizations which last forever. In any event, the fact remains that there has never been a major merger of any of the Finnish churches or religious groups along ethnic lines. The Suomi Synod Finnish-Evangelical Lutheran Church in America, of course, merged with the Lutheran Church in America, while National Finnish Lutherans joined the Lutheran Church-Missouri Synod. The other Finnish church groups, of which there are some eight or nine, have remained as separate ethnic enclaves ministering to members even in the third and fourth generations.

The socialist groups themselves exhibited the same kind of particularism. I.W.W. syndicalists still dream of one big union and revolutionary action, while the Communists presumably believe that Gus Hall will still usher in a workers' paradise.

In brief, then, patterns of Finnish life in America are distinctively different from those of other Scandinavians. In fact, the movement must be studied from the perspective of the later immigration. It appears that the Yugoslavs and the Czechs are probably closer parallels to the Finns when it comes to their adjustment to industrialized America.

I'd like to reflect a bit on the question of the relationship of ethnicity to church life as it exists today. Recent studies, of course, have indicated that the ethnic factor somehow persists, and it certainly persists in the churches. The melting-pot has not really homogenized its ingredients completely. Ethnicity will be with us until the end of the century if Andrew Greeley is on the mark, and even longer than that according to Dr. Fishman.

It seems to me that there is a viable ethnic factor still present among Scandinavians today. Many of these signs are obvious: Norwegian hymns, Danish special interest conferences, and Swedish architecture. As recently as 1961 one-fourth of the members of the Suomi Synod worshiped in the Finnish language. And the Finnish Conference of the Lutheran Church in America flourishes today, far past expectation, as a foreign-language conference, much of this activity sustained by continued immigration into Canada.

It seems to me, however, that we have hardly begun to explore other ethnic contributions that not only persist in local congregations, as Dr. Preus has clearly indicated, but that have become contributions to general church life among Lutherans or church life in America at large. For example, it has been widely observed that Lutherans have been "sleepers" on the American theological scene, that they are only now beginning to make a contribution. If there is a Lutheran theological contribution, we might ask then as to what is the indigenous, or the ethnic factor in this contribution. Religion, theology, and ethnicity are hopelessly intertwined. And yet it is very clear that theology and piety have an indigenous character, but that few theologians have examined this carefully. The literature is scarce, indeed, and I think that's a scandal. Ralph Jalkanen explored this question in an essay entitled "Certain Characteristics of the Faith of the Finns," and he found that our indigenous theology affirms, among other things, suffering, which brings not only a sense of self-identity and self-consciousness, but also potential healing. He found this to be coupled with a Christian vision of the tragic sense of life and a tenacity of faith in the midst of death. All men suffer, and all men die. But each theology and each ethnic tradition gives its own peculiar or even unique stamp to what living and dying are all about. It would be interesting to find out what other Scandinavian groups have contributed to the panorama of American Christendom. This is not clearly defined.

I teach at Augsburg College which came out of the Norwegian Lutheran Free Church tradition. The free church piety and politics have their own peculiar stamp, harking all the way back to a Hauge-like pietism in Norway and to Georg Sverdrup. Many of our students reflect this piety; it is a subtle kind of piety that is hard to define. But it is nurtured in old free church congregations and nurtured even more specifically in families which still read the old prayerbooks. I believe that this piety, as well as this political spirit that we find in our college, is in some way definable. Certainly Augsburg's free church piety is different from St. Olaf's piety and significantly different from Gustavus Adolphus's piety.

My final example concerns the Finnish Apostolic Lutheran Church, or churches (five or six separate bodies). In America they are also known as the *Laestadians*. The theology and piety of each are very different from one another and exceedingly exclusivistic. It is apparent that they have been able to preserve their theology and their way of life into the third and even fourth generations. I suppose one could best compare them with the Mennonite communities in Pennsylvania. There the ethnic factor and their peculiar kind of ethnic theology persist in a very conscious way in a viable church.

What I am suggesting is that we do indeed have an ethnic theology, an ethnic piety or life style, or whatever, and that these have been somehow preserved in the life of our churches. How, is difficult to say. Institutionally certainly, but perhaps even more so they have been unconsciously transmitted through the family. In any event, I believe that we have hardly begun to examine the question, and that as yet we have not admitted to ourselves that the ethnic factor even exists in our theology and church life. Not even today.

Ethnic Awareness Among Clergy and Parishioners

DUANE R. LINDBERG: What is the level of ethnic awareness among clergy of Scandinavian background and what is their perception of the level of interest in ethnicity among their parishioners?

My first thought in attempting to answer this question was to consult data assembled by M. P. Strommen and associates in the excellent resource volume entitled *A Study of Generations*. However, except for a few very general questions on race and nationality, I was not able to find help on the question of attitude toward ethnicity.[1] This may betray a particular bias on the part of the research team. More likely, however, it indicates a general tendency among American scholars which has been well documented by R. J. Vecoli in an article entitled "Ethnicity: A Neglected Dimension of American History."[2]

Furthermore, the data gathered by our American Lutheran Church parochial reports give no help in studying the role of ethnicity within the church. This too seems to indicate something. Does this official silence indicate an actual lack of ethnic consciousness on the part of the church members, or an official disinterest in matters of ethnic differentiation within our denomination? Could it be that in our zeal for merger the church has pursued a "let sleeping dogs lie" attitude with regard to ethnicity? Perhaps the church has assumed that the "melting pot" has done its work effectively and has destroyed all significant ethnic distinctions among Lutherans in America.

At the grass-roots level, however, there are clear signs that ethnicity and interest in ethnic matters have not passed out of the picture, even among Germans and Scandinavians. The parish pastor notices that children are being christened with non-Anglo names; young couples are showing a new interest in the "soul foods" of their people and in family tradition and history; language camps, Norway trips, and pictures generate a good deal of enthusiasm. But these are only the impressions of parish pastors. Where is the empirical evidence? How about data whereby the impressions can be either scrapped, reinterpreted, or verified?

Historically, it is relatively easy to document the significant role which ethnicity has played in the Lutheran Church. Our entire history in America is dominated by ethnic factors such as language and social-religious pluralism. Even the present organization of Lu-

1. M. P. Strommen et al., *A Study of Generations* (Minneapolis: Augsburg Publishing House, 1972), pp. 30–31.
2. R. J. Vecoli, "Ethnicity: A Neglected Dimension of American History" (unpublished), p. 2.

theranism is an example of what Milton Gordon refers to as an ethnically based structural pluralism.[3] However, today the importance of, or the interest in, ethnicity is not so easy to measure. In order to provide an empirical basis regarding the current situation relative to Scandinavian ethnicity and the awareness of it in the ALC, I prepared a questionnaire for the thirty-two clergy of the Decorah Conference, Iowa District of the ALC. Twenty-four clergymen responded to the questionnaire. My inquiry deals with these areas: ethnic character of the parish, symbolic expressions of ethnicity in terms of non-English language usage, and church architecture and decoration. Also, I included questions on social expressions of ethnicity in the parish, the pastor's subjective evaluation of ethnic awareness among his parishioners, and a section for the pastor's own expression of Scandinavian or German ethnicity.

Though the field sample is not large enough to make absolute statements, it does suggest definite patterns and correlations that I believe are pertinent to the substance of our seminar.

The statistical basis of my study is as follows:

32 Parishes of the American Lutheran Church in N. E. Iowa
21,395 Total Baptized Membership
24 Parishes Reported
   10 Norwegian-background parishes
   6 German-background parishes
   4 Norwegian-German
   3 Mixed
   1 Norwegian-Swiss
10 Pastors over 50 years (5 Scandinavian background)
14 Pastors 50 years or under (9 Scandinavian background)

To me, the most interesting fact which this inquiry reveals is the difference in responses between those in the over-50 age cate-

3. M. M. Gordon, *Assimilation in American Life* (N.Y., Oxford University Press, 1964), p. 114.

gory and those who are younger, especially in terms of Norwegian ethnicity. All were asked whether:

There seems to be a (growing) (diminishing) interest in ethnic background on the part of the people in my parish who are *over 50 years* of age.
There seems to be a (growing) (diminishing) interest in ethnic background on the part of the people in my parish who are *under 50 years.*

Among pastors serving congregations that are reported to be partially or totally Norse in background, the younger men (all nine) say there is a growing interest in ethnic background, whereas among the older men only one says "growing" while five say "diminishing."

This difference in perception becomes even more interesting when one notes that among pastors serving German-background congregations, the perception of ethnic interest is the same for both groups. In the younger group three say "diminishing" and one "growing" and in the older group seven say "diminishing" with one reporting slight increase among the younger group of parishioners.

The reported facts seem to indicate that one's subjective attitude determines what one "sees" of ethnicity. For example, in terms of the reported facts, the younger group reports a total of thirty public services in which the Norwegian language was used during 1972; whereas the older group reports only two. Even allowing for the fact that there were one and one half times as many younger men reporting, if this reported difference indicates the actual difference in number of times the Norwegian language is being used in the public services of the church, then perhaps it is renewed interest in ethnicity on the part of younger pastors which stimulates this interest in the congregations.

Other data comparing the "Over-50" and "Below-50" groups are also interesting (see table, page 75).

How, then, is the above data to be interpreted? Furthermore, what suggestions does this inquiry give in terms of the Seminar's evaluation of Scandinavian ethnicity and the church?

First, one may postulate that a local phenomenon explains the situation of a perceived growing awareness of Norwegian ethnicity. For example, the proximity to Decorah, a Norwegian-American cultural center, may cause an awakening of ethnic interest in the congregations of the Decorah Conference. This does not, however, explain the difference in perception of ethnicity between the older and the younger clergy.

Next, this inquiry may reflect a changing philosophy regarding the nature of American society. Cultural pluralism is no longer un-American and younger men may feel less inhibited by the old philosophy of the "melting-pot" and 100 percent Americanism. Also, interest in ethnicity may reflect the growing identity crisis in America and the need, felt especially by the young, to find one's roots. It is not enough today to be a "good American," we must discover who we are in terms of the "quarry from where we were digged."

On the other hand, a growing awareness of ethnicity may be simply a phase which Marcus Lee Hansen referred to as "the third generation return" and may represent only a temporary slowing-down of the "melting-pot." Whatever the explanation, the fact of a definite difference in attitude with regard to ethnicity is apparent between the younger and older clergy serving Norwegian-background congregations of the ALC.

In addition, the perception of a growing interest in ethnicity would suggest that this is a factor in attracting people to a particular congregation. In both North Dakota and Iowa some people are attracted to a church group because it is associated with an ethnic group. How often this is a motivational factor I can not say, but the factors which P. A. Munch identified in his article in 1954 are still operative: "Loyalty to the Norwegian Lutheran Church is a symbolic expression of ethnic identity for Norwegians." [4]

However, with a greater degree of allowable cultural pluralism in the rest of society, the church's function as a vehicle for the acceptable expression of ethnic diversity may be diminished.

4. P. A. Munch, "Segregation and Assimilation of Norwegian Settlements in Wisconsin," *Norwegian-American Studies and Records,* vol. 18 (1954), p. 136.

In conclusion, I would like to stress that in charting our future course of action relative to guiding the growth and expression of Scandinavian ethnicity in American society, we begin from the philosophical premise that ethnicity is a natural and positive dimension of vital and creative church life. The church, by learning to accept cultural pluralism and harness its creative potential, can provide the necessary help which our society needs to overcome its fear of difference and its mania for mass manipulation. It was the American philosopher Horace M. Kallen who pointed out the important role of "the deep-lying cultural diversities of the ethnic groups," as a defense against the regimentation of industry and the logical monism of science.[5]

In the spirit of this positive attitude toward ethnicity, I consider these words of Monsignor Geno Baroni to be suggestive of the direction the Seminar should move in charting its future course of action: "How do we transform the ethnic gift of middle-America into a creative key to the restructuring of American culture and society? Ethnicity is that gift which America has which can energize a new American dream." [6]

TABULATION OF DATA

		Clergy Respondents (ALC)	
		Over 50	Below 50
A.	Does your parish have an ethnic character?	Yes 7	Yes 8
		No 2	No 5
		No Response 1	No Response 1
B. 1 a.	Use of Norwegian in public services in 1972	2	30
1 b.	Use of Norwegian in devotions with sick, shut-ins, private communions in 1972	8	47

5. H. M. Kallen, *Culture and Democracy in the U.S.* (1924), p. 229.
6. G. Baroni, Lecture at Minnesota Consultation on Ethnicity, Feb. 1972.

2. Decoration or archi-
tecture of German
influence   Yes 1   Yes 4
                                   No   9   No 10

C. 1. How many social
functions in your
parish expressed
ethnic awareness   1   17

2. Number of persons in
parish who receive
Norwegian religious
publications   0   19

      Number who receive
secular Norwegian
publications   11   53

      Number who listen to
Norwegian radio pro-
gram once a month   33   111

4. & 5. Interest in ethnic background on part of
parishioners in con-
gregations of Nor-
wegian backgrounds   Growing 1   Growing 9
                          Diminishing 5   Diminishing (1)*

D. 1. Clergy with some
ability in the
Norwegian language   3   9

2. How many times did
clergy use Norwegian
during week in
prayers, greetings,
communications   4   26

3. Wives of clergy who
have some facility with
Norwegian   1   4

4. Pastor's children who
have some facility with
Norwegian   0   2

---

* One of the nine (9) clergy respondents below the age of 50 years indicated a "diminishing" interest in ethnic background among those parishioners who are 50 years old or younger, whereas those over 50 years were
reported to have a "growing" interest in their ethnic background.

Brotherhoods and Fraternal Organizations

Panel: KENNETH O. BJORK (Chairman), MAGNE SMEDVIG,
JOHAN HAMBRO, BERTIL G. WINSTROM, DONALD V.
EVERSOLL, VAINO A. HOOVER, K. VALDIMAR BJORNSON,
ODD LOVOLL (Student Representative)

Sons of Norway

MAGNE SMEDVIG: Sons of Norway was organized in Minneapolis on January 16, 1895, by eighteen young Norwegians. Times had been tough; there was no Social Security, pension plan, or welfare. As a matter of fact, these Norwegians were too proud for the dole anyway, so they organized a self-protective society. Only Norwegians could join and draw benefits. By 1912, they had 9,000 members who owned $2 million of insurance. They also permitted members to join without insurance. By 1930, they had 24,000 members who owned $10 million, and in 1950 the membership reached 30,000 and the insurance $16 million. Ten years later, in 1960, the membership grew to 36,000 and the insurance to $35 million. By 1970, Sons of Norway had grown to 65,000 with an insurance total of $78 million. Two years later the membership exceeded 80,000 and passed the $100 million mark. In 1973, more than 5,000 new members joined, making the total membership more than 85,000, with insurance in force at a little over $115 million.

Local branches number more than 300 across the country, and a new one is organized somewhere in the United States or in Canada every month.

At the beginning, Sons of Norway used the Norwegian language exclusively. Almost 100 percent of the new members who joined had been born in Norway. The magazine of the society was printed in Norwegian, the application, even the insurance policies, were in Norwegian. As an ethnic society, one could say that we learned rather slowly that if we were going to interest subsequent generations in our Norwegian heritage, we first of all had to communicate with them in a language they could read and understand. There was much debate about this basic change. I rather suspect that the nudge needed came with World War II, for in 1942 the last Norwegian issue of *Sønner av Norge* was printed, and in January, 1943, Sons of Norway changed to English. The war was a turning point for the society.

Sons of Norway has probably experienced three major stages of growth. First, the organizational or protection phase: people of limited means banding together for protection and mutual support. The second, as Sons of Norway grew, was the social and recreational phase; fraternities within the Norwegian-American community. Third, in the last ten years, Sons of Norway clearly has been entering the heritage phase, probably its final and most lasting objective, since it will last as long as interest in ancestry endures. Our members now ask: Who am I, where did I come from, what kind of values and lifestyle does my heritage represent?

As a fraternal benefit society, Sons of Norway has a representative form of government. Management does not dictate what should be done. Management is, in fact, the agent and the servant of the membership. Local lodges elect delegates to attend seven geographical district conventions, where the delegates elect representatives to attend the international convention. It is at these biennial conventions that the members shape the programs and the objectives of Sons of Norway. As a fraternal membership, it is naturally a participating membership. The members folk-dance, sing, ski, they trace their ancestors, travel to Norway, speak Norwegian, and they try to teach the language to anyone who will listen.

The level of serious interest in heritage is rising, and we of Sons of Norway have a responsibility to serve the interests of our members. Our rapid growth, a new lodge, and a thousand new members every month, suggests that we are doing that. We believe that Sons of Norway is now well into the heritage phase, its permanent role in American society.

What are we doing for our members? Our members wanted more programming in folk culture, arts, literature, music, crafts; so we made several motion pictures for their use, and distributed them widely. Next we took a unique step. We created the heritage series. These were complete programs—slides, scripts, posters, demonstration guides—but they had to be presented by the local Sons of Norway members. The objective was to draw out local talent on the subject of the Norwegian heritage. It worked. And now many lodges are putting on their own programs. The first series was called "Those Gifted Norsk," and dealt with the folk and fine arts of Norway. The second one was called "Discovering Your Ancestry," and dealt with the art of tracing family ties; the third one was called "Browsing Through Norwegian Folk Tales, Sagas, Songs, and Plays." We are now expanding this series into a newer format which will also be available to schools.

Sons of Norway has a growing interest in travel. Tours and charter flights to Scandinavia, arranged by all of the seven districts, have brought tens of thousands of members into personal contact with their relatives and friends across the sea. Not only tourism, but business and industry have benefited from this activity. In 1973, some sixty airplanes were chartered by Sons of Norway. When we speak of the extent to which the society supports and strengthens ties with the homeland, no other single activity could come close to the value and impact of such visits. And this activity is stimulating a reverse flow of visits of Norwegians to America to visit relatives, friends, and business acquaintances here.

Our members are interested in books about the arts, crafts, history, folk tales, the translated literature of Norway's great novelists and playwrights. As a result, we have extended our mail-order book series; purchases of books in 1973 were up 100 percent over the previous year, and publishers tell us that we are now the largest buyer and importer of Norwegian heritage books in the United States.

Our members want to learn to speak Norwegian. Sons of Norway has language classes all over the country, and they range from small study groups to conversation groups to large schools, like the 350 students who jam our cultural center every Saturday morning in Minneapolis. Perhaps the most exciting and popular new service we have developed is a package called "It's Fun to Speak Norwegian"; in this cassette there are folk songs, favorite expressions and proverbs, and more importantly, pronunciation, grammar, and vocabulary without those technical grammatical terms that frighten the beginner. It has been put to use for beginning students of Norwegian and in a number of colleges and high school labs. But the people who most appreciate it are those for whom the language is an introduction to our culture, our heritage. In order to create and produce these objects, Sons of Norway established a service arm called Heritage Productions, which functions much like a church publishing house. Heritage Productions provides our membership and others with tapes, programs, and films. In the case of the language tapes, Heritage Productions has gone beyond the Norwegian, and, discovering an unmet need, produced "It's Fun to Speak Danish, Swedish, Finnish," because so many inter-Scandinavian families are members of Sons of Norway.

Since most members think of and evaluate Sons of Norway in terms of the local lodge, the local lodge leadership and programs are of primary importance. Since local lodge leadership changes annually, it becomes a major effort to familiarize and orient that leadership to the overall program. To solve this problem, we have developed a series of officers' manuals—how-to-do-it books for every lodge officer—in which the entire approach is merely suggestive.

We are attempting to develop a community-minded approach, cooperating with other organizations, and developing meaningful programs that carry through the heritage concept. We are noticing much more activity among our youth: one example is our youth seminars; we had forty young people aged sixteen through twenty-one at a recent convention. Forty young people will visit Norway in the summer, forty more from across the land will come to Minneapolis, and they will run Sons of Norway and be executives for a day. A youth convention will be held at Banff in Alberta, Canada, in 1974. Through our membership in the National Fraternal Congress of America we have observed that ethnic fraternal societies which do not become attuned to change have discovered that their membership starts to decline. In Sons of Norway we recognized these signs early and decided to turn the corner to become a vital part of this ethnic renaissance. Our theme became: preserving a heritage, insuring the future. We are not researchers, or statisticians, but we have a notion—a gut feeling as it were—that we have a more mature and intelligent outlook today of what is and what is not 100 percent American. Actually, our values seem to be getting back to basics. We need to relate to the times. There is a searching need and desire for identity, recognition, continuity, to link the present with the past. The more people we have, the more congestion in urban areas, the harder this becomes. Since man is by nature a social animal and does seek his own kind, it seems to us quite natural that people would once again want to join a society which gave them these opportunities to do something about the preservation of a heritage, and do so in a lighthearted way. By combining our activities and publicizing them widely, we have seen an enormous interest and potential develop.

The future of Sons of Norway seems bright to us; whether the ethnic renaissance diminishes or flourishes in the future is not of primary significance. What is important is that we as a society maintain relevance. We see many exciting things on the horizon, for we intend to promote what we are, a heritage people. Sons of Norway is now seventy-eight years old; our long-range plans anticipate doubling our present size by 1980.

The embryonic Sons of Norway Foundation will grow and become an important arm in the field of scholarships, grants, and aid in those areas in which it received its charter. Gifts by members, lodges, and districts to innumerable worthy causes during these past seventy-eight years have essentially gone unnoticed. It is not generally known, but estimated investment in this effort in the past is $5 million. The foundation will serve as a vehicle for these good works and provide a historical record for them. Development of heritage centers around the country is on the drawing board for the future. Business and cultural centers are also being considered, although these two require a great deal of cooperative effort to assure their success in the local community. We are not historians, publishers, or transportation experts. But within our Scandinavian presence, we have these talents and organizations. By strengthening our cooperation and public relations efforts we can be a mighty force.

Any man who is not motivated by tradition, the deep inner glow that develops from pride in ancestry, in my opinion has missed the salt in the stew.

Nordmanns-Forbundet

JOHAN HAMBRO: In a sense I feel as if I am sailing under a false flag because the organization that I represent is not basically Norwegian-American, but a global one. The Norsemen's Federation, *Nordmanns-Forbundet,* has members in every part of the world and takes in men and women of Norwegian descent wherever they are, so in a sense we are concerned with a Norwegian presence in many parts of the world. But, of course, the overwhelming majority of the hundreds of thousands of people who emigrated from Norway over the last 150 years settled in this country and in Canada, so quite clearly the main emphasis of our work has been in this country.

Nordmanns-Forbundet is different from many of the other Scandinavian organizations because it is not a mutual aid society, and it offers no kind of direct fraternal benefits or insurance. Its creation was a direct consequence of Norway's gaining complete independence in 1905, when the union with Sweden was dissolved. And it came as a complete surprise, as a revelation to the national leaders of Norway at the time, that all these hundreds of thousands of emigrants whom they thought had left the country in bitterness and anger, had by no means turned their backs on their native land. Just the opposite; they offered to help Norway with money and supplies of all kinds, because, strange as it may seem today, it appeared likely that there might be an armed conflict between the two countries. It was felt afterwards that these strong ties and these feelings for the old country were something of very great and lasting value to both sides, and the national leaders in Norway issued an appeal that led to the founding of *Nordmanns-Forbundet* in 1907. I should perhaps add that there are similar organizations, sister organizations, in all the Scandinavian countries; we have regular meetings to exchange experiences and discuss common problems. Thus, in a sense, we are working already on the problem of the Scandinavian presence: I am sure it will not ruffle any Scandinavian feathers if I say that *Nordmanns-Forbundet* is not only the oldest of these organizations, but I think the largest and the one which has by far the broadest scope, although I think the Finnish group particularly has enjoyed impressive growth over the last decade or so.

It is fair to say that the first four decades of *Nordmanns-Forbundet* had what I might call an essentially national romantic emphasis. There was a distinctly sentimental approach in the best sense of that phrase. This was of course the period when the membership was primarily made up of the original immigrants, those who had been born in Norway and still had certain roots there. In the 1940s and in the 1950s, it was frequently and confidently predicted in Norway that such a Norwegian organization, made by and for the immigrants, necessarily would have to stagnate and then dwindle as immigration itself dwindled to a trickle. It is interesting that the opposite has proved to be true.

This is largely because the emphasis in the period since World War II has changed from the sentimental approach to practical service and cultural exchange.

Developments during the last two decades have confounded all predictions; the downhill trend has been decisively reversed and there has been a remarkable increase in interest and activities. Let us take one single item, the important role played by local chapters, where members in their individual areas, with our help, get together for whatever activities they may choose. Six chapters have been organized exclusively as a result of local initiatives and local desires. They have never been urged by the home office, in fact we have frequently discouraged them whenever we felt that there was not really any growth potential. And yet the fact is that the number of such local chapters in this country has more than doubled over the past decade or so. While the number of first-generation Norwegian-Americans has been sharply declining during the same period, and those members, of course, have disappeared from the roster, recent years have yielded far more new members than those naturally disappearing. And there has, again contrary to all predictions, again and again been a net increase in new members of the organization in this country. The approximate net increase for 1971 was 12 percent, and the corresponding figure for 1972, while somewhat lower, was still a very considerable one. These figures, of course, include members in every part of the world; indications are that other countries with very small Norwegian groups and virtually no immigration for the last decade show a decrease in membership which means that the figures for North America are in reality still higher than the figures mentioned.

The largest group and the greatest increase naturally are in those areas where the Norwegian ethnic settlement was the largest: in all the midwestern states, along parts of the East Coast, in the Pacific Northwest, and in more recent years also in the mountain states. There has been a considerable increase in the state of California, which may reflect the move towards the West, and also in Florida, and a scattering of sometimes substantial groups in other states.

Contrary to all expectations, the average age of our members is lower than it was ten or fifteen or twenty years ago. There has obviously been an awakening of interest among the younger generation, an awareness of background and roots in another country; the result has been that there is a lower percentage of old-timers and a correspondingly higher percentage of middle-aged and young-middle-aged members. And in more recent years there has been a trend which is of course encouraging: a growing interest among the fairly young and among the third and fourth generations. One reason for this development is the adoption, against strong opposition, and incredibly enough only ten years ago, of English as the second working language of the organization and of the publication. In addition to a primarily Norwegian magazine which has existed since 1907, there is also now an English-language magazine, *The Norseman.* There is a growing percentage of members who prefer the English-language magazine.

Another factor is that transatlantic travel has been brought within reach of everyone, and that neither time nor purse will be strained too much by a visit to the country of one's ancestors, whether individually or in large groups, on charter flights offered by so many of these organizations.

There are also concrete services rendered by *Nordmanns-Forbundet* to its members: free legal consultation services which obviously fulfill a great need whether it has to do with tax problems or social security or citizenship or whatever the case may be; youth exchange, concert tours both ways across the Atlantic, lecture tours, and so on; or free assistance when it comes to the tracing of ancestry. (I don't think we knew what we were doing when we offered that service because there's been a tremendous increase all the time.) There are also free travel service and purchasing service which have been very important to growth in recent years; they meet a need and they stimulate interest in the organization.

The Vasa Order

BERTIL G. WINSTROM: A hundred years ago in America there were many local Swedish immigrant groups, organized primarily to help their members when adversity struck. Toward the end of the last century, as the immigration continued, a desire arose among the leaders of these Swedish groups to increase the usefulness of these independent societies, and to become national in scope. Thus were formed the Vasa Order of America, the Order of Vikings, the Independent Order of Swithiod, *Skandinaviska Brödra Förbundet,* the Order of Runeberg with mostly Swedish-speaking people from Finland and Åland, and the International Order of Good Templars. All six organizations survive to this day; they use prescribed rituals, and their local chapters are known as lodges. They all share a common interest in the Scandinavian (especially Swedish) heritage in America.

The Vasa Order is divided into 19 districts and 360 local lodges; the membership today is 38,000 and we function in the United States, Canada, and Sweden. The connecting link between our members scattered over this very large area is the *Vasa Star,* our monthly publication. It has a circulation of 25,000 copies, and we estimate it has a reader potential of about 100,000. The Grand Lodge of the Vasa Order was incorporated in the State of Connecticut. The charter of the Vasa Order very clearly sets forth the ideals of the organization, and it reads in part as follows:

The object of said corporation shall be to render aid to sick members of the corporation, whether such sickness be temporary or incurable, and to render pecuniary aid towards defraying the funeral expense to members, and to promote social and intellectual fellowship among its members.

Although all of the initial aims of Vasa are sustained, those interests more readily associated with the cultural and heritage aspects of Swedish descendancy have become foremost in the activities of our members. This transition into the field of preservation of our heritage has been gradual, and it is continuing.

Our leaders recognized early that it was important to instill in young people a pride in their ancestors' culture and achievements, their heritage. Over fifty years ago, we established the first children's clubs. Our youth program today consists of sixty clubs with 2,000 members. In these clubs we teach our children Swedish history, Swedish achievements in the New World, Swedish songs, folk dances, and introduce them to the Swedish language. As an example of what we do for our children, we have a song book published by the Vasa Order of America. In 1924, we organized our first children's tour of the land of our ancestors. It is interesting to note that this youth trip was the inspiration for the beginning of the Vasa Order in Sweden. As a direct result of this trip, the Göteborg Lodge of the Vasa Order was formed. Many trips in both directions have taken place since 1924.

The Vasa Order also maintains an educational fund from which ten or fifteen scholarships are available annually. We also have a student loan fund without interest for our members in college.

Our adult membership consists more and more of second-, third-, fourth- and fifth-generation Swedes. We arrange many activities to stimulate their interest in their heritage; our meeting programs are geared to educational themes; and we sponsor a goodly number of annual charter tours to Sweden for our members.

Many of our local and district lodges own parks and buildings where Swedish holidays are celebrated in the traditional manner. English is, of course, the business language of our order. However, we maintain an active Swedish language study department, from which we supply textbooks and tapes. The study of Swedish is based principally on vocabulary, rather than classroom oriented study, and there is a considerable interest in conversational Swedish. Many of the students have been stimulated to visit Sweden, and they find themselves quite able to converse there. We have recently started a department for cultural groups to promote fellowship among Vasa members, both young and old. The activities include singing, dancing, music, drill teams, language study, sports, and so forth.

There are two Vasa districts in Sweden, with over fifty lodges and a total membership of 5,000. They recognize the importance of preserving a close cultural relationship between Swedish people on both sides of the Atlantic.

There are many monuments in Sweden dedicated to the emigrants who left for America; there are also two emigrant registration institutes which are supported in part by Vasa members. The office in Värmland is gathering the names of people who emigrated from that province, their descendants and their relatives in Sweden; one of the prominent present-day family trees recorded there is that of Colonel Edwin Aldrin who, of course, was the second man on the moon. The emigrant institute in Småland covers the emigration from several provinces. Both institutes have modern microfilming techniques.

Vasa members also select and organize the reception for the annual Swedish-American of the Year; this has now become a joint venture with the Foreign Ministry of the Swedish Government. The person so honored is an American who is active in the preservation of our heritage.

We have, for the most part, ceased to consider ourselves a strictly financial benefit organization. Our founders did not set up a funding system which would increase payments to meet today's needs. Therefore, we have turned to preserving the culture of our motherland and to the importance of its emigrants in American history. Swedish scientists, inventors, businessmen, and politicians, artisans, and farmers all contributed a great deal to the development of America. For many years it seemed that this ethnic identity would be consumed in the great melting-pot, but recent events in our country have created the desire among many people to affiliate with an ethnic organization. In our experience, this trend is particularly noticeable in persons of the third and later generations. The Vasa Order of America is well suited to serve coming generations. So convinced are we that our future is secure that we now feel the need to preserve our own history. We are in the process of building an archives building in Bishop Hill, Illinois, a rural Swedish community founded in 1846 by Swedish immigrants from Biskups Kulla in Sweden. Changing times passed this little community by, leaving it today the only remaining Swedish settlement in the United States such as the original settlers claimed it. Both the State of Illinois and the United States Government have given recognition to this as a historic site, thus assuring its preservation for generations to come.

The Danish Brotherhood

DONALD V. EVERSOLL: The Danish Brotherhood is people, Americans of Danish descent, who wish to preserve a proud heritage and to gather together in a fraternal society to share memories, experiences, and a bit of old Denmark. At show-and-tell meetings of lodges across the nation, Brotherhood members get together to relive memories, or, even more important, to bring a bit of Denmark to the many younger members who have never seen the works of art, the crafts, the way of life of their parents and ancestors in the old country. These meetings are demonstrations of the fraternal spirit of the Danish Brotherhood of America, a spirit kept alive in the hearts of Danish-Americans for over ninety years. Danish Brotherhood lodges can bring Denmark to the young members in many ways. The pen-pals program through National Headquarters will team up a pair of youngsters, ages five to twenty, for international correspondence. An annual essay contest on the subject of why we should preserve our Danish heritage and culture interests hundreds of youngsters, those under sixteen in one category, those over sixteen in another. And what young man or young woman doesn't like kite flying! A lodge-sponsored contest will involve children and their fathers in a wholesome outdoor activity, and creates valuable publicity for the lodge. Evenings are often devoted to authentic Danish folk dances to bring young people together and bring them closer to the Danish heritage.

The monthly magazine of the Brotherhood is the cornerstone of the fraternal services for all members. It is a valuable source for all lodges, from which they gather ideas, information, suggested activities, and news of lodges and members from other states and cities. Newsletters are part of the fraternal activities of the Danish Brotherhood. Each year the Brotherhood also provides six $1000.00 academic scholarships to encourage young men and women to further their education. This is fraternity at work.

Within the headquarters at Omaha there is a Danish archive or museum of old-country artifacts and treasures. The Brotherhood is thus preserving the culture and heritage of Danish-Americans. But fraternity goes beyond preservation; a true fraternity serves to protect its members. The Danish Brotherhood provides a choice of family insurance protection plans, certificates to protect every member of the family, life plans, term insurance, and retirement income plans, and all at the lowest possible cost. And with the basic insurance packages supplemental insurance is available.

The Danish Brotherhood is a democratic organization where every member has a voice, a voice that should be heard through the elected officers, local or national, by the professional staff at National Headquarters. So that each lodge may operate successfully, the Brotherhood has prepared large handbooks on the how-to-work fraternal lodge activities, how to conduct the lodge's business affairs, cultural activities, and even how to sponsor a Danish festival.

Open festivals and cultural activities involve many people both within and outside of the membership and often result in valuable publicity for the lodge, a logical first step in the expansion of both membership and activities. And publicity is an outstanding way to broaden the community's knowledge and interest in the part Danish-Americans are playing in building an American culture and heritage.

The Danish Brotherhood is a nationwide fraternity and is recognized as the largest Danish organization of its kind. There are 150 member lodges in twenty states. Under the guidance of the elected Board of Officers, the Danish Brotherhood is developing new ideas, creating new services, and building new programs, programs dedicated to preserving a culture as old as the Vikings.

There are certain things that help one understand the nature of the organization. The Danish Brotherhood was founded in 1882, in Omaha, and evolved from the Danish Veterans Society organized by one Mark Hansen. The Veterans Society and subsequently the Brotherhood created things new to the United States, a chance to get together and help one another over the rough spots, from finding homes to getting jobs. The need was for an organization to serve as an immigrant meeting place. Now this need obviously has been outgrown, so we need to give our prospective members some other reason for joining, and for present members to remain. Our programs are geared to this philosophy.

The requirements for being a Danish Brotherhood member have been the same for ninety years: one must have a Danish background, be married to a Dane, or related to a member. The Danish Brotherhood has recently revamped everything in its program from magazines to management techniques because the original reasons for being no longer exist. The recent response to programs like the Danish folk dance kit, the language tapes—which incidentally are developed in cooperation with Heritage Productions —and special film programs have proved that our members believe we are headed in the right direction.

The Finlandia Foundation

VAINO A. HOOVER: James Michener, in his book on Hawaii concerning the exodus of the Polynesians from Tahiti to Hawaii, mentioned in some detail the preparations for the trip and the articles that were taken along; one thing in particular that he mentioned was that the Polynesians took their gods with them. In one sense the immigrants who came to this country brought some of their physical assets—the material things—but they also took their gods with them. If one thinks of the gods in terms of institutions such as the church and the school, and that broad area of intangible values that we call our ethnic heritage, those things are hard to put a finger on but they certainly have value and they establish identity.

The Finnish people particularly, when they arrived here, like many other ethnic groups settled in colonies relatively restricted in size with a fairly high concentration of their own particular national group. Thus, they could organize along national lines their choral societies, their temperance unions, their coopera-tive purchasing societies, and also be active in such things as the labor movement. During the development that followed the initial immigration period, these island cultures that were established here by the different immigrant groups became diffuse.

People moved into different areas and the sharp identity of a particular island culture became less and less distinct. Finns began to confuse national and ethnic identity with language identity; we began to think and were told, perhaps, that essentially the American people is an English-language heritage group that will tolerate a few other ethnic groups within it provided that they are well-behaved and are not too obvious. We who live in California are particularly aware of this as we have a large ethnic group of Mexicans who are Spanish-speaking people. For many years their participation in government and other functions was rela-tively small, but they also have discovered that there is, in fact, an Anglo-American myth. The fact is that Americans are not essentially an English-language group. The American nation as a whole is composed of many different nationality groups that have no common base other than this very heterogeneous mixture of people, each of which is important in itself. In that respect, perhaps one could say it is somewhat like a tree that has many roots, some larger, some smaller, but all important. Various nationalities support and nourish the common culture that we call our American heritage but which still has room in it for the whole ethnic heritages of various cultural groups that enrich the whole. In Los Angeles, for example, the city government celebrates approximately fifty different independence dates per year.

The identity of each particular immigrant group has to disappear to some extent, but there is no reason why it needs to disappear completely. Many Americans, particularly those who have not been active in keeping in touch with their forefathers or the area from which they came, are now in search of an identity. They ask: why do I behave as I do, and what are the values that are perhaps most distinct in my personality which make me an individual, perhaps slightly different from somebody else, certainly not better but at least different, and give me a personal identity?

We had this situation in the Finnish groups some twenty years ago. The strong fraternal orders seemed to be both local and specialized in their work. We had need for an organization that would be nationwide in its operation, that could do things as a group that none of these organizations could do by themselves. This need gave rise to the birth of the Finlandia Foundation.

The Finlandia Foundation was created to fulfill an increasing need for a national organization that would be available to all people of Finnish origin and to others interested in Finland and in the Finnish culture and people. It is nationwide in character with an organizational framework for local chapters and cooperation of chapters on a state and nationwide basis. The purposes of the Foundation are cultural, educational, and charitable. The Foundation is active in raising funds for scholarships and educational projects; its activities include the supplying of information on Finland and Finnish cultural subjects to speakers, as well as the loan of motion picture films and tape recordings to interested groups. The Foundation is also active in supplying information on America and American institutions to Finland. The

Finlandia Foundation is actively cooperating as a host with local and federal government agencies to assist visitors from Finland to make the best possible contact with American people and institutions. Work is being done in creating and preserving national monuments which commemorate the pioneering deeds of the early Finnish settlers within the United States. The attention of the American people is also being directed to the contributions which have been made by the Finnish people to American culture. The Finlandia Foundation is an active and vigorous organization. Participation by interested persons is solicited, whether they are of Finnish origin or not.

The Finlandia Foundation also sponsors exhibitions of materials from Finland for showing throughout the United States, such as books, art, architecture, some of which have been circulated in cooperation with the Smithsonian Institution, some by the Finlandia Foundation acting on its own behalf. The Finlandia Foundation has exhibited in Finland such things as United States Indian arts and crafts from the Southwest Museum in Los Angeles which traveled through all the various provinces of Finland as well as some of the other Scandinavian countries. The Finlandia Foundation has sponsored Finnish artist groups in the United States and American performances of Finnish choral groups, such as the University Singers, the Helsinki City Chorus, the Helsinki Symphony Orchestra, and the National Ballet Theatre of Finland. During the Sibelius Centennial year in 1965, which marked the 100th anniversary of the birth of Sibelius, the Finlandia Foundation was particularly active in sponsoring concerts throughout the United States of Sibelius's music and the music of other Finnish composers. Women gymnasts have toured the United States on two separate occasions; we expect to continue to do this sort of thing in the future.

The Finlandia Foundation has also been active in the educational field, through gifts of materials to libraries including the United States Library of Congress of Finnish materials that are not in print and are not readily procurable in this country; they have also provided funds for the cataloguing of materials that are in the Library of Congress but have so far not been readily available. To the University of California in Los Angeles we have provided assistance in binding Finnish folklore materials and also for the purchase of additional books. We have also sent volumes to the University of Helsinki Library.

We are anxious to have different universities throughout the United States develop Finnish studies programs. This is a rather difficult area in which to work because it is subject to all sorts of budget difficulties. At the University of California in Los Angeles we had a very excellent Finnish studies program with courses in Finnish literature, Finnish folklore and Finnish language, and a first-rate library; then came a dry spell during which the university threatened to cut out some of the Finnish language instruction. The Finlandia Foundation raised some $3,000 as a gift to the University of California in Los Angeles to provide teaching salary assistance for the Finnish-language classes for that year, with the result that there was a full year of teaching of the Finnish language during 1972–73 which would not otherwise have occurred. Another area of assistance has been the procurement of professors from Finland to teach in United States universities, particularly in the area of Finnish studies or Finnish language or Finnish literature.

The Finlandia Foundation has a scholarship program which is perhaps unique in that it is in cooperation with the Sibelius Academy of Music in Finland. Here in the United States, we can give a man or woman a scholarship in music which will permit him to travel to Finland; the Sibelius Academy of Music in turn gives them a tuition-free grant for the year of their study, so that this Sibelius scholarship grant is not only from the Finlandia Foundation on the part of the United States but also a grant from the Sibelius Academy in Finland. Likewise, the Sibelius Academy recommends certain students for study in this country, and normally those students are given scholarship grants by the Finlandia Foundation for study in the United States.

In addition to these two institutions we have available a foundation created by our family, the Vaino Hoover Foundation, which supplements the scholarship gifts of the Finlandia Foundation. With the Finlandia Foundation Trust, which administers the monies of the Finlandia Foundation and the Vaino Hoover Foundation, we have a capital of some $300,000 which produces income from which scholarship grants can be given annually.

The odd thing about the scholarship grants to American students to Finland is that predominantly they have been given to non-Finnish students. It is not that we favor non-Finnish students, but the applicants who have applied for these grants have been of exceedingly high caliber, all of them being persons who are interested in supplementing their musical education with a knowledge of Finnish music and particularly wish to have the opportunity to study in such a fine musical institution as the Sibelius Academy of Music.

An Icelandic Footnote

K. VALDIMAR BJORNSON: I could be almost as brief as that old-time British encyclopedic work, in which the title of a chapter was "Snakes in Iceland" and the full text of the chapter was "There are no snakes in Iceland." With regard to brotherhoods and fraternal organizations, we Icelanders had no fraternal organizations; we had a cooperative store which started in the mid-80s approximately and lasted for eleven years in my home town of Mineota, then faded away because of financial difficulties. Otherwise, the strong cohesive factor in my childhood and adolescence was the church. I might just quickly add as a footnote that we had an Icelandic Lutheran Synodical body founded in the 1880s by a charter meeting in North Dakota; it had congregations mainly in Canada, plus two rural and one in the village of Mineota in Minnesota, six as a maximum in North Dakota, and congregations in Seattle, Blaine, and Burlingham, Washington. That body later merged with the United Lutheran Church of America. There were also a few Unitarian congregations formed by Icelanders.

The Bygdelags

ODD LOVOLL: The *bygdelags* were of an ethnic identity that is not completely national but regional. I think the Norwegians perhaps more than the other Scandinavian groups had developments that demonstrated this fact. The *bygdelags* were social organizations. They began at the turn of the century and they produced roughly fifty national societies whose main function was to convene once a year for three days to reminisce about the old country. There are still about twenty of these societies in existence; they are now very, very small, and during the three past summers I have visited a number of these groups and I think attendance has been as low as twenty, although in one group I believe they estimated about 500; I think the latter, however, was not really a meeting of these particular people from a Norwegian region, but rather a festival for a particular town. Perhaps half of those present were not even Norwegian.

The *bygdelags* were primarily a movement of the first generation, those who were born in Norway, who could take pleasure in meeting and in talking about the old country, of the valley they had come from; they were not able to any large extent to pass along this sentiment, this sense of nostalgia for the old country, to the second or later generations; still, there are people born in America who have shown great interest in these groups.

The *lags,* in spite of the fact that they have been regional, have promoted a kind of national feeling; they formed a federation which is known as the Council of Bygdelags, and this body meets once a year and deliberates on joint projects.

The Council of Bygdelags (*Bygdelagenes Fællesraad*) lists twenty-two member societies with a national following in 1970; in addition, there were seven specifically west-coast organizations. But, in spite of renewed vigor in a few organizations such as *Valdres Samband,* the pioneer society, there is every indication that within a few years the *bygdelags* will belong to history. All have small memberships, most of them show losses from year to year, and the average age of persons attending meetings is high.

The *bygdelags* have, however, influenced the present interest in genealogy and family background, *rosemaling,* and other peasant arts and crafts. They have also emphasized the importance of the common man in the ethnic community. The Council of Bygdelags has supported a research project that has resulted in the writing of a definitive history of the *bygdelag* movement, to be published soon.

Discussion

S. RALPH COHEN: The Scandinavian-American community, in the ethnic sense, has somewhere around a million-and-a-half members. A quick bit of addition would indicate that membership in the organizations of the kind we have covered is approximately 200,000. If you extend the Scandinavian-American community into successive generations, one wonders about the extent of organizational penetration of the whole of the Scandinavian-American group. Obviously each of them has shown a redirection, a concentration on heritage and on youth. At the same time, if you look at the potential target, there seems still to be a disparity between the opportunity, or the challenge, and the realization. That is not a question; I suspect it is perhaps a heresy.

MAGNE SMEDVIG: Let me comment from the standpoint of the men and women throughout the country who are organizing lodges and selling memberships; we now have sixty men doing nothing but that full-time. In any comparable organization, one of the hardest things to learn is how to prospect, where to find people. For us this problem just does not exist; the Norwegians just seem to come out everywhere; it is absolutely phenomenal. The men tell us that they won't be able to call on all the Norwegians in the United States in a generation. Granted that Sons of Norway is composed of perhaps a Norwegian Papa and a Mama of some other nationality, or vice versa, nevertheless, we like to make them think that the Norwegian heritage is the most important, so that the children will become all the more excited about it, and essentially that is what happens. We just don't sense any saturation point.

JOHAN HAMBRO: Ralph Cohen has proved himself a master of statistics; still I wonder whether the figures that he quoted should not be revised downward quite a bit. He talked about a community of one-and-a-half million, but we don't always expect that husband and wife and children all belong to the various organizations. When it comes to our organizational penetration, as I think you call it, we are quite aware of the fact that there is a tremendous potential, but we are hampered simply by a shortage of funds.

GENE G. GAGE: There's something that I have noticed. Why are the Norwegians so much more effective in organizing? In terms of absolute statistics they seem to have more success in organizing and I am curious as to why.

I don't think that they are overorganized; I think circumstances brought some fine organizational people into top positions. But in the Norwegian groups one has, whatever the reason might be, more of an awareness; that I think is perhaps the major reason. Dr. Fishman observed that he felt that the ethnic groups here were not organized before coming to America. I would disagree with him on this point because as far as the Norwegians are concerned, they had a great national consciousness before coming. Their emigration corresponded precisely to the height of national romanticism in Norway and ended, of course, with the fight for independence from Sweden. Norwegian national consciousness was certainly stronger than that of any other Scandinavian movements. I do feel that has quite a lot to do with it.

EINAR HAUGEN: At the time I was working on my book on the Norwegian language in America, I was struck by the fact that there seemed to be greater ethnic activity among Norwegians than in comparable Scandinavian groups. I found this was not an absolute fact, but relative to Swedes and Danes it was fairly clear, and it seems if you want to set up certain laws, one of them would be that the smaller the ethnic group, the greater the activity. Now that is not entirely true, but it does hold for the Icelanders who seem to have been probably the most retentive of their language in this country. The Finns have been very strong also. I think the Norwegians rank third, relatively speaking, and if I were to account for it, the explanation would seem to be the greater rural-settlement pattern of Norwegians in the United States. It has been pointed out repeatedly that the rural settlements were made early, they were stable, they developed their own culture, and thus Norwegian-ness was retained longer. However, statistics in the United States census relating to urban Norwegians and urban Swedes came out exactly alike, they were 50/50. Urban Norwegians and urban Swedes were losing their linguistic identity at approximately the same rate. Danes are the least retentive, proportionately speaking, which is not accountable in terms of their numbers since they are relatively fewer, but I think it is accountable in terms of the urban nature of Danish life in Denmark.

PETER A. MUNCH: I may offer an almost simplified explanation: if we look upon Scandinavia, the five countries, as a family, we have two big brothers, Sweden and Denmark, and three small brothers, Finland, Norway, and Iceland. And if we look at the political history of the last couple of hundred years, we find that Finland, Norway, and Iceland have each gone through an emotionally loaded fight for political independence, which Sweden and Denmark did not have to do. And I think the greater ethnic awareness among the former three is explainable in that way.

CARLTON C. QUALEY: Most of the immigrants were peasants, uneducated, loyal to their district, but they were not strongly conscious of being Norwegian nationalists. We need to focus on the leadership of the intellectual elite; this has not been adequately explored and would explain a good deal, I think, about leadership among the Norwegians.

KENNETH O. BJORK: It is interesting that with their organizational powers, business skills, etc., the folklore among Norwegians is that they are miles behind both the Swedes and the Danes in these particular respects. I'm not going to try to interpret that, but they don't think of themselves as being particularly keen in these areas.

Special-Interest Societies

Panel: FRANKLIN D. SCOTT (Chairman), NILS WILLIAM OLS-SON, CARLTON C. QUALEY, JOHN CHRISTIANSON, ERICK KENDALL, HOLMFRIDUR DANIELSON

Chairman's Remarks

FRANKLIN D. SCOTT: Special-interest societies concerned with Scandinavia and with Scandinavians in America have proliferated in many directions. In university communities there have been small ad hoc groups meeting to discuss topics connected with ancient Nordic culture, and the Society for the Advancement of Scandinavian Study is a venerable organization of deep scholarly concerns. Learned societies, musical organizations, professional groups, museums, drama clubs are usually formed on the basis of a specific national origin, as are cooperative societies and charitable and social organizations; they are multitudinous, and it would be quite impossible to do anything more than sample their variety.

Each of the treatments that follows is different in approach, for each grows out of the experience and the perspective of one person. It would be a mistake to try to cast them into a common mold, but together they make a realistic mosaic illustrating the wide-ranging diversity of interests among the Scandinavians and their friends in the United States. Each individual has been asked to comment on the character of the membership of the societies discussed, the purposes of the organizations, language usage, and the question of how much of an attempt should be made to keep alive interest in Scandinavia. Each in his own way touches on these common concerns.

102

Swedish Special-Interest Societies

NILS WILLIAM OLSSON: American Swedish groups throughout the United States and Canada include historical, cultural, and social societies representing a total of perhaps 50,000 people. Though I speak for all I admit to a certain bias in favor of the organization I presently head, The American Swedish Institute in Minneapolis.

The historical societies are: The American Swedish Historical Foundation in Philadelphia, which long has published a yearbook (under changing names); The Swedish Pioneer Historical Society of Chicago, which publishes the *Swedish Pioneer Historical Quarterly;* the Augustana Historical Society of Rock Island, which publishes occasional books. There are also a number of smaller societies such as the Swedish Historical Society in Rockford; the Swedish Pioneer Society in Austin, Texas; the New Sweden, Maine, Swedish Historical Society; and the Bishop Hill Heritage Association. The American Swedish Institute represents both the historical and the general cultural pattern, as does the Swedish Cultural Society of America. Another group of organizations is the professional societies such as the Swedish Engineers' Society and the John Ericsson Society. In addition there are a multitude of local social clubs, the largest being in Seattle where the Swedish Club has 7,500 members. In some urban areas there are city-wide joint groups, which serve as cooperative committees for a number of the smaller groups, such as the Good Templars, the provincial societies (many of them now dying out), and the men's and women's clubs. In the Twin Cities we have *Svenskarnas Dag,* in Chicago the Swedish Central Committee, and in New York the United Swedish Societies. Details on many of these organizations can be found in the *American-Swedish Yearbook* (Vol. VIII, Rock Island, 1973). All of these groups that I have mentioned share in larger or smaller degree two basic goals: (a) to broaden the scope of American-Swedish relations, mainly cultural, and (b) to inculcate into the minds of Americans with Swedish background a pride in their Swedish cultural heritage.

Several of these societies maintain significant archives, some for their own use, such as the Vasa Order in its new building at Bishop Hill, some for more general material including private letters and documents, such as the American Swedish Historical Foundation in Philadelphia and the Swedish Pioneer Historical Society in Chicago.

With regard to one of the basic questions, the structure and program of the societies, I can answer only for my own organization, but I suspect that the problems and the patterns are much the same within the Swedish community throughout the country, differing mostly in details. In those groups where there has been little renewal of content in program, but only the following of an old hackneyed pattern, the basic membership is still tied to the first-generation Swedes with little recruitment from later generations. Where attempts have been made to give the organizations new perspectives, the second, third, and even fourth generations have now begun to be involved. The membership in the American Swedish Institute, for instance, has prospered lately because of giving the younger generations an opportunity to explore their ethnicity in a milieu familiar to them. As an example, we still offer the old-timers films and coffee on Sunday afternoons, but we have also structured new groups such as a ski club, Swedish-language training for children and young people, the young ladies' ensemble, Swedish arts and crafts classes, and a number of charter flights to Scandinavia (eight in 1973).

Here it is interesting to note that the trend is away from the long summer flights, lasting from eight to ten weeks, which were desired by old-timers, ten years ago or so, who wished to see the old sod once more before they were too feeble to travel. Now the charters are almost entirely three or four, or even only two-week trips that suit busy employees, or families with limited means. The increasing number of families where children meet cousins or second cousins indicate that the younger generations of Americans of Swedish background are beginning to discover the land of their roots. Sometimes the increasing awareness of one's ethnicity spills over into serious study of family origins. Scarcely a day goes by that I do not get an inquiry by telephone or letter or personal visit from some young person of Swedish ancestry who is seeking a contact across the water. Such interest may then beget curiosity about other facets of Swedish culture—music, literature, the arts and crafts, as well as the cooking arts. It is no accident that Lilli Lorenzen's book *Of Swedish Ways* (Minneapolis, 1964) is now in its fifth printing.

Our experience at the Institute also indicates that the rings on the water are widening. Intermarriage with other Scandinavians makes our members increasingly less Swedish and more Scandinavian, and thus interested in Scandinavian culture in its entirety. Therefore, we have opened the galleries to Finnish design, modern Norwegian painting, and Danish glass. By this process we hope to cross-fertilize the American-Scandinavian community. We feel strongly that our own members, mostly Swedish in origin, should know more of their sister cultures, and by bringing in other American Scandinavians we also have the opportunity to demonstrate what Swedish culture is all about. But it is not only the Scandinavians who through intermarriage are more and more affiliating with us. We are also getting a growing number from other national groups, including a recent member with roots in Lebanon.

Finally, how do we retain these new additions to our institute? I would venture to say that the question is equally relevant for other Swedish ethnic societies. I think that we must accept the new trends, we must answer the new questions, we must heed the new interests that develop, and be prepared to meet the challenges with new ideas and new approaches. Unless we can harness this emerging interest and new thinking by servicing the demands, we shall have to see the new Atlantis recede again into the sea. I personally do not believe we can activate young people today with the folklore of yesteryear, effective as it may have been fifty to seventy-five years ago. It is up to us who have worked with these ethnic groups for many years to regroup our forces and to meet the new challenge in new ways.

One of the new departures that we hope will bear good fruit is the Swedish Council of America, started this year by the American Swedish Institute, the American Swedish Historical Foundation, and the Swedish Pioneer Historical Society. But only started by these three societies, for its purpose is to draw together all the institutions in the country interested in promoting Swedish and American Swedish culture to provide a means of coordinating activities and enhancing effectiveness. Common nationwide action is particularly important if we are to realize the goals of the Bicentennial celebrations.

Norwegian-American Learned Societies

CARLTON C. QUALEY: Two organizations dominate the field of Norwegian-American learned societies: the Norwegian-American Historical Association, with headquarters at St. Olaf College, Northfield, Minnesota, and the Norwegian-American Museum at Decorah, Iowa. The latter predates the 1925 centennial; the former stems from that occasion.

The Norwegian-American Historical Association was created by a small group of dedicated scholars, journalists, and businessmen who undoubtedly had a variety of motives. However, the danger of its becoming just another ethnic mutual admiration society was fortunately avoided by the appointment of Theodore C. Blegen to be managing editor of publications. It was also wisely determined not to infringe upon the museum operations of the Decorah institution and instead to concentrate on publication. Archives were established to be housed in the St. Olaf College Library. It was Blegen who established the guidelines for the new organization. He resisted the importunities of those who wished to use it for ethnic glorification. He even resisted the zeal of O. E. Rölvaag to make it a vehicle for the preservation of Norwegian culture. He particularly resisted too close an identification with any religious group or college. From his independent vantage point at the Minnesota Historical Society and as Dean of the Graduate School of the University of Minnesota, Blegen firmly guided the Norwegian-American Historical Association into the channel of a learned society in the true sense of the term. In his thirty-five years as managing editor, some forty of the present fifty-two volumes of publications were produced, all of high quality, making the Norwegian-American Historical Association the acknowledged model immigrant-American historical society anywhere. Blegen's prestige and personal charm were such as to gain support from a number of economically well-situated Norwegian-Americans, and in this his loyal supporter was Birger Osland of Chicago. This tradition of support has been continued. Following Blegen's retirement as managing editor in 1960, Kenneth Bjork of St. Olaf College took over and expanded the publications program. It is significant that by the time Blegen retired, his concern that the Norwegian-American Historical Association might become subordinated to a sectarian institution proved without basis, partly perhaps because the host college was itself becoming a liberal arts institution in the true sense, but chiefly because the editorial board and the managing editor maintained a policy of independence.

The significance of this independence cannot be overemphasized, and it should be instructive to those with simplistic notions concerning immigrant identity. The membership, now just under a thousand, paying modest annual dues, the generous donors of supporting funds, and the flourishing archives, now directed by Lloyd Hustvedt, testify to the viability of an immigrant-American organization which has kept itself in the mainstream of American and world scholarship. Any organization which is only parochial is by that fact limited in its appeal to new generations. The membership is still largely Norwegian-American, chiefly of the first three generations. However, the new generations are far more American than they are Norwegian. As I read their life style, they have shed all sense of being a minority, of being distinctive because they are of Norwegian ancestry, and of any lingering *"Ja vi elsker"* syndrome. Although numerically enrollments in Norwegian language classes have increased, proportionate to the total stock the numbers are small indeed. Even the much touted "identity" crisis is not measurably helped by harking back to ancestry. What these newer generations can respect is "success" in any field of knowledge, and in the Norwegian-American field publication by the Norwegian-American Historical Association represents something tangible and respected.

The Norwegian-American Museum in Decorah, Iowa, has also become nationally known and respected in its field. Despite inadequate housing, financial difficulties, problems of relationship with Luther College, now happily resolved, and crises common to museums everywhere, this museum has been developed by a dedicated group of administrators and supporters led by its director, Marion Nelson, into a truly unique institution. It is recognized among professionals in its field as exemplary, and has been accorded praise and honors for its displays and its huge collections. Artists and museum professionals from all over the continent and abroad make use of these collections. The visual appeal of the exhibits and publications of the museum exerts influence far beyond the printed word, for beauty is an international commodity. The *rosemaling,* wood carving, textile handicrafts, artifacts of immigrant life, and the innumerable other materials collected by the museum constitute an education in a life style. With a much too limited membership (ca. 2,000) its appeal must be to the general American public as much as to Norwegian-Americans.

Certain other oganizations belong in this brief record of Norwegian-American learned societies. One is the Norwegian-American Technical Society, with archives in its Chicago branch. The *Norwegian-American Technical Journal* has been the vehicle of communication within this highly specialized group, many of them among the most distinguished engineers in American history. In his *Saga in Steel and Concrete* (1947), Kenneth Bjork has recorded the extraordinary achievements of these scientists.

Although not strictly Norwegian, the Society for the Advancement of Scandinavian Study continues to promote scholarship in Scandinavian linguistics, literature, and culture. Its journal now includes an annual bibliography of publications on Scandinavian subjects, including Scandinavian-American. It is of course limited in membership and its primary concern has been literary, but it, like the organizations previously mentioned, helps keep scholarship at a high level.

In conclusion, one may be permitted a general comment on the problem posed by the organizers of this Seminar, a problem common to all immigrant-American groups. As one interested primarily in comparative history, I do not view with any great alarm the possibility of dissipation of interest in things Norwegian-American in the near future. Each immigrant-American society has reason to be proud of its ancestry, to deplore excesses of chauvinistic enthusiasm and evidences of discrimination, and to retain curiosity concerning the country of origin. But as the inexorable processes of time and change operate, reliance on ethnic identity becomes less than adequate to sustain a life style. It becomes a fringe thing. Substantively, what will survive is the scholarly, artistic, and archeological record.

Danish-American Special-Interest Societies

JOHN CHRISTIANSON: Danish-American special-interest societies are usually small, like the Norwegian-American Historical Association, but also, like that society, they are often vital, attractive to both recent immigrants and descendants of immigrants and to non-Scandinavians who share the special interest that is the focus of the organization.

Significant for our perspective on such societies is the strong support for similar groups in Denmark itself. The annual celebration of America's Fourth of July has been going on in the Rebild Park for almost half a century. The Danes Worldwide Archives (*Udvandrerarkivet*) is a collection of emigration materials located in Ålborg. *Dansk Samvirke,* which plays a role similar to that of

Nordmanns-Forbundet, puts out an excellent journal and holds an annual gala get-together at Kronborg. *Danmark-Amerika Fondet* is active as the sister organization of The American-Scandinavian Foundation. The Danish West Indies Society conducts group flights to what are now the American Virgin Islands. Strong ties continue between the Danish state church and the Danish Lutheran churches in the United States.

However, the Danish-Americans lack some of the special-interest societies found among other Scandinavian-Americans. For example, there is no Jutland *Bygdelag,* nor is there anything comparable to the Norwegian-American Historical Association or the American Swedish Institute. Danish-Americans do have local cultural societies and clubs and some characteristic organizations that are uniquely theirs. On the one hand are the Grundtvigian heritages with their folk high schools and leisure-time activities; on the other hand are the legacies from Danish colonialism in the West Indies. A few selected from the many can illustrate the problems and the potentialities that face such societies today.

Danebod Folk School, Tyler, Minnesota, illustrates what has happened to the folk high school tradition in America. Annual four-day Danish meetings are held at Danebod, and the program is still entirely in the Danish language, though much of the casual conversation may be in English. As many as one hundred people participate. For the most part, however, the old folk high school buildings at Tyler are used for congregational activities and regional meetings without specific ethnic significance. Two trends are worth noting: one, the family-centered Leisure-Time Workshops, now in their twenty-sixth year, represent a remarkable though not specifically ethnic adaptation of the Grundtvigian spirit to the English language and the North American milieu; they lack the media dimension, however, that has been exploited so effectively in recent years by some of the Scandinavian-American fraternal organizations. An example of another trend, if it may be such, was the splendid Scandinavian exhibit, accompanied by crafts demonstrations, pastries and foods, folk dancing and all, attended by several thousand people in the spring of 1972. This was part of a wider program originating at the University of Minnesota, but it revealed a grass-roots interest in Scandinavian ethnicity, as well as a widespread and growing interest in popular ethnic festivals.

Also in the Grundtvigian tradition are the Danish American Center in Minneapolis, currently flourishing as an up-to-date version of traditional Danish social vitality (as well as the sponsor of rock-bottom-priced charter flights to Denmark); and the Dannebrog Dancers, a popular and far-ranging group which performs regularly throughout a four-state area from their home base in Minneapolis. The hallmarks of the Dannebrog Dancers are a cosmopolitan membership that includes Chinese and many European nationalities and meticulous authenticity. Their leader is a Danish-speaking Puerto Rican scholar who insists upon the highest standards of costume and performance, and the result is that the members create interest in antiques, Danish museums, folk music and folk culture as well as dancing; they also cultivate interests in Norwegian and Swedish folk dance and sometimes perform programs featuring these nationalities. The interest of young people, especially college students, in this organization is worth particular notice.

Quite a different type of society, but no less vital, is *Dansk Garderforening i Kalifornien*. This cohesive group, whose members must be veterans of the Danish Royal Guard, has included Lauritz Melchior and other popular figures; they come from a cosmopolitan stratum of society and, consequently, although it is highly specialized, it maintains its vitality and readily absorbs new members. In some ways it is the type of professional organization which has existed among Scandinavian-American engineers, journalists, and others. There are similar chapters of *Dansk Garderforeningen i Udlandet* in New York City, Chicago, Buenos Aires, and three Canadian cities; Danish is always the language of regular meetings.

One of the most active areas currently, with respect to special-interest societies, is the United States Virgin Islands. Here in what were the Danish West Indies until 1917 interest in Denmark is still strong among Danes, Danish-Americans, and some of the older colored families (the population is heterogeneous, with over 89 percent black), as well as among recent migrants from the North American mainland. An institution like the West Indies Company plays its part in assuring the continuity of a Danish presence in the islands, and in Denmark the *Dansk Vestindisk Selskab* gives institutional focus to interest in the islands.

This society cooperates with the Friends of Denmark Societies in St. Thomas and St. Croix, arranging exchange visits in both directions for people to stay in private homes. It also works with the St. Croix Landmarks Society that dates from 1948 and now has some 450 members and a substantial annual budget, one quarter of it contributed by the Virgin Islands government. With these funds comes public responsibility, and the Landmarks Society has met this responsibility with a vigor and imagination that should be an inspiration to other Scandinavian-American groups. The society is dedicated to the preservation and interpretation of landmarks from the Danish period of the islands' history. It took the lead in the establishment of the National Historical Site in Christiansted under the present supervision of the United States National Park Service; it maintains its own impressive sugar plantation museum at Whim, conducts annual House Tours, publishes a newsletter and a handsome series of histories and guidebooks, and sponsors special projects such as the reproduction of an authentic Danish sentry box to be set up outside Government House. At the present time the society is working to promote an environmental open space project in St. Croix. In addition to public service the society has created interest in Denmark and things Danish as well as in the Danish period of West Indies history.

With regard to historical organizations in the United States something seems to have gone wrong among Danish-Americans. The Danes have not suffered from any lack of source materials nor any absence of competent historians. There are possibly more than enough depositories for historical materials, and such men as Enok

Mortensen, Paul Nyholm, Kristian Hvidt, and Carlo Christensen testify to the high quality of Danish-American history. What seems to be lacking is a unifying institutional structure like that provided by the Norwegian-American Historical Association. The Danes have been burdened by the legacy of an energetic and brilliant start that was headed down the wrong track. The Danes World-wide Archives, founded in the years 1930–1932, was originally well endowed and handsomely housed in a castle surrounded by a park on the outskirts of Ålborg; it was financed largely by a group of Chicago businessmen. But it was built in Denmark, not in North America. It has had through the years an excellent and dedicated staff, but it has suffered various vicissitudes—for example, the house was used by the Nazis for a headquarters during World War II and was left in such a shambles that it could not be reoccupied. It has failed to acquire a viable base of continued support, while its very existence has destroyed the possibility of developing a similar archive or depository in the United States. Danish-Americans have been reluctant to give wholehearted support to an institution that is located overseas. Hence the organization has pursued no publication program, no program of systematic research or exhibitions as has the Emigrant Institute in Växjö, Sweden; it has even been forced to curtail its cooperation with the Rebild Festival. Thus, despite a number of archives and collections on both sides of the Atlantic (such as those at Grand View College, Dana College, and Lutheran School of Theology in Chicago) the Danes lack a unifying central organization in North America. This has been a serious detriment to Danish-American historical scholarship.

May I return to an important aspect of ethnic activity in the present day? Ethnocentricity is no longer regarded as a virtue, and it is rapidly vanishing in our cosmopolitan culture. Ethnic organizations that want to survive and function must justify themselves according to the values of a cosmopolitan and shrinking world, better educated, more sophisticated, more heterogeneous. An individual now has an opportunity to choose his interests, his associations, his cultural traits from the bewildering variety that is made available to him, not so much by his friends and neighbors and family but by the wide range of media. As has been seen earlier, the Brotherhoods have been sensitive to the chance to present traditional values in new and exciting forms through contemporary media. Those who affiliate with ethnic organizations today, particularly the special interest groups, do so by choice, not just because they are born into a group. The focus is upon the interest exemplified or cultivated by the society concerned, not necessarily on the ethnic background of the individual members. This tendency opens up, then, a wide range of Americans to our sphere of activity, Americans who may not be of Scandinavian descent.

Finnish-American Societies

ERICK KENDALL: The Finnish presence in America has been numerically small, less than 300,000 during its height in the 1930s and 1940s, with half of these concentrated in the Upper Midwest. This is the area, therefore, where flourished the Finn Halls, each busy with choral groups, folk dances, amateur dramatics, and mass meetings at which orators declaimed in the Finnish language.

It was here also that the Finnish-American cooperatives made their greatest impact on American life, an impact that has created what is probably the most lasting image of my compatriots, recorded in scores of reportorial books and scholarly studies of the American cooperative movement. Most of these Finnish-American cooperatives were organized by Marxian Socialists. The leaders of that group considered cooperatives a very important branch of working class action, outranked only by Socialist Party politics and labor unions. Exceptions were a few co-ops in rural areas into which Finnish peasants had migrated directly from Finland, without exposure to the growing militancy of American industrial centers.

The conditions on the Upper Midwest frontier were ideal for

cooperative action by the language-locked Finnish settlers. In many cases they were in virtual economic slavery to their business-men compatriots, getting paid for their produce in the store-keeper's private chits that were acceptable in trade only at the store of their origin.

It is difficult, almost impossible, to pinpoint the exact size of the Finnish-American regional cooperative when it was still 100 per-cent Finnish. The process of Americanization started gradually: people of other origins elbowed their way in despite the language barrier, the main reason being the obvious economic advantages of buying in a co-op. But in the early 1930s, before Americanization had become a studied policy, the Central Cooperatives, Inc. had about a hundred mostly small local co-op affiliates with some 20,000 individual members. CCI did an annual business of over $1,000,000, and the retail co-ops had sales of $40,000,000.

In the late 1920s and early 1930s these Finnish-American co-ops went through a traumatic factional struggle that ended in the total ousting of Marxist influence from their affairs. In the worldwide split of socialism following the Russian Revolution the pro-Communist radical wing gained control of *Tyomies,* which had earlier espoused democratic socialism. Then, in what the radi-cals believed to be a period of imminent American revolution, they sought to solidify their loosely-affiliated locals and to exploit the cooperatives' considerable economic resources to finance revolutionary activities.

But the vast majority of the Finnish-American cooperators had learned to value a cooperative for its own sake. In a bitter strug-gle lasting into the mid-1930s they rallied around those leaders of CCI who advocated the Rochdale principle of political neutrality. The radicals and their influence were ousted from the wholesale and from all but a half dozen local co-ops. The strident militancy of these few co-ops quickly alienated all but the true believers, and the businesses were eventually liquidated.

Motivated by a conviction that cooperatives are the needed democratic countervailing force to monopoly capitalism, the younger Finnish-Americans saw that they must Americanize the movement if it was to have significant impact on the region's economy. In the mid-1930s a systematic Americanization effort was launched, against determined resistance by some of the more ethnic-minded elders. English became the official language, and the major publicity thrust was directed through the regional's English-language tabloid, *Cooperative Builder*. However, publication of *Tyovaen Osuustoimintalehti* (Finnish Cooperative Weekly) was continued into the 1960s, mostly out of sympathy toward the gradually vanishing ranks of pioneers.

And finally, to match the ever-growing wave of consolidations among its private profit competitors, CCI was merged in 1963 into the large, five-state Midland Cooperatives, a regional organization with more than a third of a million members of many ethnic origins. Finns were still the dominant majority of CCI's merger-time membership of 75,000 individuals, but a large minority of members and staff consisted of other Scandinavians and Americans of various ethnic origins.

The Finnish influence on Midland and other American cooperatives continues. Many ranking leaders of large cooperatives are second- and third-generation Finns. And even the "non-Finn" co-op executives readily acknowledge the valuable contribution of the Finnish pioneers.

Not being a psychologist I am not qualified to make motivational judgments, but I have occasionally speculated that the energetic push for *total* Americanization could have been at least partially motivated by a subconscious desire to bury the radical skeleton in the image of the larger American cooperatives.

In the years following the factional struggle in the co-ops, several thousand Finnish-American leftists emigrated to Russian Karelia, a Finnish-speaking province bordering on Finland. This mass emigration of former immigrants to the United States was promoted by the Karelian Communist government so as to draft the agricultural and industrial skills of the Finnish-Americans for their technically undeveloped province, and also to get some hard currency from the new settlers. The actual recruitment of the emigrants was done by some of the discredited and ousted pro-Communist former leaders of Finnish-American cooperatives.

The once powerful leftist wing of the Finnish-American press atrophied after the struggle in the co-ops and is today virtually nonexistent. And although the emigrants to Karelia totaled only a few thousand, Elis Sulkanen, historian of the Finnish-American labor movement, notes that it consisted of the most enthusiastic rank-and-file supporters of the leftist press. This weakening of their base, plus their World War II support of the Hitler-Stalin pact, hastened the demise of these papers, Sulkanen concludes.

Other Finnish-American ethnic activities such as the Finn Halls have vanished from the scene because of the disappearance of their linguistic need and the recent vast changes in American social and cultural life. But vestiges of Finnish ethnic organizations remain, such as the Minneapolis-based Finnish-American Society, Inc., which claims 2,500 members in several states. However, most of its activities seem to consist of membership picnics and the organization of low-cost round-trip flights to Finland. These for-members-only flights are undoubtedly the main attraction of the group for new members.

There are other Finnish ethnic groups, such as the Finlandia Foundation and the various Lutheran churches, but they are well represented at this seminar by their knowledgeable leaders.

Finnish ethnic feeling in the Upper Midwest is probably strongest in the Upper Peninsula of Michigan, where an estimated 60 percent of the population is of Finnish origin. But even there I have found that aside from the Suomi College circles and a weekly Finnish-language TV show aired from Marquette, cohesive Finnish cultural activity has vanished. There as elsewhere a linguistic mish-mash which I would term "Finglish" is occasionally spoken by descendants of the immigrants and could probably be considered an expression of ethnic pride.

Such pride does persist, and is probably stronger among the second- and third-generation American-born. To end with a personal example: my only son is of mixed parentage and does not speak Finnish. And yet, when he was serving in Vietnam, he wrote home about his delight in meeting "another Finnish-American Marine." And now he and his part-Swedish wife of similarly mixed parentage are planning to vacation in "the two old countries." But like the Finns and Swedes of the New Sweden Colony on the Delaware of the 1600s, their descendants will be absorbed into the polyglot American stream.

I may not like it, but I must accept it.

Icelandic Special-Interest Societies

HOLMFRIDUR DANIELSON: Icelanders in Canada and the United States are few and scattered, but from the establishment of the first settlements societies have been formed to preserve the Icelandic heritage. Strong emphases were placed on education, law, religion, literature, and citizenship in the new land. Schools and churches were built immediately, a newspaper was started, and where necessary, as in Manitoba, a special government district was created. The Manitoba settlements date from 1875 and by the turn of the century twenty-nine scattered communities had libraries and reading circles. The libraries were good, and the most famous Icelandic-Canadian poet in Manitoba, Stefán Stefánsson, who had no formal schooling, called the local library his university.

In 1918 a number of the local societies formed the Icelandic National League (INL) in Winnipeg; now it has about 900 members and there are ten chapters, seven in Manitoba, two in Alberta, and one in North Dakota. Some strong local organizations remain outside the League, such as the 400-member society in Vancouver, and others flourish in Toronto, Montreal, Seattle, Chicago, New York, and Northern and Southern California. The League is attempting to gather these groups together for more effective work, but they already cooperate in many ways. The INL has sponsored scores of eminent visitors from Iceland, cultural and political, and they usually make the entire circuit of Icelandic groups in both Canada and the United States. They usually come at the time of the INL convention in the winter or for the Icelandic Festival in the summer.

The INL and the many other clubs, church groups, Ladies' Aids, drama groups, share the same general goals in the preservation and passing on of Icelandic culture, but they pursue their purposes in a great variety of ways. They support six homes for senior citizens (four in Canada and two in the United States); they show innumerable films on Iceland; they organize choral groups; they produce plays, and so on. From the early immigration years down to the present, literary productivity has been impressive—books, magazines, pamphlets. Publication was of course in Icelandic. But now the *Annual* of the INL, which existed for fifty years, has been discontinued; the *Icelandic Canadian Magazine* is published in English, and the one remaining newspaper is partly in English. Increasingly the language of meetings and conventions is English, though we tend to speak whichever comes out of our mouths most naturally. We probably attempted too long to hold on to Icelandic and this hampered our work; membership seems to increase as we shift to English. Drama has been one of the most popular activities, and our drama groups have won prizes in all-Icelandic competition, and in provincial meets in Canada. Recently students of the Icelandic Department at the University of Manitoba formed a drama club and they have produced some excellent plays both in Icelandic and in English translations of Icelandic works.

The interest of young people has been one of the most encouraging developments of late. Very few of the first generation of immigrants remain, but the second and third generations are taking over. The Icelandic Festival committee, for instance, is now entirely second and third generation, and they do everything in English. Youth participation has been stimulated especially by the creation of the chair of Icelandic studies at the University of Manitoba (Professor Haraldur Bessason), funded by $200,000 raised through the cooperating Icelandic communities. Each year various cultural groups in Canada give scholarships to thirty or more high school and university students, and send one student to Iceland. Students from Iceland come on scholarships to study in Canada. Last year a folklorist from Iceland visited Canada for six months on a fellowship provided at the University of Manitoba by an individual gift. Language instruction is expanding and increased efforts are being made to get it recognized in the schools.

A general upsurge of interest in liaison with the old country is in evidence. The Icelandic classics are being translated into English and are opening minds to the value of our heritage. The 1974 celebration of the 1100th anniversary of the settlement of Iceland will command a large number of charter flights, and the 1975 observance of the 100th anniversary of the Icelanders' coming to Manitoba also will attract widespread attention. The volcanic disaster in the Westman Islands has opened hearts and pocketbooks, aid being channeled through the Canada Icelandic Foundation. The Icelandic Festival at Gimli, now in its 83rd year, is a great cultural occasion, with essay contests, music, poetry, sports, displays of arts and crafts, all ending with a big dance. In 1972 the Reykjavík City Band graced the Festival, and in 1975 the Male Choir of Reykjavík will sing, along with other groups. Plans are under way for an Icelandic Museum to be founded at Gimli.

My philosophy with regard to our opportunity and our task is expressed in my foreword to the book *Iceland's Thousand Years,* the first paragraph of which reads:

Great thinkers and educators tell us repeatedly that it is a grave mistake for people who emigrate to a new land to toss into the discard their ancestral culture and traditions. The flower of Canadian culture is still a young and tender plant. It would do it immeasurable harm and stunt its growth for years to come were we to cut it off from its roots—those racial roots that lie deep in the soil of many lands.

Discussion

WALFRID ENGDAHL reminded the assembly of the Liberty Party in the United States during the early part of this century and of its remarkable magazine. He spoke briefly of his hope that his descendants for many generations to come would be able to read the rich literature of the Scandinavian lands in their original languages. This Seminar itself had given him deep satisfaction and trust in the future.

MICHAEL G. KARNI: My Finnish friend Erick Kendall and others are negative about the persistence of ethnicity. But he and I see things differently—it is an illustration of that prism effect mentioned by Professor Scott. In Mr. Kendall's vision is the memory of that tight-knit Finnish-American culture at its most intense in the 1920s and 1930s in northern Wisconsin, Minnesota and Michigan; he is dismayed, naturally enough, by what he sees remaining.

I see it from a different perspective. I grew up with one foot in that culture and it was fragmenting, dying. I learned how to dance and to pitch woo and to drink home brew at the dances on Saturday night, and to sing Finnish songs and so forth. But I also had another foot in the small-town culture of northern Minnesota and in the public school system of the United States—two institutions that were not very kind to Finns. As a result I rejected with a vengeance that small part of Finnish culture that I had inherited. I am told that I was fluent in the language when I was five or six years old; I lost it deliberately; I could not stand to be a Finn. For many years this went on. Then, a few years ago I thought I had become a victim of Marcus Lee Hansen's third-generation syndrome; today I am happy to report that I am also the victim of Joshua Fishman's mid-1960s social crisis syndrome.

I did rediscover the past that Erick Kendall was part of, and I did come along at a time in the mid-1960s when all the alternatives seemed to have been wiped away. There was nothing to do, there was no place to turn, it was like "the burnt-out end of a smoky day," as T. S. Eliot has said. And so, just by accident, I discovered Finnish immigrant culture; it fascinated me, and I began to admire my forebears because they had sought, it seemed, through their major institutions to remake America into the paradise they had come here to find. There was a great deal of idealism. The church pushed vigorously to redeem what they considered a lost America, especially the conservative congregation I grew up in.

Given all the stereotypes of Finnish drunkenness you are probably not aware of the strong temperance movement among the Finns—four national Finnish temperance brotherhoods; as late as 1960 they wrote Hubert Humphrey and John Blatnik protesting the establishment of a cocktail lounge across the street from the Capitol. That is an idealism that is persistent. I came to admire that, and to admire also the idealism of the radical labor movement. There were good lessons to be learned from the Socialists, from the old Wobblies who still persist in Duluth, dreaming, as Doug Ollila said, of the day when the workers' paradise will be ushered in. And the cooperative movement was another source of inspiration, something to inform the dead life I was leading. I rediscovered myself.

Recently I have been collecting material for the Finnish collection at the University of Minnesota, and that really showed me how vital immigrant life still is. There are tons of material out there, and for weeks one summer I actually swam in Finnish culture: I could not believe there were that many Finns still kicking around in northern Minnesota and Michigan. But I found two things happening: certain organizations, including special-interest societies, are dying; the surviving three labor societies (the Duluth IWW group, the Superior Communist group, and the group in Massachusetts) are of course dying because they made little appeal to the second generation—the vilification was too much for the newer generations; and the temperance movement is just about dead. But groups such as Dr. Hoover's Finlandia Foundation and many others on my long list are very much alive. I know this because I have had the privilege of addressing at least a dozen of them in the past year-and-a-half or so, and I find the interest amazing; the people in these groups are delighted to see a third-generation person do some work in the field. And they are keeping a kind of ethnic identity alive at least as a base for social and charitable programs and for the ubiquitous flights to Finland. Hence I think the future of these organizations is good because of the surprising number of second- and third-generation Finns involved (there aren't yet many fourth-generation Finns here), and I think they will continue as Finnish organizations for a long time to come.

Vaino A. Hoover: I came to this country with my parents— or rather they came here a year before I was born, and I was thus a new American. Other people have investigated the Finnish heritage as students, or like those who watch a ball game, but I took part as a participant in that heritage. I learned Finnish and English at the same time, and I was about twelve years old before I found out that some people were so stupid that they spoke only one language. What is the benefit of having two languages? Well, of course one can read one or the other, but I found that perhaps the greatest advantage of having two languages is that enjoyed by my wife. Her grandmother came to this country in 1865, her mother was born here, she was born here, but she speaks and reads Finnish exceedingly well. So when she complains about me she criticizes my behavior first in English, and when she runs out of words she switches to Finnish—but I must say that English is ample for my life!

Franklin D. Scott: The special-interest societies differ from the other ethnic institutions we have so far considered in a rather fundamental way. The ethnic churches gather together people who have inherited or created a particular religious faith and organization and who share a basic language bond. Brotherhoods and fraternal organizations build to a lesser extent upon language but are founded to hold together people who stem from a common locality. The special-interest societies, whether historical, musical, professional or even social in emphasis, are less definitely tied to the traditions or place of origin of their members; their focus is on a subject of common concern. Hence we see that as the language bond melts away in the heterogeneous American community the churches tend to wither or to merge, for their primary reason for existence is religious, and the religious purpose can better be served by amalgamation. Fraternal organizations may survive the impact of intermarriage and scattering, but to the extent that they do so they tend to lose their ethnic character. The special-interest societies may, on the other hand, be diluted with non-ethnic membership from the beginning, for it is the common interest, not the language or the locality of origin, that brings their members into association. Nordic culture has literary and artistic and social values that attract individuals from wide segments of the American population—wider in each decade as indicated by the increasingly diversified enrollments in university classes, for example. Because of this difference in focus the special-interest societies may continue without change of character or purpose as long as people are interested in the study of the language and the culture of the Scandinavian countries, in genealogical research, or in the processes of migration and the new hybrid culture created in the western hemisphere. It is therefore probable that the special-interest societies will be the longest-lived of all the different kinds of ethnic organizations.

EDUCATION AND THE
SCANDINAVIAN PRESENCE

Panel: NILS HASSELMO (Chairman), C. PETER STRONG, GENE
G. GAGE, WALTER JOHNSON, LLOYD HUSTVEDT, ERIK
MORTENSEN, RALPH J. JALKANEN, HARALDUR BESSA-
SON, DAVID A. WARD, B. R. EGGAN (Guest Informant),
LARS JOHNSON (Student Representative)

Chairman's Remarks

NILS HASSELMO: In an act of March 2, 1883, the Minnesota
Legislature specified that "There is hereby established a professorship of Scandinavian Language and Literature in the State University. . . . It shall be the duty of the Board of Regents . . . to
appoint to said professorship some person learned in the Scandinavian language, literature, and at the same time skilled [in] and
capable of teaching the dead languages, so-called." I do not know
the specific circumstances surrounding the passage of this, to me at
least, very interesting piece of legislation. However, I think that it
may be safely concluded that it was not an intense desire on the
part of the university itself to fill a serious gap in its offerings that
prompted the passage of the bill in question. Rather it appears that
we have here an example of Scandinavian ethnic self-assertion in
the field of education. Maybe the Departments of Scandinavian at
Minnesota and elsewhere should be viewed as forerunners of such
additions from the 1960s and early 1970s as the Departments of
Afro-American, American-Indian, and Chicano Studies at Minnesota.

Secondly, since 1965 the Scandinavian program at Minnesota
has been one of 103 federally supported area centers for the study
of critical languages and neglected world areas, in the company of
centers for East European, East Asian, South Asian, Middle East,
African, and Latin American Studies.

127

These two glimpses of the history of a Scandinavian department in this country may seem to represent two fundamentally different views of Scandinavian studies, but are they entirely different? The act of 1883 represents a presumably somewhat forced recognition on the part of America of its internal diversity. The establishment of the federally supported center in 1965 represents a recognition on the part of America of the diversity of the world in which we live. As Professor Fishman has suggested in his book, *Language Loyalty in the United States,* America's recognition of internal diversity may indeed be closely linked to its recognition of external diversity. The ethnic and the international components of Scandinavian studies may not be opposites but rather different sides of the same coin. Both are worth exploring. C. Peter Strong's report and the report by Gene G. Gage are the two basic factual studies that will launch this exploration.

Educational Exchange

C. PETER STRONG: The history of opportunities to study abroad until recently has been one of growth in size and in variety. According to the Institute of International Education publication, *Open Doors,* a record 32,209 American students studied abroad in the academic year of 1970–71. This is up from less than 10,000 in 1955. There seems to be no end to the desire of Americans to study abroad, although this desire is always subject to the vicissitudes of history, economics, and politics. The reverse pattern, the number of foreign students received here, has leveled off, particularly during 1971–72, reflecting the high cost of education and the unfortunate image of the United States abroad. Both problems will no doubt be with us for some time. The figure is holding at about 140,000. From 1965 until 1971, the annual increase was between 7 percent and 11 percent. These figures relate to visiting students who are fully enrolled in recognized colleges and universities, and thus may overlook many relevant educational programs. I point to the comparison between students coming and going, as it may be a straw in the wind. If the U.S. image continues to deteriorate, and the cost of inflation continues to escalate, will this holding or reversed trend not also be reflected in study abroad programs for Americans? Another question is: what effect will the Common Market have on United States-Scandinavian educational relations?

For the most part foreign students take courses in technology and the physical sciences, while 39 percent of Americans abroad study the humanities. The number of fully matriculated American students in Scandinavia—these are 1970–71 figures—is about 915, of which about 190 were in languages and literature. The breakdowns by country are: Denmark, 74; Finland, 91; Norway, 250; Sweden, 490; and Iceland, about 10. The programs offered Americans who study abroad range from high school level to postgraduate. They involve almost every kind of curriculum desired. One can study as an individual, as part of a student body from a United States accredited institution, or in a free-swinging group, travel-cum-curriculum. You can work on the Bergen railroad, free of charge, for no credit. There are Junior Year abroad programs, homestay (living with a family), seminar summer programs in Scandinavian studies generally, at the University of Oslo for instance, or in specific areas such as architecture in Finland, design in Denmark, or environment in Sweden. Illinois State, Washburn, and Whittier Colleges have academic programs in Copenhagen, and the University of California gives you the option of Lund or Bergen. California State, on the other hand, offers Uppsala in the summer. The Scandinavian Seminar utilizes the folk high school system throughout Scandinavia, with excellent functional language training assured, and individual cultural homestays can be arranged at the high school level through the American Field Service and others. The list is too long to go into.

What opportunities are there for support? Scholarships, fellowships, and travel grants can be obtained for structured study from many different sources, depending upon the program design.

Foundations and fraternal organizations are good sources. One should also stay abreast of government programs. Care should be taken in matching the application for support to the potential source of funds. Nothing drives the foundation executive up the wall faster than the applicant who has not taken the time to make sure that his request for funds is in line with the policies of the donor institution. "My mother came from Denmark. Can you pay my tuition to Suwannee State?" The answer is no. It is wise to seek advice or consult standard references in the field of educational support. There are also educational experts to be consulted before a program is decided upon. This is most important because often students studying abroad return to find that the courses they took, or the institute at which they were studying, do not qualify them for credits in the United States. This is particularly serious in the professions. I refer here particularly to medicine. There are some cases where credits are applied, but the program is so carefully prescribed that the student might better have stayed home, there being minimal exposure to the culture of the host country. Things have loosened up considerably in this respect, but I date myself by recalling the exquisite exercise in logistics posed by the problem of returning a Smith College junior to her Paris residence —read nunnery—after hours, that is after 10 P.M.

Finally, I think we would all do well to take the large view of education. We should remember that the trend is toward a continuum, that education less and less stops with graduation, that individual growth is a life process, that a well-structured tour under the guidance of experts is a fine educational experience for young and old, credits or not, and that there is no substitute for a primary experience. What the Scandinavians read and hear about us today is unfortunately distorted, and we no doubt are misinformed in our view of them. The result is deleterious to people on both sides of the ocean. It is important to all of us here to realize that through our programs of study abroad, no matter what their structure, understanding and friendship are promoted, and without these essentials mutual trust and cooperation are impossible.

Scandinavian Studies in America

GENE G. GAGE: There is another kind of Scandinavian presence in America that is not the cultural heritage that so many of us represent. It is not the new ethnicity that Professor Fishman so ably describes. It has always been here, in fact it may even have been here before the Scandinavians themselves. If I too may use a metaphor of Atlantis, this presence broke the surface sometime in the mid-nineteenth century, rose periodically, never quite disappearing at the low points, never quite reaching the metropolitan stage at the heights. Our imaginary city popped up here and there, often in quite unlikely places, for a generation or two, and then in 1875 in Madison, Wisconsin, was finally incorporated and has been with us ever since. Since this is not a historically oriented seminar, we are forced to jump over some ninety years, over two world wars, over social upheaval of the first order, over the incredible migration from the old world to the new, all of which changed the face of Atlantis which was still, for the most part, a nice, midwestern town of churches and grocery stores, perhaps a small college, maybe even one or two saloons where the farmers and the bakers and the stone-cutters could meet and talk about the old country. Like so many American cities, Atlantis was to be changed and changed dramatically in the mid-sixties. Somehow or other in that mysterious process which sociologists try to describe, and only partially succeed in describing, cultural heritage, antiestablishmentarianism, the new ethnicity, pot-smoking hippies, and many other powerful forces entered the city center of Atlantis and introduced some urban renewal projects. Though this urban renewal is still going on, with unfinished buildings and dirt streets here and there, the new skyline of Atlantis can clearly be discerned through the smog. I submit, along with John Christianson, and I believe along with Professor Qualey, that as far as we are concerned, Atlantis has been, is, and must remain the presence of Scandinavian studies in American colleges and universities. And I further submit, indeed I think it is self-evident by now, that our new Atlantis is inhabited by more Jews and Italians and WASPs and mongrels than by Norwegians or Swedes or Finns or Danes or Icelanders. And I further submit that it is a better place to live because of it.

Professor Fishman is probably right; Women's Liberation will pass, and ethnicity will still be with us. But I do not think he is right when he wags his finger at us and says: "Don't be afraid." The more extreme ethnic spokesmen, and I am not limiting my comments to the Panthers, the Jewish Defense League, or the Italian Anti-Defamation League, terrify me. For the first time in my life, I find myself on the conservative side of a great social debate. That is terrifying to me also. I haven't quite got it all straight in my mind.

Three or four years ago I got involved in a project that I assumed would take me a couple of months, and which ended up taking two years, and will still take a good number of additional years, since I am rather deeply committed to it. This project was an attempt to describe "the state of the art" of Scandinavian studies in America. The original study was more or less foisted upon me, as there was no one else willing to do it, and the Society for the Advancement of Scandinavian Study asked me if I would be willing to do it. My boss at the foundation has been extremely generous in his support as were, I suppose, the donors of the various funds to the foundation which paid me while I was working on this project. In addition, I originally received a grant from the Council for European Studies that allowed me to tour the campuses of various colleges and universities to do in-depth research, interview students and faculty members, examine libraries, and so on. I would like to talk about the future, so if you want to find out what is going on at present I refer you to my book, available from The American-Scandinavian Foundation, or from the Council for European Studies. In it I have tried to describe what has happened in the last four or five years, with some historical references, such as who teaches what, where it is taught, how many students are taking the courses, the academic qualifications of the faculty involved, and so on.

There were some things that emerged clearly in the first study. Scandinavian studies undeniably is becoming more American and less Scandinavian. Of the students whom I interviewed, well over half have not a drop of Scandinavian blood in their veins, and some of those who are one-fourth or one-half or one-eighth Scandinavian say it played no role in their decision to pursue the subject. Quite a few graduate students in the area of Scandinavian studies have come to the discipline not from Scandinavian studies departments or from the Scandinavian colleges and so on, but from disciplines like linguistics where they might have been studying Italian or Hebrew or German, or from straight history as I did; I came to Scandinavian studies through European history. There are a great number of people coming through the social sciences. It is indisputable. There is a fantastic increase in students from sociology, political science, and, to a lesser extent, economics. There are people who simply discover the phenomena of the welfare state, the unique Finnish geopolitical situation, Danish pornography, Norwegian fjords, or whatever.

Another tremendously important thing is that the emphasis has shifted away from the past to the present. I think any study along these lines will show that you have relatively fewer (not on an absolute basis, but relatively) people studying the sagas, studying immigration, studying Ibsen and Strindberg, and many more students studying contemporary Swedish literature, contemporary Finnish politics, contemporary Norwegian history, etc. I think it is a good sign.

In 1970, when I did the basic statistical work, there were some 4,000 enrollments across the United States in courses in Scandinavian studies. If we computed a whole year instead of one semester the total enrollment for one year would not just be double 4,000, it would come closer to treble that number, because there seems to be a unique situation where the Scandinavian faculties always have larger enrollments in the spring. We may have as many as 15,000 "enrollments," which does not mean "students," because obviously some students are enrolling in more than one course. Recently I did a survey based upon the ten universities that have the largest enrollment, and there were only two colleges among these ten that have gone down: Berkeley and UCLA. And for anyone who is aware of the California educational crisis, that is easily understood. Berkeley's situation was complicated by the fact that they had lost two senior faculty members; they had been cut in half. On the other hand, and on the positive side, the three biggest programs, at Washington, Minnesota, and Wisconsin, have experienced healthy jumps upward. Minnesota, in the fall of 1970, was at 550, dropped off to 365 in the winter of that year, and then rose to over 700 in terms of enrollment. At the University of Washington, it was 550 in 1970, and is now well over 700. The University of Chicago has held pretty steadily through the years at about 100; the University of Chicago is remarkable because of the fact that it produces not only absolutely, but also relatively, by far the greatest number of Ph.D.s. The University of Texas, which has a rapidly growing enrollment, is a new phenomenon which is probably not based on ethnic heritage at all, and only based to a small degree on beginning language courses. Its real strength is in literature and the social sciences. The enrollment at the University of Wisconsin has increased from the mid-300s up to around 600, and close to 700 at times.

Graduate Studies in Scandinavian

WALTER JOHNSON: Graduate studies in Scandinavian can and will be one of the strongest guarantees of Scanpresence in the years ahead. At no other time in the history of Scandinavian studies in the United States has the situation been more favorable or more firm that it is at present. Before 1947, there were only (1) George Flom's one-man effort at the University of Illinois to train Scandinavianists through to the doctor's degree, and (2) Chester Gould's training beyond the master's in Scandinavian at the University of Chicago. The master of arts degree in Scandinavian studies had been awarded occasionally, of course, at such universities as Minnesota and Washington.

But the coming of Assar Janzén to Berkeley in 1947 marks, I believe, the beginning of a development that will assure Scandinavian studies a respectable place and role in academia. Assar Janzén took it for granted that a basic function of a department of Scandinavian is to train university and college scholar-teachers of Scandinavian. That is, he took it for granted that a department of Scandinavian should train qualified graduate students all the way through to the doctorate in Scandinavian. This he proceeded to do in terms of faculty, library, programs, and student body. Since then, the much older university departments in Scandinavian at Minnesota, Washington, and Wisconsin have made the leap of faith, and they now offer the Ph.D. in Scandinavian; at least two private universities, Chicago and Harvard, have programs that lead to the doctorate. In addition to these six, there are several other universities that do offer some graduate courses in Scandinavian; one university for example, UCLA, offers many.

The development of many undergraduate programs in Scandinavian is a closely related *major* means for realizing the hopes of continuing and sustaining the Scandinavian presence in the United States. Through these programs we do have the promise and the possibility of fulfilling what probably should always have been the proper, that is the realistic rather than the sentimental, goal of Scandinavian studies from the beginning: the acceptance of Scandinavian on the same level as Romance, German, and Slavic, and along with those and English the acceptance of Scandinavian as an essential part of the American exposure not only to our European heritage, but also to our contemporary European competitors and critics.

There is nothing new in asserting that Scandinavia and its civilization are a major segment of the world, and its civilization is essentially comparable to the English, the French, the German, or the Spanish, in every way except that of population numbers. There is nothing new in asserting that surely it is a must to have a goodly number of Americans study foreign languages and foreign civilizations which conceivably can contribute a great deal directly and indirectly to the enrichment of American life. There is nothing new in asserting that Scandinavia, past and present, still has every potentiality for serving America as a major resource in terms of intellectual and esthetic stimulation, social experimentation, and technological advance.

What is striking for many of us in Scandinavian studies is that an ever-increasing number of graduate students with no Scandinavian blood ties are coming into Scandinavian, and that they are doing so for such largely non-sentimental reasons as those that I have just suggested. It is from among such graduate students as much as from graduate students of Scandinavian descent that the future faculties of departments and divisions of Scandinavian must be recruited. Until recently, universities have been able to build up effective faculties in Scandinavian largely because some natives of Denmark, Iceland, Norway, and Sweden have been willing to transfer their academic activities to the United States permanently. That, as probably all of us in Scandinavian know, is becoming increasingly difficult, if not impossible. The answer obviously lies in the training of young Americans to become professional Scandinavianists. There is, fortunately, no lack of competent American applicants for admission to our programs.

If the various departments and divisions of Scandinavian continue to develop and strengthen their programs all the way from a strong undergraduate major through a carefully planned doctoral program in terms of a trained faculty and highly competent students, there should be no question about the survival of these programs, certainly not at the state universities.

There will be problems, of course. The matter of the replacement of professors of my generation, because of death or retirement, may be difficult, because of failure to train American Scandinavianists ten to twenty years younger, and because of the difficulty in persuading Scandinavianists from Scandinavia to settle here permanently. But we have a very able group of young American Scandinavianists in their thirties at all these universities; they should be mature enough within a very few years to replace the men now in their early or middle sixties. From then on there should be no problem about replacement, if the departments and divisions produce an adequate, but not excessive, number of highly dedicated and trained Scandinavianists. There may be, at times, some difficulty in placing all Ph.D.s in Scandinavian, as there is difficulty in placing Ph.D.s in general these days, but there will be less, I think, in Scandinavian than in most other fields if the preparation has been carefully planned and carried through, and if the faculties in Scandinavian are willing to use their common sense and imagination in working with both candidates and with colleagues throughout the country, colleagues, that is, not only in Scandinavian but in related fields as well. A young Ph.D. in Scandinavian studies trained to teach Old Icelandic, one modern Scandinavian language, Scandinavian literature, and, say, German, will obviously have an advantage when it comes to placement. There will, moreover, be every good reason for active cooperation between and among the various departments and divisions in Scandinavian. Having observed the effects of recession and war and sudden shifts in academic fashions, I believe that the prospects for Scandinavian studies in this country are decidedly favorable. The growing body of Americans trained as Scandinavianists by the faculties of departments and divisions in Scandinavian can, and should, assure Scandinavian a position of equality in the American academic world. And Scandinavian already has achieved that, certainly at Berkeley, Minnesota, Washington, and Wisconsin.

Norwegian Studies in America

LLOYD HUSTVEDT: Ole E. Rölvaag, in a letter to J. Jorgen Thompson, wrote: "What you and I must aim for and never lose sight of as an ideal is this: The department of Norwegian at St. Olaf College must be made the strongest of its kind in this hemisphere. Nothing else and nothing less will do, or can possibly do. And by Jove, we have to make it go." There are days when I wish Rölvaag had not written this.

We do not view the Department of Norwegian at St. Olaf College as an ethnic attachment to a liberal arts program, and we believe that this view is shared by the other colleges who have thriving departments of Norwegian. These departments are an integral part of the larger college curriculum leading to a B.A. degree.

As is true with Norwegian departments elsewhere, we have seen an increase in enrollment. Currently we have an annual enrollment of approximately 500 students spread over two semesters and an interim. Not all of these students study the Norwegian language, for there are four Scandinavian literature courses in translation and a Scandinavian culture and civilization course which is currently quite popular. As far as percentages go regarding total college enrollment, we, in all likelihood, attract more students per square head than any other institution.

Important to any department of Norwegian is a favorable hinterland. We believe this holds true for Luther, Augsburg, and St. Olaf. At St. Olaf we enjoy a sympathetic faculty, the library collection is a generous one, the Norwegian-American Historical Association and its archives are located there, as is the Admissions Office for the International Summer School in Oslo. The radio station with its regular Sunday Norwegian church services is of much help. Professor Howard Hong, who has specialized in the philosophy of Søren Kierkegaard, provides valuable expansion. Professor Kenneth O. Bjork through his courses in migration makes a similar contribution in the Department of History. We would like to see courses treating Scandinavia in the Departments of Sociology and Political Science. At the moment, at least, we are clearly deficient. The Departments of Music and Art have high curricular interests in matters Scandinavian. Contributing to a healthy hinterland is also the fact that we receive annually eight to nine students from Norway who receive full scholarships. A stipulation for receiving this scholarship is that they work three hours a week within the Department of Norwegian in one capacity or another.

Immigrant colleges are at once fortunate or unfortunate, depending on how they interpret their roles. Those who have built their Norwegian (or whatever other ethnic origin may be theirs) departments on immigrant sentiment alone can expect that such departments will fall when that sentiment vanishes, and at best can only hope for a resurrection when and if a new wave of ethnic interest should appear. Departments that have built on solid academic foundations and that have positioned themselves firmly within the liberal arts concept will survive the whimsical ebb and flow of ethnic interest. When this is done, the emphasis is inevitably placed on values like quality, integrity, humanity, critical thinking, and self-examination. In a word, the department then becomes tied to durable values, the very essence of culture itself.

Study in Scandinavia

ERIK MORTENSEN: There are two problems concerning the possibilities for American students to study in Scandinavia. First, the need for better information about the opportunities; and second, the need for improved modes of measurement to assess the Scandinavian language competence of students who have participated in such programs.

It has been noted that there is a growing interest in contemporary Scandinavia in this country, especially among young Americans who seek to identify with something outside the environment in which they live, or who feel sympathetic toward social and cultural developments in Scandinavia. Where can such students turn to obtain information about programs for foreign students in Scandinavia, and how can they find out whether a given program would correspond to their fields of interest and academic aspirations? The most important information sources are: the study-abroad advisors at colleges and universities, the cultural and information offices of the Scandinavian governments in the

United States, and a variety of handbooks and publications about studies abroad.

I have examined a number of these study-abroad publications to determine how well Scandinavian study programs are described. First of all, I found that there is a lack of uniform information about different programs. The same programs are sometimes described variously in different publications.

Publications also differ in the number of programs listed for each Scandinavian country. In most instances, handbooks list three kinds of programs: semester and academic year programs, interim programs (e.g. Kierkegaard's life and philosophy), and summer programs. The *Whole World Handbook,* published by the Council on International Educational Exchange, 1973/74 edition, lists the following totals of academic, interim, and summer programs: Denmark 16, Finland 2, Norway 4, and Sweden 7. On the other hand, the American-Scandinavian Foundation monthly bulletin, *Scan,* January-March 1973, lists for corresponding categories these totals: Denmark 10, Finland 8, Norway 3, and Sweden 8. The Institute of International Education (1973) lists the following summer programs alone: Denmark 10, Finland 4, Norway 3, and Sweden 2. As you can see, the information is quite uneven and incomplete. This is particularly evident with respect to study possibilities in Denmark. According to a publication by the Danish Information Office entitled *Study in Denmark—Courses for Foreigners '73,* there is a total of 44 different such programs in Denmark alone.

What is therefore needed is some kind of clearinghouse operation that will insure complete and uniform information about studies in Scandinavia for interested American students. This information should also be distributed to such organizations as the Institute of International Education and the Council on International Educational Exchange.

The second problem I would like to touch upon is that of accreditation. How can we translate academic and intellectual experiences gained in Scandinavia and apply them to programs at

home colleges? Some skills and knowledge are admittedly very
difficult to translate into a credit system, whereas other achievements lend themselves more readily to such translation. An important part of this latter category of achievements relates to
acquired skills in one of the Scandinavian languages. In our experience at the Scandinavian Seminar with our ten-month program, most students acquire language skills that are equivalent to
at least 12–15 hours of academic credit. Part of this knowledge is
acquired by means of regular classroom instruction; but a large
portion of the language skills is gained through everyday personal contacts and communication with people in the foreign culture. However, most language tests tend to emphasize such matters as literature, vocabulary and structure and knowledge of
grammar, all of which are typically part of classroom learning and
exclude those functional skills that are acquired through everyday conversations, television, newspapers, and simple day-to-day
activities in the foreign country. Therefore, a great part of the
Scandinavian language competence achieved by American students in study-abroad programs is of a functional nature which is
rarely, if ever, measured by schools in Scandinavia or by colleges
in the United States.

Scandinavian Seminar is presently exploring with several interested parties how functionally oriented Scandinavian language
tests can be developed. This should be a collaborative undertak-
ing by academic institutions in the United States and in Scandinavia. We are presently exploring two kinds of tests: (1) an
oral interview test of approximately twenty minutes' length ad-
ministered to students on an individual basis, and (2) a series
of tape recordings of dialogues involving native speakers of Scandinavian languages dealing with a variety of subject matters.
These tapes can be played to large groups of students furnished
with test booklets with multiple-choice questions, keyed to the
taped presentation.

It should be emphasized that the proposed type of Scandinavian
language tests would serve several different groups: (1) Amer-

ican students studying in Scandinavia who will need reliable measurements of language competency upon their return to their colleges in the United States; (2) American students in this country engaged in various kinds of Scandinavian studies; (3) immigrants to Scandinavia who must learn to function in a Scandinavian language.

Finally, it should be emphasized that the proposed new test package would not duplicate the present kinds of language tests reflecting formal learning of language, grammar, culture, etc. Rather, the new tests are viewed as an important supplement which will enable us to obtain more complete information of total language gain in Scandinavian languages.

Finnish Studies in America

RALPH J. JALKANEN: There is a strong interest in learning about ways in which people of the Scandinavian tradition have learned to cope with the process of enculturation and how the new ethnic develops and views life. In studying the preceding work we find ourselves changing our ideas not only about ethnicity, but about ethnic research as well. As the "ethnic years" pass we must change our primary questions and our method of observation and research. For we discover that changes brought by the new ethnicity create an interaction in society which changes the nature of the very process we were studying: change is becoming endemic to American society; in part it is taken for granted by those understanding it as a natural and essentially inevitable experience, and it becomes a conscious concern and an experience deliberately sought by the new generation; change itself has taken on a positive value.

For example, the study of Finnish in America takes place in the following colleges and universities:

Language, Literature—University of California, Los Angeles; Columbia; Heidelberg College; Indiana University; Northern Michigan University; University of Minnesota; New York University; Suomi College; University of Texas; University of Wisconsin.

Mythology—University of California, Los Angeles; Indiana University; University of Minnesota; University of Wisconsin.

Culture—Columbia; University of Kansas; University of Minnesota; University of Texas; University of Wisconsin.

History and Geography of Finland—University of California, Los Angeles; Columbia; Indiana University; Northern Michigan University; University of Minnesota; Suomi College.

Finnish Folk Art and Technology—University of California, Los Angeles.

Finnish Folk Song and Ballad—University of California, Los Angeles.

Although the above statistics are the result of a recent survey, they may not include all American institutions of higher learning offering instruction in Finnish studies.

Opportunities for American students to study in Finland are offered by the Fulbright-Hayes Act; the Finnish-American Society, Helsinki; Suomi Seura Exchange, Helsinki; Finland's Ministry of Education through Suomi College; the Council for Instruction of Finnish for Foreigners—Ministry of Education at Helsinki and Turku Universities; and the Trainees Exchange, Helsinki.

Perhaps the most unusual educational exchange between countries began in 1949 when the 81st Congress made available the sums of all subsequent payments by Finland on her postwar relief debt to the United States dating back to 1919–20 for educational exchange between the United States and Finland through the so-called ASLA Program. The loan payments will be completed by 1984. Under this program some eighty students study in America annually.

The Fulbright-Hayes Act in 1952 provided for the United States to send lecturers, research scholars, and graduate students to Finland. Between 1952 and 1966 this group averaged 25 per year. The courses attracting Finnish students to America form a continuum from American history, literature, and civilization to psychology and business administration. Finland's achievements in architecture, music, art, the theater, mathematics, and forestry have undoubtedly drawn a significant number of American scholars to Finland.

Finland has the most extensive Slavic library outside of Russia. This is probably the reason why so many Americans going to Finland devote themselves to Slavic studies. Also, Finland's geographic and political situation is no doubt intriguing to students involved in international relations.

Although ethnic heritage may provide a basic motivation for many of the Fulbright scholars, the statistics indicate that only a small fraction of an estimated total of well over 400 Fulbrighters did have Finnish-American parentage. An appendix provides a sampling of the number of Fulbright scholars involved in studies in Finland.

Informal instruction in Finnish culture and language takes place in at least 30–50 cities and towns in America. It appears that the Finns have always engaged in non-traditional studies. The early Work People's College at Superior, Wisconsin, focused on the life style of students wherein business skills and language were only a means to an end. The entire atmosphere was one of total immersion. In the cooperative movement the educational section had first priority, profits second, viz., until about 1935, when a clash occurred with profit-oriented teaching, constituting for some a breakaway from the cooperative ideals of the past. These stood against the supermarket concept and held to the Rochdale ideals of the movement. The saving in dollar purchases was acceptable, but education of youth and children in cooperative ideals was basic. It was the same with the church summer schools, in which children were taught not only Christian truth, but love of the Finnish ideals. The Kalevala Society had its summer camps for training the young. For the Temperance Movement, as well as for the Socialists, education was the prime experience and all else followed. "Hall life" was rife among Finns, whether it was that of the Communists, Socialists, or Temperance groups,

with the programs typically aiming at the total life styles of the
participants.

Today, when the National Endowment for the Humanities un-
derwrites as innovative the "Courses through Newspapers" project, it is good to know that Scandinavians as a group, and Finns
in particular, are of a society in which illiteracy was virtually
unknown. They were avid readers of newspapers that carried on
debates and featured propaganda attacks, speeches, and lectures
on the issues of the day in order to educate all readers in the
common ideals of their particular positions. The crusading spirit
was in evidence in over ninety newspapers circulating among a
people with an immigrant population of only some 330,000 persons.

The arts also flourished in the halls where drama, music, bands,
speeches, and the reading of poetry were regularly offered. Public speaking was highly regarded among a people for whom, from
time immemorial, the word had been freighted with a mystical
magic of primitive myth and a symbolic significance far beyond
its literal meaning. And there was a deep wisdom among the common folk who had a rich treasury of proverbs and myths from
which to draw.

We tend to agree with Professor Fishman that enculturation in
a diverse culture provides a depth perception otherwise lacking
on the homogenized American scene.

Finally, to return to the primary theme, it is unlikely that we
will actually see a new societal stance ensuring the right of all
ethnics to play out their role "as strangers and non-Yankee Pil-
grims" in America. In spite of evidence to the contrary—Federal
programs, social permission for Blacks to find integrity and identity and to catch up on the benefits and the evils of the Industrial Revolution, allowing white ethnics to have a "replay" of
ethnocentrism—the cast and directors of our society led by the
liberal (and radical) scholarly leadership of our nation are in-
herently quite opposed to ethnic emphases by virtue of the tacit
assumption that the basic struggle of every society is a class

struggle, all ethnic considerations notwithstanding. Although Blacks may have opened the door for other ethnics to legitimize their particular ethnicity, the long-term historical perspective inveighs against its prolongation once the fad and fashion of the moment are past.

Appendix

LECTURERS, RESEARCH SCHOLARS, AND GRADUATE STUDENTS ON THE FULBRIGHT PROGRAM IN FINLAND FROM 1953 TO 1966.

Area	Lecturers	Research Scholars	Graduate Students
Agriculture	2		
Architecture	2	6	14
Art and the Theater	2	4	22
Botany	1		
Business Administration	11		1
Chemistry	3	1	2
Economics	8	2	5
Education	2		1
English	5	2	
Forestry	1	2	11
Genetics	1		
Geography	2		
Geology			2
History:			
American	13		
General	1		6
Russian	1	5	3
Home Economics	1		
International Relations	1		2
Journalism	1		
Law	2		1
Linguistics		1	2
Literature:			
American Literature and Civilization	28		
English	10		
Finnish:			
Finnish			1
Swedo-Finnish			1
Swedish			1

Area	Lecturers	Research Scholars	Graduate Students
Mathematics	1	3	
Medicine	3	2	
Music		5	2
Nursing			1
Philosophy		1	
Physical Education	6		
Physics	4	2	
Physiology		1	
Political Science		3	4
Psychology	12	2	
Slavic Studies		3	2
Social Work	2		
Sociology	5	3	1
Technical Science	2	1	1
Theology	1		
Zoology	1		
	135	49	86

Icelandic Studies

HARALDUR BESSASON: The sensible policy of bringing new life to the study of Old Norse/Icelandic by introducing students to the living language of Modern Icelandic is only one reason of many why, from the linguistic point of view, it has become important for North American students of Old Norse to study in Iceland.

If one can judge by its calendar, the University of Iceland has recognized this fact by offering a program in Icelandic specially designed for foreign students. The university awards a degree in Icelandic philology to students from abroad who have successfully completed the examination required. The entire curriculum is designed as a four-semester or two-year program of study.

Since 1949, the Icelandic Ministry of Culture and Education has annually awarded a number of scholarships to foreign students for study of the Icelandic language, Icelandic history, and literature at the University of Iceland in Reykjavík. The Ministry decides, every year, in which countries these scholarships are to be made available, and requests the Ministry of Culture and Education in each of the recipient countries to select a candidate for the award. These scholarship awards are calculated to cover full maintenance, board, and lodging for the period of study, that is, from October 1 to May 1. The Ministry makes available accommodation and board for the foreign students in one of the university dormitories.

There are perhaps various other ways in which North American students can obtain support for studying Icelandic in Iceland. In Canada, a rapidly growing organization called the Canada-Iceland Foundation plans to give substantial support to Canadian students who wish to study Icelandic in Iceland.

Recently, conditions for the study of Icelandic at the University of Iceland have been improved. Of particular interest is the newly founded Arnamagnaean Institute at the University, which concentrates on research on Icelandic manuscripts, including many of the old Icelandic vellum manuscripts which are now being returned to Iceland from Copenhagen. Furthermore, attention should be drawn to a growing emphasis on linguistics at the University of Iceland and the increased quality of the teaching of this subject there. The University has now launched its own series of publications on linguistics in English. Therefore, one may conclude that in the years to come Icelandic linguistics in Iceland will prove to be a growing attraction for North American students and scholars.

Specialized Studies

DAVID A. WARD: As has been indicated previously, there is a substantial shift in interest at American colleges and universities away from some of the traditional areas such as business administration and the hard sciences to the social sciences and to law. This is demonstrated very dramatically in the shift of majors at American universities from Harvard to Berkeley. This turning of students toward social sciences coincides with the growing recognition of the critical social problems that exist in American society. Students and faculty are interested in the issues; courses are becoming issue-oriented. To give you a specific example, the criminal justice problems in this country are critical. We are in a crisis state in this area, and I think the points I am making about criminal justice could apply in Scandinavia to health, housing, welfare, and environmental problems, to a wide variety of issues. I am certainly not limiting the application of these points to the criminal justice area, but that is the one that I am involved in and the one with which I am most familiar.

In my experience with American criminal justice administrators, university teachers and students, there is not a great deal of interest in the criminal justice practices, policies, and institutions of France, of Germany, of Italy; there is great interest in those of Scandinavia. The Swedish model of prisons—and, when they become better known, the experiences in other Scandinavian countries—is really very much in the minds of American criminal justice practitioners as well as those who study criminal policy. At the University of Minnesota it is possible, for example, to offer a course that focuses on Scandinavian penal policy on a regular yearly basis drawing as many as two hundred students who are interested in studying very specifically criminal policies, practices, and institutions in Scandinavia. And it is my hope to expand their horizon somewhat, from their rather exclusive interest and concern with the Swedish correctional system, to other aspects of criminal policy.

An opposite point to be made is that there must be a realistic assessment of the political implications of being an American student in the social sciences in Scandinavian universities. If an American student studies in the Department of Sociology at Lund, or the Sociology Institute at Helsinki, or most of the other universities, he must be prepared to spend a good deal of his time debating and defending, if that is possible, American domestic and foreign policies on a wide variety of issues. And there can be some rough times for students who are not prepared, even though many of them will share the criticisms of American domestic and foreign policy that they will hear from their colleagues at Scandinavian universities.

Finally, I should like to take up Mr. Strong's important consideration of education in its broader context, that is, continuing education for people over a lifetime that does not necessarily involve instruction in a college or university. There is substantial interest in the Scandinavian criminal justice area on the part of the people who run all of our criminal justice institutions from courts to prisons, as I found after publishing an article in a journal that is widely read by criminal justice people, lawyers, judges, and others. Many of them desire to see firsthand those things that they have been reading about for a long period of time, in the wake of the tremendous effort by Torsten Eriksson to spread the gospel of Swedish correction throughout the world. And the desperate situation in the United States is prompting them to view the experiments made in other countries where they can find some similarity in cultural tradition, history, and social institutions to the United States. I think that the problem for the Swedish Institute and the Ministries of Justice in the Scandinavian countries is the number of people who would like to do this. Unless they want to have special institutions that will just cater to touring American students, academics, and criminal justice practitioners, there will be serious problems regarding the invasion of privacy of the prisoners. In my experience, this is particularly true in Norway and in Sweden. There is also a very real danger, I feel, that short study tours, unless they are carefully conducted, will give a superficial view of how it is possible for these kinds of prison systems to exist successfully in Scandinavia. It is not just having an ombudsman, it is the question of how these societies permit such an institution and others to operate. Therefore one must understand the economic, historical, cultural, and political context within which these institutions function. I think that in the criminal justice area, as well as these other areas of social concern, the opportunities for commerce between Scandinavia and the United States are extremely valuable. I think that the Scandinavian countries can perform a great service to the United States as social laboratories for programs with which we desperately need help.

Scandinavian in the High Schools

B. R. EGGAN: As far as I can discover, there are now only five high schools in the Midwest offering either the Swedish or Norwegian language. Three of these have added the languages recently. Lindstrom, Minnesota, added Swedish to its curriculum three years ago and this year has an enrollment of forty students. Last fall two high schools in Grand Forks, North Dakota, started classes in Norwegian. When I checked the two high schools in Minneapolis where Swedish and Norwegian have been offered for some 63 years, I found that they are not losing ground, they are gaining slightly. This fact is rather surprising since the total enrollment in the other foreign languages in the state of Minnesota dropped about 2,000 last year, and the enrollment in Minneapolis alone dropped about 200 during the same period.

How is it then that the Scandinavian languages are, at this moment, holding their own better than other foreign languages? There are a number of new developments that seem to carry over into the high school situation. We have had a tremendous increase in the interest shown by adults, especially by parents of the second, third, and fourth generations. When Sons of Norway started to offer classes in Norwegian for children and adults thirteen years ago, there were only three institutions in the Twin Cities area offering evening classes in Norwegian or Swedish, namely, the American Swedish Institute and the YWCA in Minneapolis and the International Institute in St. Paul. Now there are six junior or senior high schools and six other institutions—including those that I have mentioned—offering evening classes in Norwegian or Swedish.

We also have another development that I think has helped to maintain the enrollment in our regular high school courses, namely the rapid growth of the language camps. When Concordia College in Moorhead started its first Norwegian language camp eleven years ago, there were only nineteen students registered. In 1972 we had 350 campers. In 1972 also, there were four Norwegian language camps in operation, one in Minnesota, one in Montana, and two on the West Coast. Two more will be added, one of which will be conducted in Norway and sponsored by Sons of Norway. You may be interested in knowing that although the camp to be held in Norway will cost each student $500.00, we have had 69 applicants, and the camp has been planned for only forty students. The Vasa Order started to offer adult classes in Swedish eight years ago and they are also operating camp programs.

In connection with the language programs, there is another matter which may prove to be of considerable significance. Five years ago a high school credit course was added to the Norwegian language camp program held at Bemidji, Minnesota. The results of the first three years have been as follows: In 1970 eighteen students were enrolled, and of these thirteen qualified for one year's high school credit. In 1971 we had sixteen who earned one year's credit and six qualified for a second year's credit. In 1972 twelve earned one year's credit and two a second year's credit. Still another feature was added to the Norwegian language camp at Bemidji. A graduate student from Concordia College took her practice teaching in the high school credit course. Our recommendation and a rather detailed description of the work this student had completed during the four-week course resulted in her being granted a teacher's certificate in Norwegian by the North Dakota Department of Education. She is now teaching the Norwegian classes just started at Grand Forks.

In discussing the teaching materials now available, I shall limit myself to the most recent additions. Mr. Smedvig mentioned the five language tapes—with texts to go with them—published by

Sons of Norway Heritage Productions, called *It's Fun to Speak Norwegian*. This year Heritage Productions will have available similar tapes for Swedish, Danish, and Finnish.

I hesitate to make any predictions about the future of the Scandinavian languages in our high schools. There are so many changes in the curricula, and the foreign language teachers find it difficult to compete with or adjust to the new priorities that are constantly added to the high school programs. However, having observed the new developments mentioned above, I feel rather optimistic about the future.

Comments

LARS JOHNSON: My background is Norwegian, but my interest and involvement in Scandinavian matters did not begin until 1964. At that time I took a class in Beginning Norwegian under the direction of Professor Walter Johnson. Needless to say, I did not know what I was embarking upon. I took the course, and by the completion of the first year the Sons of Norway lodge in Seattle had awarded me a scholarship to the University of Oslo International Summer School. I, of course, accepted this stipend. I went to Oslo, enjoyed the experience immensely, and decided to remain at the University of Oslo for the following academic year. Following this sojourn in Norway I returned and earned a Bachelor's Degree the next year in History and Norwegian. Thereupon I continued into the graduate program in Scandinavian studies under Professor Johnson and completed a Master's Degree in Scandinavian Language and Literature two years later. I returned to Norway in 1969–1970 for further study, and now here I am at the University of Wisconsin in a different field—Scandinavian History.

My first experience at the University of Oslo was a meeting with the foreign student advisor. She looked at me—aha, a potential draft dodger. This was in 1965 and she had reason to be cautious; however, she was a very pleasant person. I later discovered that there were male students at the institution who were taking advantage of the situation, and who were avoiding the draft, not really studying and not learning anything—the language, history, literature, culture, political history, and so forth. Later, after the completion of that school year 1965–1966, I went to visit with her. We talked for an hour and a half in Norwegian, which I felt was not so bad for me, and she was quite impressed, too. We parted good friends, and when I returned to Norway in 1969, one of the first persons I went to see was the foreign student advisor. I can only praise and recommend the University of Oslo. My experiences there—working with Professors Ingrid Semmingsen and Magne Skodvin, among others—were nothing but enjoyable and enriching.

The summer school at the University of Oslo, I found, was truly international. Originally, it was known in the early postwar years as the American Summer School, but now the administration is limiting the number of participants from the United States and Canada to approximately half the enrollment. The growing numbers of foreign students from Africa, Asia, the Continent, and the Soviet bloc countries are partially subsidized by the increasing tuition charged the more affluent students from across the Atlantic. The academic environment is English and the school an English-speaking island. As interested as I was in Norwegian, I discovered I could do very little to expand my language capabilities. I took the advanced Norwegian course and learned as much as I could, but since all the activities were conducted in English, my Norwegian stagnated for the duration of the session. Not until I came into everyday contact with the people again—buying gasoline, bumming, sleeping in youth hostels—did I feel I was making headway.

One thing that I did not encounter in 1965–66 or during my last stay in 1969–70 at the University of Oslo was much student reaction against Americans. If students tried to provoke me, I usually answered, "I do not know much about the subject," or "I am not in agreement either," or "Let us talk about something else." Other students who have recently been in Scandinavia—especially Sweden—have shared their experiences with me; i.e., others' reaction to their being American and the American involvement in Vietnam. Some people take the criticism personally while others are able to shed it and to say, "Well, this is my government, my country, I am not necessarily in agreement with it, it is a democratic country," and so forth. They let it go at that.

At the present time there is a question arising about maximum enrollments at the University of Oslo in the liberal arts faculty. I read *Aftenposten,* Norway's largest newspaper, to keep up-to-date, but lately I have not heard of any further developments concerning this issue. Whether this trend will result in a quota being placed on foreign students at this institution is hard to determine. The Norwegians are reaching a point now where they are training more people for certain jobs than are actually required; the jobs no longer exist. Are these priorities correct, should they continue unchanged, or should people be moving in another direction toward other occupations which require less expensive training? There are other alternatives which might also cause change and reorientation.

Are there other educational institutions in Norway besides the major university in Oslo? I knew little about such alternatives before I spent my second year abroad. In August, 1969, I attended Nansenskolen in East-Central Norway; it was a delightful experience. Everything was taught in Norwegian, and I think I probably learned more Norwegian there in the space of four weeks than during any other equivalent period.

Another alternative is the small teachers' schools, which are scattered throughout the country in both rural and urban settings. In addition, there is the University of Bergen, which is expanding but still has less than five thousand students. In Trondheim the Norwegians are expanding the national teachers' college and hope to create another formal institution of higher learning—the University of Trondheim. The latter will also share some facilities with the Norwegian Technical University. These are all viable alternatives.

I speak the Oslo or Eastern Norway dialect as a result of studying at the University of Oslo and meeting a young lady in the reading room of the American Embassy. She is now my wife. She is also a native of Oslo, so I hear that dialect day in and day out. I cannot get away from it. I have learned how to be reprimanded in two languages, to accept it, and to understand it.

One of Dr. Erik Mortensen's statements concerned the evaluation of credits and study earned abroad. I have discovered that there are some problems involved in this translation of credits to American equivalents. These stem, however, from the experiences of other students.

When I came back to the University of Washington in 1966, I did not have to take tests to determine my proficiency and what I had learned. Professor Johnson knew my capabilities and ability in the language. There was no difficulty. When I returned to the University of Wisconsin in 1970 after coming back from Norway, I talked to my major professor and was able to bypass certain course requirements. It was all handled informally and very easily.

Other universities, especially those that do not have Scandinavian departments or connections with Scandinavia in general, probably have real problems equating work and study done in Scandinavia with the American system of credits. And I do believe the draft and the Vietnam war did not make the situation any more flexible. I myself had difficulty explaining the European system of fewer class hours with more independent study. In the early fall of 1965 my draft board and I carried on a hectic correspondence to clarify this issue. I stated the case roughly as follows: one cannot set our credit system on a par with the Norwegian educational system. If one takes fifteen credit hours at the University of Wisconsin, the University of Washington, or any other American university, this means more or less fifteen contact, or classroom, hours per week. If a Norwegian or Swedish student assumed that hour-load with the equivalent amount of reading and study required in the Scandinavian university, he or she would not have time to eat or sleep, much less anything else. One could not participate in all the extra trappings of the Scandinavian system—ski trips, opportunities to take occasional short-term substitute teaching jobs for supplemental income, and so forth.

Discussion

RICHARD B. VOWLES: Scarcely a year passes at the University of Wisconsin that we are not reminded that the Department of Scandinavian Studies is a luxury item. In point of fact it is the big courses that carry our small courses; in other words, a course like "Scandinavian Life and Civilization," which is taught in translation to the general public, is able to carry Finnish, for example, where they may have three students in first-year Finnish and two students in second-year Finnish and one student in third-year Finnish. What's going to happen? Can we continue to generate the big courses to carry the small courses? We are doing so, carefully and not desperately, with a course in "Scandinavian Twentieth-Century Drama and Film," a course in "Scandinavian Mythology" and conceivably a course in "Women in Scandinavian Literature." But the program is being threatened, and, while Norwegian has high enrollment, and Swedish next, I think it is quite conceivable that Danish and Finnish are going to be phased out. I don't know how seriously we are threatened, but I'm raising some questions. Is this happening at other institutions? What is the solution? Can funds be found from the home countries, or from foundations or businesses? And does it matter? I think it does.

JOHN CHRISTIANSON: Just one question that perhaps I should address to Professor Ward. In pursuing an interest in a technical subject in Scandinavia such as, say, penal policy, or for example, physics, something like that, how much of a fluency in the Scandinavian language concerned is necessary?

DAVID A. WARD: I think that depends on—obviously—the amount of time one has and also on the country. My own experience in visiting thirty prisons in Norway, Sweden, Denmark, and Finland was that the situation varied extremely. I met with one inmate council consisting of eight prisoners, all of whom spoke English, and only one of them was an American. But at a smaller institution in Finland I was not able to talk with any prisoner. At one institution in Sweden I did have a chance to help an English-speaking prisoner who was in a facility for twenty people where no one spoke English. He was from Czechoslovakia, and he had a serious legal problem involving deportation. Thus on one occasion, at least, I was able to assist despite my limited knowledge of Swedish. I would say that if people want to get really immersed in the correctional system outside the major prisons, and something more than under the leadership or guidance of one or two people from the ministries of justice, that if they're going to do the kind of sociological or criminological research that is done in this country, knowledge of the language is essential. And I think that for what they say to be credible, they must have the language facility.

TORE TALLROTH: This is a rather important question. Must we foresee a future where there are, let us say, special courses in Scandinavian criminology at all universities, or could there be some sort of division of interest? I know how difficult it is to get some sort of division established at the Scandinavian universities, but this is a more broadminded country.

NILS HASSELMO: I think we are dependent on the availability of people like Professor Ward, who actually came to the university in a different capacity but who had the specialization in Scandinavian criminal justice. There exists an arrangement between some universities in the Middle West, including the Big Ten and the University of Chicago, for exchange of students in specialized programs. It may be possible to share some experts through C.I.C.'s "traveling scholar" program.

GENE G. GAGE: Something really dangerous we might be falling into now is overemphasizing Scandinavian studies departments. My experience in Sweden taught me that we often become a little too isolated; for instance, Scandinavian history is probably more effectively taught at a Department of European History and a course in Scandinavian linguistics is equally effectively taught in a Department of Linguistics and obviously broadens our appeal. This goes for any discipline whatsoever, except perhaps beginning language instruction.

FRANKLIN D. SCOTT: We have concentrated very much on the concept of ethnicity and the connection of university studies with ethnicity. I have been connected with some African studies programs for a long time. We don't look to African studies programs for experts. The African studies programs throughout the United States are staffed by WASPs and the students are WASPs or their like. You don't have to be an ethnic to be interested in an important subject. Professor Johnson touched on this in a somewhat different way. I think this is extremely important for us to keep in mind, and to give us a different perspective; as a matter of fact, I even think that perhaps the present, if not the future, of Scandinavian studies has been hampered by the ethnic connection. This is not expected for African studies; it is not expected for French or Greek; and I don't know why we should think of it quite so exclusively for Scandinavian studies.

COMMUNICATIONS AND THE
SCANDINAVIAN PRESENCE

The Immigrant Newspaper

Panel: NILS WILLIAM OLSSON (Chairman), GERHARD T. ROOTH, SIGURD DAASVAND, PAUL NYHOLM, TOPI HALONEN, HARALDUR BESSASON

Chairman's Remarks

NILS WILLIAM OLSSON: The immigrant newspaper was the first institution established by the arriving newcomers, antedating schools, colleges, hospitals, fraternal organizations, and other societies and, in most instances, even the churches themselves.

The immigrant newspaper was the window to the outside world for most arrivals whose knowledge of English was nil, or at best, very sketchy. I don't have the data on the earliest newspapers published by Scandinavian immigrant groups, except that the first Swedish newspaper, begun in New York in 1851, was aptly enough named *Skandinaven,* for it had a liberal sprinkling of Danish, Norwegian and even a little German. Let us see what the status of the Scandinavian-American press is today.

The Swedish-American Press

GERHARD T. ROOTH: *Skandinaven* was the first Swedish newspaper established in this country and it was followed by several hundred others. Of those few that remain, our own paper, *Nordstjernan,* the Swedish *North Star,* is now the oldest, and, in 1971, we celebrated our one hundredth anniversary.

The next oldest is the *Svensk-Amerikanaren Tribunen* in Chicago, which will be one hundred years old in 1976. The *Svenska Posten* in Seattle and *Vestkusten* in San Francisco are both more

163

than seventy-five years old. In Los Angeles, we have the *California Veckoblad* and a small paper called *Texas Posten* is published in Austin, Texas, really as a travel agency paper.

As the largest of the Swedish-American papers, *Nordstjernan* has a circulation of 5,200 subscribers as of October, 1972. Approximately 75 percent of our readers came to the United States between the two World Wars and their average age is about sixty years. Of the remainder, those of American stock, the first generation born in this country, constitute about 15 percent of our readers and the next generation 10 percent. You can figure out for yourself what is going to happen to the newspaper.

What is the main purpose of the newspaper? Of course, it is to inform. We don't inform about politics, we stay on the fence. We don't want to fall on either side, because we don't want to lose any of our subscribers who may have different opinions concerning Sweden or Swedish or American politics. We maintain, as the Swedes do, a neutral position.

How much text material do we get from the old country? I'm happy to say about 60 percent, thanks to the Swedish Information Service and the Foreign Office in Sweden. A Swedish-American wants to know what happens in his home town. That's the most popular reading.

We now run about 25 percent of our content in English, but that does not mean that we are going over to the English language. I also don't believe that if we have a national newspaper, as a union of all five of the existing Swedish-American papers, that it would be possible to concentrate as we all do on local news. It just wouldn't do.

The Norwegian-American Press

SIGURD DAASVAND: When I left Norway in the beginning of January, 1971, I was a well-paid old-timer after twenty-five years at the Norwegian News Agency with five weeks of paid vacation. And then when I came over here, I suddenly found myself as the youngest in the Norwegian-American press, with no limit as to working hours, and just a few days of paid vacation. We are two men on the editorial staff: besides me, it's 79-year-old Carl Søyland, the editor emeritus. It certainly was a great upheaval for me, with very little training in English. I had to answer the telephone and make important decisions in English the morning after I landed at Kennedy because my predecessor had left before I came.

I am fully aware that this Seminar is not concerned with history, but I have to mention a few things in order to draw a line from the beginning of the Norwegian press in America up, or down, to the present situation. The Norwegian-American press in this country celebrated its 125th anniversary last year. The first Norwegian newspaper in the United States was *Nordlyset,* which appeared in 1847. Since then some 300 such newspapers have been published together with several hundred periodicals, monthly and quarterly publications in the Norwegian language. Most or all these went out of business after ten to fifteen years, more or less. The first big blow came when the oldest of them all, *Skandinaven* in Chicago, died in 1940 after it had been published since 1865. *Skandinaven*'s subscription list was taken over by *Decorah-Posten* in Iowa. At that time the number of Norwegian-American newspapers was reduced to ten.

The next, and second big blow, and a sad one, was when *Decorah-Posten* had to give up at the end of 1972, some eighteen to twenty months before this great newspaper would have celebrated its centennial as the first, and perhaps the only one, of the Norwegian-American newspapers to do so. Since its demise there are now only four Norwegian-American newspapers left in this country, and one in Canada. These four are all weeklies and all of them come out on Thursday. They are the *Western Viking* in Seattle, the only one on the West Coast; *Minnesota Posten* in Minneapolis; *Vinland* in Chicago; and *Nordisk Tidende* in Brooklyn, the only one on the East Coast. *Western Viking* had a circulation of about 3,000 before it took over the subscription list from *Decorah-Posten,* and according to a recent letter from its editor and publisher, the circulation is now 7,400. *Minnesota Posten* is said to have 3,200 and *Vinland* in Chicago, 1,800. The circulation of *Nordisk Tidende* is considerably higher than the biggest of the other three, and it is increasing. I have reason to believe that this growth will continue, and it is encouraging to be editor of a paper under such circumstances.

As for *Nordisk Tidende,* about 75 percent of our readers are among those who were born in Norway. The rest are from the second generation. We have subscribers in 48 of the 50 states in America, and *Nordisk Tidende* is sold on 150 newsstands in Greater New York. The average age of the readers is, as the weather man says about the temperature, "low in the high 50's."

The main purpose of our newspaper is to provide news from Norway and the Norwegian colony, and about Norwegians all over the United States. We have twelve pages each week, sometimes more; about nine pages are in modern standard Norwegian and the rest are in English. For the last ten years we have had a rather big special issue in February or March called "Travel in Norway." These inserts are all in English. In addition to this, we have started a series of special issues presenting Norwegian industry, and we have finished number two in this series, devoted to the Norwegian oil exploration in the North Sea, which has 48 pages, all in English.

The Danish-American Press

PAUL NYHOLM: Very recently the University of Michigan published an excellent doctoral dissertation entitled "The Danish Language Press in America." (Available from the Microfilm Department of the University of Michigan at Ann Arbor.) As far as the present situation is concerned, there are only two Danish-American newspapers left—*Bien* and *Den Danske Pioneer.*

I am not able to say how many of the subscribers were born

overseas, but I am sure that the great majority are over the age of 55, so for that reason the future does not look bright for the papers.

Before looking at the papers still being published, let me mention certain other publications. First there is the *American Dane Magazine,* published by the Danish Brotherhood of America. This magazine mirrors the Brotherhood's approach to young people. Then you have the *Dana College Review*. In both of these you will find quite a few columns devoted to Danish activities. I think that we can say that the *Dana College Review,* more than any other medium, reflects best Danish-American culture. This is owing in no small part to the excellent work done by Norman Bansen, head of the Department of English at Dana College.

Next we have the *Grand View College News* and finally, the *Dansk Kirke og Folk,* which is the only Danish-American paper printed partly in Danish and partly in English. It has a subscription list of between 800 and 900, but the financial future looks quite optimistic, for though the paper has a small circulation, many of the subscribers send in gifts to keep the paper going. It is published by the Danish Interest Group, of which Enok Mortensen is the chairman.

Concerning the two newspapers, *Bien* and *Den Danske Pioneer,* I do not expect a great or expanded future. But on the other hand, when I wrote my first article in the *Pioneer* back in 1923, just fifty years ago, everyone thought that it would fold in just a few years. Last year it published a beautiful one hundredth anniversary edition. With each issue we see new subscribers added.

On the other hand no one mentions lost subscribers. There are some encouraging signs about the *Danish Pioneer,* primarily because of its editor, who took over in 1958 when the paper was doomed and moved it from Omaha to Chicago. He has been able to inspire a number of people as coworkers, who love to work for the paper and who make it the success it is today.

It is my fervent hope that when the four Danish-language papers die, which I believe will be in the next generation or so, that we shall have an English Scandinavian newspaper. There is much to be said for this and I have great plans and desires for this project. It seems a great tragedy to me that we can gather as many as 50,000 people at annual Scandinavian festivals, but we do not have the answer to this problem of keeping alive a newspaper which can communicate its ideas to these very people. Perhaps we shall find a man who, like Thomas Edison, labored hard at finding a solution, even if he only succeeds after the fiftieth attempt. If we are really interested in the problem, I am confident that we can find a solution.

The Finnish-American Press

TOPI HALONEN: The Finnish-American press had its beginning in 1876, so that soon we shall celebrate our one-hundredth anniversary. Altogether there have been some ninety-three Finnish-American newspapers. Here we find a little discrepancy with the statistics, but educators are bound to exaggerate a bit, just as we newspapermen used to do.

Even though the crest has been reached so far as immigration of Finns is concerned, there are still dozens of Finnish-American newspapers. The most popular of them, amounting to a half dozen, have a combined circulation of about 60,000. The Finns in America have never been more than a few hundred thousand. But the story goes of two Finns, stranded on a desert island, one of whom founded a temperance society and the other a workers' movement; soon they also started two fiercely competing newspapers in the Finnish language.

There are some Finnish-language newspapers in the United States which are yet not finished. Their total circulation is about 12,000. *Amerikan Uutiset* happens to be by far the greatest and I can modestly claim that we have one distinction in common with our famous competitor, *The New York Times:* we both have subscribers in every state in the Union. Of our 4,500 subscribers, 80 percent came from the old country and the other 20 percent were born here. The average age of our readers is estimated to be seventy plus. A remarkable portion is ninety years old, which is balanced on the other hand by those who emigrated to the United States and Canada in the last twenty-five years.

The main purpose of my paper is to serve as a bond between Finns in California and New York, from Maine to Florida as well as the Middle West, telling everything possible about their doings, social as well as statistical, from birth to death. We are trying to communicate with Finnish-American retirees in Florida and in California, and we place a special emphasis on news related to senior citizens and their problems.

About 20 percent of our newspaper text comes from the old country. As a paper enjoying a national circulation, our local coverage is rather limited, and our public enemy number one is party politics. If we stress the achievement of the Democratic Party, all of our Republican readers would terminate their subscriptions immediately, and vice versa. We cannot afford to lose any of our friends.

Is the publication of a foreign-language newspaper essential, even if most readers understand English? It seems to me that our readers prefer to read about the latest price of beef or what the unions will be negotiating in the Finnish-American press. So far as combining all of the Scandinavian-American newspapers, including the Finnish ones, into a collective publication in the English language, I would give this idea my unqualified endorsement. In the long run this would be particularly for the benefit of those born in this country.

A publication, combining the latest news of the political, scientific, social, and cultural developments in all of the Scandinavian countries would appeal, if not necessarily to the first generation readership, to other generations and in the long pull would be a great boon to those born here. It might prove successful also in providing the lighter side of the lives of all of us Scandihoovians.

The Icelandic Press in North America

HARALDUR BESSASON: I shall only discuss the Icelandic immigrant newspaper. Therefore, I shall not describe the *English-Icelandic Canadian,* the English publication, nor the *Icelandic Canadian* magazine, published in Winnipeg four times a year. *Lögberg-Heimskringla,* the Icelandic newspaper, published in Winnipeg, is a fifteen-year-old amalgam of its almost ninety-year-old component which long ago outgrew its function as an immigrant newspaper since immigration from Iceland to North America virtually ceased during the early years of this century.

The role of the Icelandic newspaper is therefore complementary rather than substitutionary in character. It is no longer designed to replace the English-language press, rather it attempts to reach beyond it. Stability of circulation during the last ten or fifteen years seems to indicate that the paper has been achieving this difficult but worthy objective. This implies, of course, that in recent times the editorial policies of the paper have changed or have been modified considerably. A good example of this is that the newspaper has been able to eliminate all political and religious discussions from its pages, in order not to offend diametrically opposed political groups or different religious views. Some of the older members of the Icelandic community felt that this was unwise and a step backward. Others hailed it as a sign of maturity.

In going through fifteen or twenty issues of the newspaper, the following conclusions are reached. In literary content the newspaper is quite traditional, and prefers the writing of Icelanders with a rural background to the literature of the new urbanized Iceland. The emphasis is on alliterative poetry, and only limited attention is paid to the post-1930 revolutionized poetic form. The paper diligently reports matters of historical significance and devotes more space to obituaries than to birth announcements. It is the most important link between the various Icelandic organizations in

North America and contributes a great deal to the maintenance of their relations with Iceland. The publishers have experienced considerable financial difficulties, but a large portion of the deficits are absorbed by voluntary contributions. English is on the increase in the paper, which is one way of preventing a decrease in circulation. It is, I think, virtually certain that the newspaper will continue for many years to come, even though its form and content may have to be modified from time to time.

A Student's Comment

LAURENCE BERGE: We are not specifically concerned with history, I understand, but I think we should be. I think it would help the circulation of the Scandinavian-American newspapers in the United States and Canada if they were to be more concerned with the immigrant heritage and I would like to suggest a few simple ways of doing this.

It is very difficult, considering the bibliographic shortcomings surrounding the Scandinavian-American press, to know a great deal about what went on in Minnesota or Wisconsin and all of the small Scandinavian towns around the United States. I believe that the local readers are interested not only in what is going on today, but that they are also interested in their ancestry. This is particularly the case with those who do not read a Scandinavian language.

I would suggest that one might translate articles from the older newspapers and reprint biographies from the old press; *Norden,* for example, in Chicago, carried a lot of good biographies of prominent Scandinavians from the 1880s and the 1890s, which would be of interest to contemporary readers. Something else that could be done is to reprint advertisements from the old newspapers. These are very good art. There is the Johnnie Johnson plow or reaper, and ads for Dr. Kuriko's liniment. Also it would help to establish a closer contact with our immigrant past if the editors were to reprint material from the more ephemeral journals, some of which only lasted a couple of months such as the fascinating *Rothuggaren* in Minnesota. There is a sizable bit of literature in the Scandinavian-American press which now is difficult to get at but which should be rediscovered. Some of the newspapers have been microfilmed, but there are many which have not.

I am particularly interested in the older, more inaccessible material. Some of the more recent material, certainly that of this century contained in the larger newspapers, has been preserved for posterity through the microfilm process, but the smaller, more inaccessible and certainly transitory publications deserve to be made available to us all.

Discussion

CARLO CHRISTENSEN: There is an observation that might be of interest particularly so far as the Danish-American newspapers are concerned. As their circulation dwindles into practically nothing, we have been asked again and again at the Embassy in Washington if it would not be possible to support the Danish-American press with Danish Government funds. Years ago we looked into this matter, and were informed by the Department of Justice in Washington through the Department of State that of course it could be done, but if the newspapers accepted financial aid from Denmark they would be considered agents of the Danish Government. When we forwarded this observation to the Danish-American newspapers, they obviously did not wish to be considered agents of a foreign government, since they were indeed American newspapers, printed in the Danish language.

Now, since the Danish-American newspapers that we have left are getting smaller and smaller, my hope is that there is some way, much like Scanpresence here, in which concerted action, perhaps through an institution such as The American-Scandinavian Foundation, may be taken to found a medium which can bring news of Scandinavian culture and politics, science and education to the Scandinavian-American people.

TATU TUOHIKORPI: All of us Scandinavians are facing today the same problems and difficulties. It might be called the Scandinavian dilemma. We at the Finnish Embassy are well aware of the difficulties the Finnish-American newspapers are having in this country. What can be done in the future is a question which is being taken up in Helsinki. I hope that out of these discussions will come some kind of hope to my friend Halonen and his colleagues.

BJØRN JENSEN: My Danish friend has reminded us of a very important fact, that when an American newspaper accepts grants from a foreign government, it indeed becomes a foreign agent.

I am not ready at this time to offer advice on how to cope with the difficult problem of keeping a Norwegian-American newspaper alive in this country. I shall therefore deal with it on an *ad hoc* basis. As I see it, it is not solely a problem of language. It is a problem of survival. The question is whether the Norwegian-American newspaper should publish in Norwegian or in English or in both languages. All foreign-language newspapers face this real dilemma, for they will both gain and lose, whatever solution they choose. If, for instance, *Nordisk Tidende* in Brooklyn were to publish in English, a goodly number of its readers would drop their subscriptions, since they buy the paper for its language flavor and its local news from Norway, most of it in the Norwegian language. Additionally, if *Nordisk Tidende* were to publish in English, it would be in direct competition with American newspapers and periodicals and in that competition it would lose out immediately.

I see no pat solution to the problem, but I do feel that the newspapers should try a period of transition, during which they should attempt to be bilingual, publish more material in English, and select the language of the story to be published according to its context and possible impact. The real problem, as I see it, is not so much a problem of language as the problem of reaching out to new groups of readers. I think, for instance, that Norwegian-American newspapers would do well to cater more systematically to the business community. *Nordisk Tidende* is certainly making definite efforts in that direction and I believe that this will pay off in the long run, in fact I believe that it has already begun to pay off.

Above all, I think that the Norwegian-American press should cater more regularly to the academic community, in the first place to the universities and colleges with Norwegian and Scandinavian studies. What I would like to see is Norwegian-American newspapers developing into general-interest publications, presenting material from Norway for interested English-speaking Americans. At the same time they should maintain a minimum coverage of the ethnic community. One possible favorable side effect of such a development would be to make the Norwegian-American newspapers more attractive and more worthy of support by the authorities in the home country. So far as merging the Scandinavian language newspapers, I will only say this; so long as the Norwegian-American newspapers are unable to agree to a merger, I just cannot see any possibility of a larger Scandinavian merger.

HåKAN BERGGREN: My organization has been in business since 1921, when it was organized mainly to support the American Swedish press and the American Swedish element in this country. Already in the 1930s it was quite obvious that its scope had widened, and over the past five years in which I have had the pleasure of working with Gerhard Rooth of *Nordstjernan,* we have tried a number of devices of material effort to dodge the problems of the Foreign Registration Act. We feel that what we have done has been indeed a very small thing, but we wanted to demonstrate our appreciation of the fantastic efforts being made within the framework of the American Swedish press.

This is the first time that I have had the pleasure of being in a group-oriented Scandinavian-American meeting. I hope this will last and continue in the future. I also think that Professor Fishman gave us all something to think about with regard to ethnicity and the new definition. With those two facts in mind I would suggest that we have to realize that there are also new definitions of ethnic groups and related problems. This means that the new definitions and the new perspective will of necessity present new and different demands on the Scandinavian-American news media, particularly the press which for two, three, and even four generations has served the immigrant community. The platform which dedicated journalists and reporters have built across the years must be admired, but there is still sufficient room for a new and fresh approach which I see as not restricted to one medium but as a series of multi-media communications processes.

To begin with I conceive a joint effort by the existing ethnic newspapers to publish a national biweekly, or even a weekly with insert pages covering local stories and announcements. Obviously this could be discussed forever and a day, but I sincerely believe that the plan is realizable. Obviously, it should be published in English.

Secondly, I believe that there is a natural tie between an effort of this type and a magazine program, such as the *Sweden Now* program, as well as similar programs in our sister countries. What I am trying to say is that there should be a natural and easy way to attain the goal of cooperation between the ethnic-oriented and the heritage-oriented organizations. It is a matter of finding the right format and the ideal form of communication between members of both groups. If we use this line of approach, the problem will be easier to solve. Already a number of these newspapers are functioning as membership forums. To that degree I believe that a successfully changed newspaper should serve one of the purposes of this meeting, finding the heritage aspect within the ethnic framework.

I will, however, stubbornly advocate that a communications program, embracing newspapers, journals, books, pamphlets, and films, has to be based upon actual professional needs. It should be

closely tied to the needs of educational and cultural exchange between the United States and Canada on the one hand and the Scandinavian countries on the other. We have touched upon this earlier
in this conference, particularly in the discussion of educational exchange. This is the concept which has come to all of us as we have
worked in the United States with American-Scandinavian problems
during the 1960s. Therefore I firmly believe that organizations,
newspapers, and other media must identify their needs and if
necessary restructure their programs in order to find a workable list
of priorities between heritage organizations and professional
groupings. This is not a problem of either-or, it is rather a
problem of both-and, and we must come to the realization of this
fundamental need.

I hope that this conference will end its deliberations by adopt-
ing consensus suggestions for a long-range follow-up on the matter
of identifying both the heritage need and what I have termed the
professional need. Thus we shall eventually find rational solutions
for a communications program which makes sense and where the
past is past and the present is present. It may signal the decline
and fall of the ethnic joke, but we might survive that also.

KENNETH O. BJORK: At least two members of the panel have
mentioned the fact that one of the great services of the foreign-
language newspaper in America has been to serve as a bond to
hold Finns, Swedes, Norwegians, Danes, and Icelanders together. I
could not agree more with this point of view. One of the valuable
parts of the Scandinavian-American press was the section devoted
to letters from the subscribers. They were often dubbed letters to
the editor. With all due respect to the gifted editors of these newspapers, the most valuable thing in the paper was not the editorial,
not the big story, but the letters from the simple people—not all of
them so simple, and certainly not simple-minded—which came
to the newspaper from the rank and file of the readership.

These letters correspond in value to the letters that were written
back to the home country, the so-called "America letters." To the

historian, therefore, the immigrant press is of almost unbelievable value and I would like to urge that while thinking about the future, we include a serious plan to complete the collections of newspaper files and absolutely guarantee that these valuable documents be adequately housed and preserved for future scholars.

S. RALPH COHEN: I would like very strongly to associate myself with what the Icelanders have done, what Bjørn Jensen has suggested, and what Håkan Berggren has so well elaborated. Obviously we are faced with two basic needs—one is the need to serve the older generation, the second is to reach out to the newer. Essentially this is a matter of editorial policy and organization, but it is also a problem of economics. I have a feeling, however, that either on an all-Scandinavian basis or on a selective national basis, it is possible to put together the sort of thing that has been suggested, to do it as an insert for existing newspapers and as something which can on its own appeal reach people who are not interested in an immigrant newspaper as such. Because it will thus become a more useful publication to a great many people who are interested in the people whom we are talking about, it may well be possible to support it through the normal processes of advertising.

VAINO A. HOOVER: In regard to an English-language Scandinavian newspaper, we have an excellent example on the Pacific Coast. We had the *Pacific Coast Viking* out there for more than thirty years. Unfortunately, it died with the owner of the paper, but he published an English-language newspaper which took care of all of the Scandinavian societies, churches, clubs, etc. It covered news from the Scandinavian countries and, while it was a predominantly English-language newspaper, it nevertheless had special articles in Scandinavian languages. The editor had good advertising support from the Pacific Coast area, the various industries, stores, restaurants, etc.

It was not a daily newspaper, it was in fact in the nature of a periodical. The idea is not impossible now and I believe that it could work very nicely. The coverage of the *Pacific Coast Viking* was neutral and impartial—there was news of all Scandinavian-American groups. The editor also included such local news, which though not essentially of Scandinavian-American origin, yet would appeal to his readers.

One other aspect of the foreign-language press which I should like to point out is the inclusion of complete obituaries, telling us the complete story of the immigrant. We learn where he was born, the time when his parents arrived in this country, and, if he was born in the United States, the area in which he settled. A student researching immigration into the United States and the whereabouts of immigrant settlements, could use old Scandinavian-American newspaper files with good results.

GENE G. GAGE: Something which I have talked about at The American-Scandinavian Foundation and of which I don't think we are oblivious, is the fact that even if the possibility exists that some day we might have a daily or weekly or some kind of popular publication different from the present *American-Scandinavian Review,* there is a legion of problems which must be met before such an idea is realized. Some people have hinted at this idea, and I am convinced that no Scandinavian organization would want to get involved until basic disputes among the various ethnic groups have been settled. I think that any organization attempting to realize such an idea would be committing suicide. We are very much aware of the problem at the foundation and while I do not wish to speak for the foundation now, I believe that we would be willing to listen to any legitimate suggestions in this regard.

The Presentation of Scandinavia in America Through Books, Periodicals, and Nonliterary Media

Panel: HARALD S. NAESS (Chairman), ERIK J. FRIIS, CLAES DAHLGREN, NORMAN C. BANSEN, HOLMFRIDUR DANIELSON, BENT VANBERG, RICHARD B. VOWLES (Guest Informant), SOLVEIG ZEMPEL (Student Representative)

Chairman's Remarks

HARALD S. NAESS: We shall now hear about the presentation of Scandinavia in America through books, periodicals, and nonliterary media. I think it will appear again that our editors, publishers, directors and broadcasters are catering to very different markets, old markets with clients who have blood ties to the Scandinavian countries, and new markets with clients who do not have such ties, but who have somehow been converted to Scandinavian ideology or a Scandinavian way of life. As Mr. Gage pointed out, more than 50 percent of our students belong to this latter group. I think this situation makes it necessary for our editors and publishers to look for new approaches.

I hope that after the presentation of the facts of our present situation, members of this panel and of the Seminar will have time to address themselves to a problem which might be called cultural engineering. Is it possible—and is it desirable—to try now to bridge the gap between interests in *Rosemaling* on the one hand and Edvard Grieg on the other?

The Publications of The American-Scandinavian Foundation

ERIK J. FRIIS: The American-Scandinavian Foundation, founded in 1910, was indeed one of the earliest organizations on either side of the Atlantic Ocean that embodied the idea of Scandinavian cooperation, and it was held that one of the best ways to inform Americans about Scandinavia was to institute a program of publications, including a magazine and books. *The American-Scandinavian Review* was started in 1913 and is thus in its 61st year. It started out as a quarterly and was later published about six times a year; in the early 1930s it became a monthly and, in the late middle thirties, again became a quarterly. During those sixty years the magazine has had only three editors, Dr. Henry Goddard Leach, Hanna Astrup Larsen, and myself. I for one cannot look upon *The American-Scandinavian Review* as an ethnic magazine. It is an American magazine whose objective is to present Scandinavia to American readers; its main purpose is to present Scandinavia past and present, with emphasis on the present and on cultural affairs, and with a subject matter that appeals to both the older and younger readers. From its beginning, three of the Scandinavian countries, Norway, Sweden, and Denmark, were naturally included in its coverage, but Iceland also was treated separately at that time even though it was united with Denmark. Since 1944 Iceland has been a member of the foundation and of course the coverage has continued. Finland was included in the work of the foundation in 1961 and since then it has received full coverage in the magazine and has been represented in all publications. The magazine is in good financial position, since all ASF associates get the magazine as part of their membership. The membership cost is $15.00 for regular associates and $25.00 for the sustaining associates, who, in addition to the magazine, receive a free copy of all publications. We also have about 750 subscribers who pay $7.50 a year for the magazine alone. Most of these subscribers are probably libraries, not only in this country, but also in Scandinavia, and even as far away as the Soviet Union. We now print about 6,000 copies of the magazine, which is not enough to my mind. I believe we could make some progress here, considering that one quarter of our readership is non-Scandinavian or at least have non-Scandinavian names.

As for the coverage in the magazine, it has always been a problem to give equal weight to the five Scandinavian countries. It is also difficult to distribute articles of equal weight to different kinds of subject matter. I am fortunate in having representatives in each of the Scandinavian capitals who will help me get articles for the magazine. Quite a few articles come in unsolicited and I am also in touch with authors myself, both here and in Scandinavia. I now pay $75.00 for full-fledged contributions. Advertising income has been declining for the last few years, probably because of the business recession, but it will undoubtedly climb again before long. I think there is a great future for the magazine, but it depends to a large extent on the money that is made available for promotion in the years to come.

The American-Scandinavian Foundation's book publications program has been in existence since 1914, the first volume being *Comedies* by Ludvig Holberg in Oscar Campbell's translation. All in all we have published 125 books and our present rate of publication is three or four books per year, including reprints of all our publications. As in the case of the magazine, the book publications program is fortunate in being supported by roughly one thousand foundation members, the so-called sustaining associates, who pay $25.00 dues in advance and for that money receive the two new books that are published each year. Thus we have a built-in sale of about one thousand copies of every new title. As some of you must know, we have published quite a few sagas. We are no doubt the biggest saga publisher in America, in the world perhaps, excepting Iceland. At any rate, we have done our share of saga publishing, and we have published also in many other fields, including biography, essays, numerous plays in translation, and a series of histories of the Scandinavian countries; Norway and Finland are the two available so far. We are also publishing a series of histories of literature; in that series the Norway, Denmark, Sweden, and Iceland volumes have appeared, and Finland's literary history will be ready this year. We have published some anthologies of poetry and many volumes of fiction in translation, both classical and modern. As you know, there are many ways to skin a cat. Some books that we have published were originally brought out in English in Scandinavia and we imported them for our use and sale over here.

It may be difficult for a small organization with a very small staff to act as an independent publisher, which is what the foundation did in the beginning. Soon, however, it was found advantageous to cooperate with a larger publishing house, and in the early thirties we published our books in conjunction and cooperation with W. W. Norton and Co. Later we had a copublishing arrangement with Princeton University Press, and since 1967 we have copublished quite a few of our books, though not all, with Twayne Publishers.

I am also happy to report that many of the old books, long out of print, have been reissued by reprint houses. Kraus Reprint Company has put out a series called "Scandinavian Scene" in which about a dozen of our old titles were given a new lease on life. I must not forget our textbook project, which is going to be a very important one. This project will provide complete and modern texts for the study of the five Scandinavian languages, Norwegian, Swedish, Danish, Finnish, and Icelandic. Lappish, Faeroese, and Greenlandic have so far been left out, but whenever there is a need and a demand, we might perhaps be able to consider those too.

We ought not to lose sight of the fact that many American publishing houses do a yeoman job for Scandinavian literature. Quite a few publishers take a very special interest in the literature of Scandinavia; I might mention Alfred A. Knopf, Random House, Pantheon Books, Seymour Lawrence, Praeger, and many others. Pantheon Books has over the last few years published many books relative to Sweden; Praeger has issued Finnish art books and four Scandinavian volumes in the "Nations of the Modern World" series; Kraus Reprint Co. has reissued more than forty titles in its "Scandinavian Scene" series; in fact, most publishers are greatly interested when offered first-rate material, in the original or in translation. In compiling the book review and book notes section in *The American-Scandinavian Review,* I find that on the average I mention at least twenty-five American books relative to Scandinavia in every issue. That makes over one hundred books a year, fiction as well as nonfiction, and I think that is a respectable number of books on Scandinavia to be offered the American reader in the course of a year.

Swedish Broadcasts in America

CLAES DAHLGREN: Before I go into what the Swedish Broadcasting Corporation is doing in the United States, I think I should briefly describe who we are. Sveriges Radio is the name of the home organization, which is Sweden's non-commercial radio and television network. There is no commercial radio and television whatsoever in Sweden. The international program service of the Swedish Broadcasting Corporation is a department called Radio Sweden which produces radio and television programs in Stockholm in six languages besides Swedish. Radio Sweden broadcasts directly from Stockholm to North America on short wave several times a day, both in English and Swedish, as well as in Spanish and French. These programs feature news and commentary. To listen to these broadcasts you must of course have a radio receiver with a short wave band, and since that is not standard in the United States there might not be too many of them, whereas in Europe and many other countries short wave is standard on most radio sets. Nevertheless, my friends at Radio Sweden in Stockholm tell me that they are receiving a substantial letter reaction from short wave listeners in the United States.

The other program activities over here are the ones that I am in charge of at the Swedish Broadcasting Office in New York which, besides other duties for the home organization, handles the transcription service for Radio Sweden. This means making taped radio programs and television films available without cost for broadcasts on local stations in this country. As a matter of fact, we provide a similar service for Canada, Mexico, and Puerto Rico. As I mentioned, all the programs are produced by Radio Sweden in Stockholm and all of those intended for the United States are in English, as there is not enough of a market among the stations here for Swedish-language programs. We use American and sometimes British announcers from our staff in Stockholm.

My office in New York receives one master tape of each radio program, and the necessary number of tape copies for the American stations are made here; as for the television films, we get directly from Stockholm as many prints of each as can be afforded. We offer the programs to stations around the country and they are sent by mail as well as by personal delivery whenever this is possible. We never send out tapes or films unless they have been actually ordered by the station.

On the radio side we have two regular monthly programs, each of thirty minutes, one being "Sweden Today," a magazine-type of program that contains eight or nine separate items of two or three minutes each, usually interviews or commentaries on current Swedish events in the fields of science, music, sports, social conditions, medicine, and other topics. "Sweden Today" presently goes out to about 140 radio stations, and of these as many as 65 percent are affiliated with universities. Most of the others also are non-commercial stations, but there are some commercial stations that use excerpts from the "Sweden Today" programs. The other monthly thirty minutes program is "Swedish Spectrum," which deals with all the areas of the arts in Sweden: theater, literature, movies, music, and so on.

We have a little over 100 stations subscribing to this program, and here the percentage of university affiliates is still higher—about 80 percent. Altogether we distribute 3,000 of these two monthly programs a year. Copies of a program called "Weekly Press Review" are airmailed from Stockholm directly to around 35 stations. From New York we also have available a number of more timeless standard programs, for instance an excellent music series with commentaries on classical music, contemporary music, folk music, music of the twentieth century and so on. And there are spoken programs, we have "Highlights in Swedish History," discussions with Nobel Prize winners, and many others. I would estimate that we will place around 1,000 such special programs with stations this year, which would bring the grand total of radio programs to around 4,000. There used to be many more, but we have seen some drastic cuts in funds this year, especially for the music programs. Nevertheless, we are still hoping that some money can be found, so that we can fully utilize these station contacts that have been developed over a number of years. Meanwhile the present 4,000 broadcasts per year reach audiences that total in the millions.

When it comes to television, this is of course a much more expensive medium to operate in, both from the standpoint of production and making film copies, so our statistics are more modest. We have a series of thirteen half-hour programs called "Focus on Sweden" which in 1969 had some 850 individual showings in the United States. A 13–15-minute program called "Swedish Closeup," which has had some 200 individual telecasts since 1972, covers many different areas. Among the titles are: "Atoms for Peace," "Ombudsman—the Protector of People's Rights," "The Royal Collector," "Arctic Countdown," "From Fire and Air" (which deals with Swedish glass), "Carl Milles—Swedish Sculptor," and "The Artificial Kidney." We also have several television programs dealing with environmental protection but we have not had many showings of these as yet. Our television catalog includes quite a number of standard programs on various subjects. Most of the showings are on public television stations, including many of the big ones, Los Angeles, Boston, San Francisco, Chicago, and of course, Channel Two in the Twin Cities. There is also collaboration with the Public Broadcasting Service Network which has shown some of our programs on all of its 233 stations.

Danish Culture in America

NORMAN C. BANSEN: It is a rare public library in which one will find any Danish literature in English if one looks beyond Hans Christian Andersen or Karen Blixen (Isak Dinesen). Add to these names that of Kierkegaard and one can say the same about most university and college libraries, except those in institutions that have courses in Scandinavian.

Texts useful in courses that include Danish literature are all too quickly out of print. In the 1960s Hallmundsson's *An Anthology of Scandinavian Literature,* Corrigan's *Masterpieces of the Modern Scandinavian Theatre,* and Sprinchorn's *The Genius of the Scandinavian Theatre* appeared; two are already out of print. Mitchell's *A History of Danish Literature,* 2nd augmented edition, is available from the Kraus Reprint Company in a 1971 reprint. In the same year the bilingual edition of *Anthology of Danish Literature,* edited by Billeskov-Jansen and Mitchell, was published by Southern Illinois University Press.

Several clusters of books have appeared. In the fifties within a matter of a few years four books on Grundtvig were published—those by Koch, Knudsen, Lindhard, and Nielsen. In the fifties and early sixties Mitchell's translation of *Selected Essays* by Holberg was published by the University of Kansas Press, followed by the University of Nebraska Press publication of the same author's *The Journey of Niels Klim* and *Peder Paars.*

In addition to The American-Scandinavian Foundation and Twayne Publishers, the presses of the Universities of Wisconsin and Washington have published Danish works in English translations. In spite of financial losses reported, Wisconsin's Nordic Translation Series gave us two long overdue translations, Paludan's *Jørgen Stein* and Kristensen's *Havoc,* as well as the short stories of Branner. Word has just come from Twayne that this year Branner's *The Story of Børge* will appear; it is a translation by a gradu-

ate of Dana College and the University of Minnesota, Kristi
Planck.

A few reprints have appeared, among them, fortunately, Jacob-
sen's *Niels Lyhne* and Hansen's *The Liar.*

There is much immigrant history of recent decades in the histories of the two Danish Lutheran Synods by Enok Mortensen and
John M. Jensen and in Paul C. Nyholm's work, *The Americanization of the Danish Churches;* these are cultural history as well as
church history; all were published in the 1960s.

In the area of the immigrant novel, the Grimsen trilogy of
Danish-born, American-reared Sophus Keith Winther, *Take All
to Nebraska, Mortgage Your Heart,* and *This Passion Never
Dies,* published by Macmillan in the mid-1930s, has been unob-
tainable for years. The trilogy is available in Swedish and Danish,
the latter translated by no less a novelist than Hans Kirk. Des-
mond Powell, for a decade chairman of the Department of English
at the University of Arizona, wrote in 1948 in an article in *The
American-Scandinavian Review,* "One finds it strange . . . that
people who profess to like Theodore Dreiser and the earlier Sin-
clair Lewis ignore him. . . . At any rate it is with such writers . . .
that he should be compared." He then suggests that a one-volume
edition of the Grimsen trilogy should be published by Modern
Library "or any other publisher of masterpieces." That was
twenty-five years ago!

Danish films are relatively scarce when one considers the
Swedish films available in America. In the Macmillan Audio Bran-
don Films catalog for 1974–75 one finds listed thirteen films from
Sweden, four from Denmark, the Danish films being *The Deserter;
Ditte, Child of Man; A Stranger Knocks;* and *Weekend. Day of
Wrath* and *Ordet* have not been available for some time.

Productions of Danish dramatic works in this country have been
few in the past decades. In 1942 Kaj Munk's *Ordet* was presented
in the original Danish at Dana College and toured six states. A
decade later the same play in translation was produced by West

Virginia State College and Howard University, both predominantly black. Abell's *Anne Sophie Hedvig* was produced at the University of Illinois in the 1940s and at the University of Minnesota in the 1950s. In 1962 Dana College produced Munk's *Herod the King;* it was directed by a German-American, Herod was played by a Hungarian-American, Salomé by a black American; it is evident from this that colleges of ethnic background had by then become cosmopolitan. Dana, in 1970, produced Holberg's *The Christmas Party.* We can scarcely hope for more until the Danes produce a playwright as well known as Ibsen or Strindberg or there is a Holberg revival—and then we would have to share that with the Norwegians!

The Danish presence is felt this year in a new Danish gymnastic team at Dana College; it is directed by a young Dane and his Icelandic wife and includes students from both the college and the high school. The Grand View and Dana folk dancers have been active for many years and bring this aspect of Danish culture to audiences across the country. Both are student-organized and student-directed; less than a third of the dancers at Dana are of Danish ancestry.

The choirs of Dana and Grand View Colleges include some Danish music in most of their programs. Grand View College should also be given credit for the promotion of *A World of Song,* which contains a large selection of Danish folk music, much of which has been reprinted in various folk song books published in America in recent years. A selection of these songs is now available in a recording by the Grand View College Choir.

Icelandic Publications and Cultural Programs in Canada

HOLMFRIDUR DANIELSON: Right from the beginning of their immigration (they settled in Manitoba in the fall of 1875, somewhat earlier in Ontario and Nova Scotia) Icelanders emphasized education, law, religion, literature, libraries, etc. It may be of interest to note that even the tiniest settlement of Icelanders in Manitoba, as well as in North Dakota and Saskatchewan, had a formal library for the use of all its residents, which was looked after by a literary society or other cultural groups. Before and just after the turn of the century we know of at least 32 such library societies in various small settlements, and very likely there were many more that have not been "dug up" as yet. Many of these small localities are now devoid of Icelanders, and most of the libraries have gone, but it was a fabulous beginning for education and learning.

The output of books, magazines, poetry, pamphlets, biographies, periodicals published here in the Icelandic language has been prodigious from the very beginning. The first newspaper was started in New Iceland less than three years after the first settlers arrived, and that in a year when scores of people were dying from a smallpox epidemic, with everybody quarantined and cut off from the outside world. Today, however, publications in the Icelandic language have virtually ceased. We have one weekly newspaper, which is mostly in Icelandic, though usually with one page or so in English.

In recent years some good material has been published in English on our history here. The Icelanders in Saskatchewan have been treated by W. J. Lindal (about 1955), the Icelanders in Manitoba by W. Kristjanson (1965), the Icelanders in Canada by W. J. Lindal (1967). Of pioneer reminiscences, mention should be made of two readable and illuminating accounts by Magnus G. Gudlaugson and S. B. Olson, both published privately. Unfortunately, like *Iceland's Thousand Years,* these books are now out of print.

Iceland's Thousand Years was published as a result of the efforts of the Icelandic-Canadian Evening School which I established in 1944. This was a unique situation among the ethnic groups in Canada, being the first effort to offer regular classes where people could learn about their own history, literature, and language. During the first year there were thirteen lectures dealing with the history and literature of Iceland from the first settlement in the ninth century down to 1944, when Iceland regained its former status, becoming a full-fledged republic. Following each lecture there was an hour of instruction in the Icelandic language at three levels. The first year's lectures were published in the above-mentioned book, *Iceland's Thousand Years,* which has found its way all over the world, mainly to universities and libraries in Russia, South Africa, South America, Australia, and most of the European countries; it has been valuable in disseminating information about Iceland, and, more important, in stimulating people to acquire more knowledge about that interesting country. Also in several other places study groups were formed on the pattern of the Icelandic-Canadian Evening School, with *Iceland's Thousand Years* used as source material.

In connection with the 100th anniversary, in 1975, of the coming of the Icelanders to Manitoba, there were plans for two anthologies of Icelandic-Canadian literature, containing poetry and prose written in English or translated from the Icelandic. Also planned was a book on the history of the events that were part of the celebration. We also planned a series of biographical sketches of the leaders of the past in various fields which, later, we intended to follow up by articles on the present generation. The 100th anniversary of Icelandic immigration to Utah (1955) was given the most wonderful and extensive publicity. Practically every paper of any consequence in the whole state carried pages and pages of pictures of historical and current events. In Salt Lake City there were numerous TV appearances and the highlight of the three-day Festival in Spanish Fork was the presentation of the elaborate historical pageant *The Symbol of Iceland,* written and produced especially for the occasion by Mrs. H. F. Danielson of Winnipeg.

The Icelandic Canadian magazine was started by the Icelandic-Canadian Club of Winnipeg in 1942. It is an English-language quarterly and has collected a tremendous amount of current and

pioneer history about the Icelanders in America, besides presenting valuable literary material. There is evidence that members of
the younger generation are now becoming more interested in the
magazine which has only about a thousand subscribers; younger
people have recently inquired about subscriptions and full sets, and
for the last few years a number of university graduates have been
serving on the magazine board. From Iceland we receive a new
quarterly magazine, now ten years old, *Atlantica & Iceland Review,* which has a beautiful format and color photography, with
a wealth of information about every aspect of Icelandic life. Iceland has also produced many lovely picture books on the country,
with text in English as well as other languages, including pictorial
accounts of the spectacular volcanic activity in 1963 which formed
the island Surtsey and, quite recently, a book about the terrible
eruption in the Westman Islands.

An outstanding effort of the Icelanders here during the last
years has been the establishment of the chair in Icelandic at the
University of Manitoba. We have an excellent head of the department in Professor Haraldur Bessason, through whose influence the
department has been expanding and community interest growing.
There is a large library of some 16,000 items, constantly used, and
containing all the titles published here about Iceland; all the literature produced here by Icelanders, both in Icelandic and English;
all the books and periodicals published in Iceland since the library
was established in 1951; all the translations that have been done
in English, from the Golden Age Icelandic Classics and other
translations; and tremendous collections (some full sets) of periodicals published in Iceland through the years, as well as all available books of value published in Iceland.

Professor Bessason has also been influential in starting a publications series of Icelandic texts in English translations at the University of Manitoba Press. The first work, in 1972, was a translation of the *Landnámabók. Eyrbyggja saga, Grágás* and a history
of Iceland are now in preparation. There also has been a revival of

Icelandic language classes outside the University. Four districts that I know of have been pushing the teaching of Icelandic in the public schools and two of them already have courses in operation.

A series of Icelandic cultural programs which I coordinated, was presented over CFRW/FM, Winnipeg, featuring Icelandic artists in Iceland and America and lectures on various aspects of Icelandic culture. We had the famous Male Choir of Reykjavík, an Icelandic-Canadian pianist playing with the Icelandic Symphony Orchestra, and many other well-known soloists from Canada and the United States, as well as choirs from various Icelandic communities. There were twelve sessions altogether.

Films of Iceland have been shown throughout the years and there have been numerous showings of color slides by visitors to Iceland. People flocked to see the spectacular films of the Surtsey eruption and in January, 1973, we were able to see films of the Westman Islands eruption. The Canadian Film Board sometimes cooperates by showing films which are of interest to Icelanders.

Drama has flourished in the Icelandic settlements from the beginning. Though naturally amateurish at first, it nourished the artistic and creative spirit of the newcomers at a time when all entertainment had to be provided by the people themselves. In some districts the art of drama developed high standards, competing with the best of theatrical activities in Winnipeg.

Although drama died down almost entirely in the settlements and Winnipeg around 1940, it was revived in 1955–56 with an excellent production of Lauga Geir's prize-winning play on the Icelandic pioneers, presented eight times in Winnipeg and nearby towns, and by another cast in North Dakota. The students in the Department of Icelandic at the University of Manitoba have also become enthusiastic about drama. They performed Stefánsson's classic, *The Golden Gate,* at the Icelandic festival and the convention of the Icelandic National League, and have since done other plays, after formally organizing themselves as "The New Iceland Drama Society." Paul Sigurdson, of Morden, Manitoba, who is president of our Icelandic National League chapter there, has written a play,

The Icelander, which was performed in a Winnipeg theater, with good reviews, as well as at the Icelandic Festival at Gimli, Manitoba. A young man in Vancouver, R. J. Asgeirson, who heads Photon Productions and who planned a movie for the 1975 centennial, has traveled in the Icelandic districts gathering material. Two folklorists from Iceland, Mr. and Mrs. H. O. Eiríksson, spent six months here on a fellowship, gathering Icelandic-Canadian and American folklore. They took back with them sixty hours of taped talks with 166 individuals. The result will undoubtedly become a number of articles or possibly a book, and we hope that some of this material will be translated into English so that our people here may read it. Finally, there has been quite a revival of singing groups—adult choirs and children's choirs in various places.

I get hundreds of requests for material on Icelandic matters—songs, essays, masters' theses, costumes, food recipes—from clubs and schools all over the country whenever they are putting on some program with an ethnic flavor, or doing a social project in school. Our efforts are made easier by the fact that in all these years there has been constant liaison between the cultural leaders in Iceland and our Icelandic National League. There have been exchanges of speakers, artists, invitations to choirs, etc.; the Male Choir of Reykjavík has toured the United States and Canada twice, in 1946 and 1960, and was co-sponsored in Canada by the I.N.L. and the Fred Gee Celebrity Series. Every year at our annual convention we have a guest from Iceland, who is usually booked to tour all the main Icelandic centers from coast to coast and, in cooperation with the University of Manitoba, is also invited to speak at universities and colleges in various cities. The Icelandic Government likewise invites leaders from Canada to be its guests in Iceland. It also subsidizes our weekly paper *Lögberg-Heimskringla* and has bought a large number of *Iceland's Thousand Years* for distribution to its embassies and consulates, and to foreign diplomats.

The editors of *Atlantica & Iceland Review* waged a vigorous campaign to promote subscriptions in Iceland to *Lögberg-Heims-kringla,* and we do the same for their journal. All through the years the Government of Iceland has subsidized the efforts of the Icelandic National League to bring noted leaders from Iceland to tour here, and Icelandic Airlines, Inc. in New York, has contributed many free passages for important visitors. Individual contacts between people in Canada and Iceland are becoming more and more important, as visitors in increasing numbers flock both ways. Whenever we have charter flights from Winnipeg, Vancouver, or other places, the Cultural Organization in Reykjavík extends generous hospitality at many centers in Iceland and elaborate plans were made for us when we visited Iceland in 1974 to celebrate the eleven-hundredth anniversary of the founding of Iceland.

Two years ago the I.N.L. completed the microfilming of all papers, periodicals, etc. about Iceland published here from the beginning of immigration down to 1969. A set of this film was presented to the Government of Iceland. Iceland, on the other hand, sends a free copy of every book published in Iceland to the library at the University of Manitoba.

The outlook for the preservation of our heritage in Canada is rather bright. We seem to have more young people participating in our cultural activities; Icelandic language classes are flourishing in several places, and Icelandic has been put on the curriculum of some schools.

There is also the hope that the multiculturalism program of the Federal Government in Ottawa will provide financial aid to some of the worthwhile projects of ethnic groups in Canada.

Finally we are making considerable progress in our efforts to unite all cultural institutions among the Icelanders into one cooperative organization. The Centenary Celebration Committee has gathered the names of individual groups all over America, as well as names of current officers, with a view to being in constant liaison so that we can see what is going on and how we can possibly help each other.

The Viking

BENT VANBERG: The fraternal organization, Sons of Norway, publishes *The Viking,* which now has a printing of 72,000 copies. It goes out to the homes of all our 88,000 members, and since our membership is increasing we expect in the near future to reach a circulation of about 85,000. In my opinion, *The Viking* has become the prime spokesman for Norwegian America. This is mainly because of the sad fact that not only the Norwegian-American press but other Scandinavian papers are declining sharply. *The Viking,* thus, is moving to a key position, reflecting as it does Norwegian cultural and educational values in America.

I shall limit myself to one rather important aspect of this magazine, an aspect that was touched upon briefly by Professor Bjork, namely the section known as "Letters to the Editor." I have noticed that numerous letters in this section deal with family research, not only by elderly members of Sons of Norway, but more and more by younger members, which means that we can look forward to even greater interest in this subject in years to come. The letters keep asking how to go about tracing one's ancestry in Norway, and in the end, to save time, I developed a little booklet, a guide to family research, called *So Deep Are My Roots,* which has been a substantial help to several hundreds of our Sons of Norway members.

The Nordic Translation Series

RICHARD B. VOWLES: In its Nordic Translation Series, at the instigation of the Nordic Cultural Commission and under the general editorship of Einar Haugen, Harald Naess, and myself, the University of Wisconsin Press has published three authors for each of the five Nordic countries, a total of fifteen volumes in 5,000 copies each, or 75,000 individual books in the period of 1965–1970. As of now, 15,814 bound copies remain unsold and 30,000 unbound copies are in stock. In other words 61 percent of the original printing remain unsold and continuing sales have averaged fewer than 100 copies each over the past two-year period. Press expenses, less a subvention from the Nordic Cultural Commission, ran to a total of $171,000. After deducting a sales income of approximately $86,400 you come up with a loss of $84,600, or an average loss per book of $5,640. Now let us try to look at the happier side of things, moving away, for the time being, from figures to the authors and their works.

The Icelander Gunnar Gunnarsson's *Black Cliffs* is the top seller with almost 3,000 copies (2,993); Gunnarsson's *Ships in the Sky* was a book club choice in 1938 and, if his name does not linger on, publicity was able to stimulate memories of the earlier book. The Finnish Nobel Prize winner F. E. Sillanpää comes next. Known slightly for *The Maid Silja* (1933) and *Meek Heritage* (1938), his *People in the Summer Night* has sold 2,900 copies. Then comes the Swedish author Karin Boye's *Kallocain* with 2,700 copies, presumably selling because it is one of those frightening utopian novels like George Orwell's *1984*. Sales have run as low as 816 copies, as is the case with Falkberget's *The Fourth Night Watch*. Clearly the market does not extend very much beyond libraries and sporadic gift and textbook sales. Prices, ranging from $4.00 to $7.95, are in line with book prices generally and hardly prohibitive. The cheaper volumes have sold better than the more expensive ones. Hence the deduction that, other things being equal, it is easier to publish and market small books than big fat ones.

There is no reason to assume that any one of the Scandinavian countries is more popular than another. Sales figures by country are dictated by the popularity of the authors within the country. That sales figures for Norway are the lowest of the five countries merely suggests that with authors like Sandemose and Vesaas not selling better than they are, something is seriously wrong with cultural transmission in this less than one world of ours, and that too much depends on advertising and publicity arrangements for which university presses have very limited funds. On the other hand, I have not observed that the commercial presses have been marketing Scandinavian books notably better except in those cases where the authors are already very well known, like Strindberg and Knut Hamsun.

In Wisconsin we went through elaborate measures in 1968–70 to prepare for a second and more exciting series of fifteen titles. We were in consultation with professors, journalists, publishers, and others on both sides of the Atlantic in drawing up such a list. Unfortunately a crisis occurred, not merely at Wisconsin, but at most university presses; we had to cut back over 50 percent and as a result the new series was not embarked upon. What could make a difference, what could reactivate the project? A subvention somewhere between $75,000 and $100,000. It ought to be noted though, that fine books like Paludan's *Jørgen Stein,* which won a national book design award, lost as much as $11,240 and Laxness's *World Light* $9,300. A subvention of $5,000 per item would insure the publication of the smaller books in the series. It would make the picture a little less bleak and we hope that we can locate somewhere a business or cultural agency that might be interested in extending this Scandinavian reach.

Let me say finally that there is still a market chiefly among libraries. The book market otherwise consists very substantially of (1) book clubs and (2) paperback trade. It is difficult to break into a club with a Scandinavian book, I would guess, unless it dramatizes Vikings, food, or sexual gymnastics, or some combination of these. And unless a large volume sale is guaranteed, paperback issue is out of the question. Several of the Nordic Translation Series books would have a steady textbook usage at the reduced price of a paperback, but it is still unlikely that the necessarily large printing would pay for itself. At Wisconsin we are going to spend a lot of time Xeroxing books, which I guess is illegal, but we depend on that kind of reproduction to teach a course the way we want to. Even so our enrollments, I think, are curtailed because students don't have the books and have to use Xeroxed, mimeographed copies in departmental libraries. This is a special and somewhat separate problem, I admit, but I wanted to raise it as a concluding point. I think it deserves a conference all of its own.

Comments

SOLVEIG ZEMPEL: I have two comments that I would like to make concerning the students' point of view on the questions of books and publications. First is the problem of availability which has been mentioned before. Good translations are not available, and it is awkward to try and order these things from Scandinavia since one cannot see beforehand what there is to choose from. There is a need for more variety in textbooks, in language and literature, as well as in the fields of history and culture, textbooks both in the original languages and English. There is a great lack of graded readings for the language courses; this is a particular problem that I am concerned with, because I am teaching Beginning Norwegian. Also, with regard to the Nordic Translation Series, I should add that it is not available in the bookstores, a fact which discourages students greatly from buying it.

They don't see it on the shelf, and that is the end of that.

There is one rather personal observation I would like to make. Students probably would not agree with me on this, but I feel very strongly that professors should not be afraid to ask students to buy books. Books are the tools of students, and it is ridiculous for professors to go around saying, "This book costs $5 so we can't order it, our students won't want to pay for it." If you were in the Institute of Technology you would be paying $15 for every book you bought and you would be buying maybe two or three books for every course. Why the literature students can't buy books, I don't understand.

Secondly, I think there is a need for quality in publications, as far as translations are concerned, in choosing the material and perhaps the methods of organizing the translations. There is a need for standards to be set, for there is a great range in quality in the translations available and, since a bad translation can kill a book very fast, when I deal with students that can't have the book in the original language, a high quality translation is simply a must. And you people who are in the publications field should try to set up some sort of controls here. I know there are problems and compromises involved, nevertheless, if you expect students to use the books, the translations have to be as good as possible. This I think is of major concern.

Discussion

HARALD S. NAESS: Since Finland was not represented on the panel, would someone comment on the presentation of Finnish literature in this country.

MICHAEL G. KARNI: I believe a Finnish best-seller list here would begin with *Kalevala,* most recently translated by Professor Magoun from Harvard. Next in line, I think, would be Linna's *Unknown Soldier,* which has been available in Finnish newspaper offices here, along with such teaching materials as dictionaries and language textbooks, for instance ABC books which they are stocking and restocking—basic ABC books that were used in the Finnish communities in this country at the turn of the century. The Finnish newspaper offices also serve as an outlet for recordings and an occasional film from Finland. I can't give more details, but I would say that we are doing quite well, as well as could be expected, in having Finnish materials made available in English here.

VAINO A. HOOVER: If there are some universities that would like to obtain modern periodicals relating to Finland, there is *Look at Finland,* an excellent monthly publication, very well illustrated and of the size of The American-Scandinavian Foundation's quarterly journal. I am sure you can get this publication by writing to the Finnish consul general's office either in San Francisco or New York. Then there is another monthly journal, a trade publication, which you can get simply by writing to the Finnish Foreign Trade Association in Helsinki, and there is also a quarterly, published by the Finnish-American Society in Helsinki, which again you may want to write for. This quarterly is mostly in English, although it may have some material in Swedish and Finnish. I am sure all of those periodicals can be obtained by writing to these particular agencies. In regard to recent publications regarding Finland, there is a book published by Charles Scribner and Sons on the winter war, which may be of some historical interest to you.

ERICK KENDALL: I might add that the Pioneer Publishing Company of Fitchburg, Massachusetts, has shown an interest in the presentation of Finnish literature in English.

S. RALPH COHEN: Is there in existence any sort of consolidated list of Scandinavian books that have been translated into English, whether in or out of print, here and in the United Kingdom and Canada?

HARALD S. NAESS: As far as the field of literature is concerned, I cannot think of any consolidated list except such things as the pamphlet containing all the publications of The American-Scandinavian Foundation. I don't know that it has been updated, but it was of some use in the past. There are, of course, separate national bibliographies that list books published in English, even current publications, like *Dania Polyglotta* and, more recently, *Suecana extranea*. But the only consolidated listing of current titles in English is the bibliography published every year in the periodical *Scandinavian Studies*.

LLOYD HUSTVEDT: I would like to add the title of Erling Grønland's book, *Norway in English,* which has been out for about ten years.

FRANKLIN D. SCOTT: There are some interesting bibliographies, not only from the point of view of detail, but because they indicate the trends that are coming. One of the most progressive of these is a very thick bibliography by Sven Groennings dating from 1970, *Scandinavia in Social Science Literature: An English Language Bibliography.* A tremendous search for new books in the social sciences is underway; the panel here has been concerned primarily with literature, but other subjects are advancing to a considerable extent. Regarding Swedish literature in English, a bibliography by Bure Holmbäck appeared about three years ago in the periodical *Sweden Illustrated,* and has since become available in a separate edition.

CARLTON C. QUALEY: I submit that a very high impact will come from certain kinds of non-academic sources. One is movies such as *The Emigrants,* which has had a greater influence than perhaps anything that has happened in a long time in the American community, and I think if we could get more of that sort of thing, it would go far to solve the Scanpresence problem. The other one is a very humble thing which could solve Mr. Vowles's financial difficulties. I don't know if you consider cooking to be an art form, but the publication of cookbooks is a great American success story, the cookbooks of Scandinavian recipes actually sell tremendously, and probably a tummy-full of *rømmegraut* has as much impact as anything else. These non-academic channels belong perhaps in Scanpresence no less than some of the other categories.

RICHARD B. VOWLES: I think too many university presses are repelled by the idea of a best seller. They might well emulate Yale University Press, which has a couple of best sellers. They are not going to hurt any reputations; they can be academically respectable. I just don't know about the cookbook market, as I think several publishers have beaten us to it.

EINAR HAUGEN: I do think that one of our major problems all these years has been that of getting adequate books, and this is so because the whole publishing business has been so fragmented. We have been dependent on ethnic and religious publishing houses like Augustana or Augsburg, and bookstores in Brooklyn, Chicago, and elsewhere which have folded after a while because they were not economically viable. And, as Mrs. Zempel said, trying to get books from Scandinavia is—she didn't say it quite this way—like pulling teeth. One does it on an individual basis, one writes to Scandinavia and gets some books over, pays for them oneself and then sells them to one's students. This is utterly uneconomical, it's absurd that we should have to do it, but over and over again I've had this experience. There is no support, virtually no support, from Scandinavia for this activity, there is not an adequate market in this country, it is one point at which the Scandinavian countries could put in some money, could help us out in various ways.

However, not all initiatives from Scandinavia have been equally happy. When Dick Vowles reported on the series from Wisconsin, he probably did not tell you about the origins of that particular series. The Nordic Council through its committee on cultural affairs proposed that a series of Scandinavian classics be translated into English and distributed on the world's markets, specifically America and England. A list was drawn up by Scandinavian professors of literature which, from a Scandinavian point of view, was excellent in the sense that it included works of great importance and classic quality. However, at least one-third of them had already been translated, which immediately raised questions of copyright, and the quality of translation, and so on. Another third were books that were, quite simply, impossible, in terms of the American or English market. And so the result was that there was a tiny little list of books left, none of which were contemporary, all of which had been out at least 50–60 years by the time the list was drawn up. In other words, it was drawn up by people who knew their specialty, but did not know the American market, or anything relating to the teaching of Scandinavian literature in American universities where we have to face students with certain presuppositions and certain expectations. Eventually the series was cut down to fifteen volumes, three from each country, and even so these volumes were not the volumes that we at Wisconsin would have wanted to translate. Some of them were too long and, therefore, terribly expensive, like Laxness's *World Light,* which is a beautiful book, but you know it cost us $10,000 to print that book with perhaps $2,000 in sales in return. So the whole thing was bad in some ways, but at least it worked. We got the books out and the only thing that is necessary now is that the University of Wisconsin realize its loss and give up the idea of getting its money back and, instead, put the books out as paperbacks so that Mrs. Zempel's suggestion of making the students buy them can be effectuated. And I heartily approve of her venture in that respect. I have a tendency to ask my students to buy quite a lot of books and find that, while they don't always do it, at least they know what they ought to have bought.

HARALD S. NAESS: I would like to insert here that we have received considerable help from the Scandinavian governments, at least at Wisconsin. I could mention gifts of books and newspapers from the Swedish Institute, and, in recent years, similar gifts from the Norwegian Information Service in New York.

RICHARD B. VOWLES: To amplify Einar Haugen's commentary, we had misgivings about, in fact we had problems, with some of the titles in the first series, which is why we took the initiative with the second series. We canvassed about eighty people on both sides of the Atlantic in order to pick the next fifteen books, and were flattered to be asked by the Nordic Cultural Commission to do this. The only right they reserved for themselves was the right to veto titles. As I recall, they never did make use of this right.

GENE G. GAGE: I just have a brief addition to Professor Qualey's comment about the impact of non-academic materials. I happened to pick up an academic dissertation the other day and found a statement to the effect that SAS, our host here, has published 72 percent of all the words in the English language that present Scandinavia abroad. That is something to think about.

HÅKAN BERGGREN: I would like to add to the commentary on the book situation, but first a few words about a project which I believe is Ralph Cohen's creation. It concerns the short film, the information films for example, of which I think we have at least 100 titles, if we combine the total Scandinavian output. This production has been reviewed, thanks to SAS, and I was happy to learn that the oldest film distributed dates from 1938, and that it is indeed a Swedish one. A major problem with regard to these short films is distribution. Since each of the companies behind the films is too small to get a first-class professional distributor, the idea was that we should try to pool our resources and get a good one, and that we should concentrate on distributing them to the business community, for meetings followed by pictures, whether they be travelogues or more directly informative films about special institutions, such as the ombudsman. The short film project is, I think, an excellent initiative which deserves a lot of attention.

Secondly, a couple of years ago, when several of my former colleagues at different universities started courses in comparative social history, including Swedish history, I discovered the need for good translations and good American versions of Swedish social science research. I think there have been many developing efforts from The American-Scandinavian Foundation, from Wisconsin, and so forth, but they have been scattered. A couple of years ago we tried at the Swedish Information Service, to get in touch with a dozen different American publishing companies, hoping to invite their representatives to a conference with Swedish publishers, in order to see if we could facilitate the flow of information about publications, and indeed at such an early stage that we could get the greatest advantage out of a program or the planning of a book. This was worked out with one representative from the University of Minnesota Press and one from Doubleday & Company. The main result of this effort has been that, several times a year, a group of eight to ten Swedish publishers visit the United States on a competitive basis, in order to sell their products and pick up new ideas.

I brought up the short film issue because I think it is a good and concrete example of how we could pool our resources, and I think that publishing is another area where we together, and within the framework of the conference, could try to do something. The main problem is that there are so many publishers here. What we need in each case is to get a couple of chapters of various titles translated, in order to see if the companies would be prepared to consider the book in question. I have asked the SASS organization [Society for the Advancement of Scandinavian Study] to provide us with suggestions for translators, but it is very difficult, in my experience at least, to get names of volunteers here. I believe, however, that there is money available—from Research Councils and other funds—for supporting such a program of trial and error translation.

MARION J. NELSON: I would like to see the rest of the discussion concentrated on an interpretation of directions. In spite of the great deal of information that has come from this panel, I have no feeling of what the directions are. Perhaps it is something in the situation itself; perhaps there are no clear directions as yet. What kind of literature is there a demand for, is film and television in a sense replacing the demand for literature and, if so, what should our policy be? These are ideas I would have liked to have seen discussed, and if people have something to contribute in this direction, I would like to see it come out.

C. PETER STRONG: I believe that a very appropriate move for us at the foundation would be to do a survey among academics with regard to Scandinavian literature in English, to see if there is some recurrent opinion as to what is needed and how this might influence the foundation's publications program.

DONALD V. EVERSOLL: I hope this is not too presumptuous of me as the editor of the *American Dane* but is not one of our goals to identify and appreciate some of the Scandinavian-American influence in America? We have discussed the immigrant newspaper for Scandinavian-Americans, we have discussed the American influence in Scandinavia, and I would suggest that in the future we discuss the presentation of Scandinavia in periodicals and nonliterary media, and that we hear more about the young, the second and third generations of Scandinavian Americans.

RICHARD B. VOWLES: I agree with Marion Nelson that we need to bring things into some kind of focus. What we want, I think, is the broadest possible audience and, of course, we have a potential audience at all times in certain university courses, not just Scandinavian department courses, but comparative literature courses, social studies courses, and so on. I think there has to be some kind of concerted effort to make available inexpensive but good reprints and to make new things available. If we can do this, through whatever publishing channels and whatever channels of support, I think it is one way not of culminating, but of continuing a major effort.

S. RALPH COHEN: Mr. Dahlgren is getting a great deal of exposure and circulation with his television and radio programs and he is able to do this because it is a subsidized operation. Is it possible and is it worthwhile for the Nordic Council to undertake to subsidize the reprinting in paperback form of those volumes which are considered most necessary and which would be most appealing to American students and American readers?

RICHARD B. VOWLES: I think that should certainly be explored, and you know, of course, that the fifteen titles we did bring out were subsidized by the Nordic Council, which paid for the translations.

ERIK J. FRIIS: The discussion is out of balance by concentrating on the Nordic Translations Series to such a great extent. I think we have paid too much attention to a program that was unsuccessful, and, unfortunately, not enough attention to the successful programs. I would like to mention not only the ongoing publication program at the foundation, but also all the new books put out by commercial houses today. There is much production if we would take the trouble to look at it. I can make a list for you, the field is wide open, and there is much going on.

RICHARD B. VOWLES: It might be said, though, that books like Meri's *The Manila Rope* and Göran Palm's *As Others See Us,* came and went. The sales were not adequate for the commercial market. I think it was Bobbs-Merrill that published Palm and I think it was Knopf that published Meri. At least one of those books was reviewed and advertised in *The New York Times,* but they have disappeared completely from sight. They never went into paperback and are virtually unavailable, as far as I can tell, for classroom usage. I might add that I applaud The American-Scandinavian Foundation's intent to publish the series of paperback reprints. I would make every effort to make translations fresh and vital throughout, because this is, as has been indicated, a very important factor.

JOHN CHRISTIANSON: I might emphasize again the importance of getting things into the hands of commercial publishers. The University of Wisconsin, pretty much at the recommendation of and under the guidance of Dr. Einar Haugen, put out a book over twenty years ago on the folk arts of Norway. They were afraid to begin with, and they were totally unreceptive to a new edition when the old one was sold out. We have had so much demand for that book at the Norwegian-American Museum that I got in touch with Dover Publishing, who puts out this kind of paperback, telling them that here is a book we could easily sell in 500 copies, and they took it on. That book came out less than a year ago and is already in its second edition from Dover. I haven't heard the exact number sold of the first edition, but Dover does nothing in small numbers, they can't afford to. So these things can succeed, only there is somehow something wrong in our relationship to the buying public.

HARALD S. NAESS: I had hoped our discussion would have offered more of the kind of conclusion Professor Nelson called for, and I am sorry it has not. But I think we have to be eclectic, which means putting down some of the useful facts that have come up here and there to see if they do take us in a certain direction. I think, for instance, that we now feel a definite need for serious market research in our area, which would again call for consolidated book lists and directories of literary advisers, translators, distributors, and so on. We have also been told not to neglect the commercial publisher and to pay more attention to the younger generation, which leads me to mention that prolific literary category known as children's books. It could be a life saver for many an academic publishing venture. I agree with Erik Friis that too much has been said here about the Nordic Translation Series, but it has been a useful reminder of what we often tend to forget, that idealism needs badly to be backed by money. And if some of the rich among us ought to raise their level of idealism, so, also, some of the moneyless ought to lower theirs. That means selling *Pippi Longstocking* to pay for *World Light*.

SCANPRESENCE AS SEEN FROM
THE MOTHER COUNTRIES

Panel   Tore Tallroth (Chairman), Lars Ljungmark, Reino Kero,
Ingrid Semmingsen, Erik Høgsbro Holm, Rolf Bergendahl, Audun Toven (Student Representative)

Chairman's Remarks

TORE TALLROTH: Obviously we are not going to be able to answer all the many vital and interesting questions that have arisen in this seminar so far. There are also problems of great importance in this country and in the Scandinavian countries for the people who represent the more official side, or the Establishment, if this word is permitted. How are we going to finance the necessary work and the new initiatives flowing from the discussions at this conference? Then there is the question of who will carry the ball of cooperation among all the organizations working in the field of cultural relations and exchange between Scandinavia and the United States.

These problems will stay with us and will have to be solved, not immediately but gradually. This aspect should not prevent us from taking new initiatives, from discussing new ideas along with the constant search for ways of improving the present structure of our work, of our cooperation with the United States and among our own countries in Scandinavia.

It might be useful to get some ideas about the attitudes in Sweden and in the other Scandinavian states toward Americans of Swedish, Danish, Finnish, and Norwegian descent, toward the Scandinavian communities in the United States. What do we think of an American of Danish or Swedish descent? How does he appear to us? Is there a general consensus of views about opinion and ideas in the Scandinavian communities here in the United States?

Another aspect is the work now being carried out in the field of information and cultural relations between the Scandinavian countries and the United States.

It is just a coincidence and not a nationalistic ambition that I call first upon my countryman, Docent Lars Ljungmark, of the University of Gothenburg, a specialist in the history of Swedish emigration to the United States and particularly to this area.

The Scholar's Overview

The Scholar's Overview from Sweden

LARS LJUNGMARK: It is not so easy to say what a Swede today thinks of the present status and the future of the Swedish group in the United States, or for that matter of the Scandinavians in the United States as an ethnic group. I can only talk about Sweden, and when I talk about what the Swedes think, I mean the ordinary man and woman, the man in the street, so to say, not the specialists or experts or people with a special interest in these matters.

I don't think the people in Sweden see the modern American of Swedish descent as a member of a distinctive Swedish-American ethnic group or see him in a modern context. If there is a general view in Sweden of the Swedish-American, it is focused on or shaped by the first or second generation of Swedish emigrants of the nineteenth century or early twentieth century. This is a fact of great significance. A Swede's view and knowledge of this now dead or dying generation also forms his ideas about how the *modern* Swedish-American is thinking, behaving, and functioning. The present Swedish-American is therefore generally considered to be rather conservative, sometimes even reactionary, and also to be a rather primitive person with little knowledge of or understanding for modern Sweden, more or less with a way of thinking similar to that of his father or grandfather. This old Swedish-American with his often false picture of Sweden, which often comes through in the Swedish-American press, is a surprising phenomenon to the Swedes. But such is the standard image in the Swedish press and mass media, in TV and radio. It is also the image dealt with by the Swedish tourist business. The Swedish-American would himself, I am sure, be surprised to see this simplified and overgeneralized picture.

A good example of the kind of information about the Swedish-American community that its press gives was a lengthy article in one of the papers about the Snoose Boulevard Festival in Minnesota. It was an article dealing with numerous Swedish-Americans who knew the old traditions and songs by heart and about young Swedes coming to Snoose Boulevard in their search for the old American heritage. The young modern Swedish-Americans are not there, only the old ones, very quietly listening, with tears in their eyes, to the old songs!

An interesting question is of course what the schoolchildren in Sweden learn about Swedish America. Here I have a history book for the elementary school in Sweden. There are almost six pages devoted to Swedish emigration to the United States. One can learn how the waves of emigration to the United States started in Norway, how the Swedes followed suit. There is also a description of the Swedish background, of the various parts of the Swedish countryside where the emigrants came from, and where there was not enough land suitable for agriculture to keep them alive.

Another part of this text deals with the life of the immigrants in the United States. Here we meet the Swede as a farmer out in the wilderness in the Middle West, some of them also building Chicago. There is also something about Swedish girls as housemaids in American families.

In the pictures, which dominate this chapter, you meet the Swedish-American of the nineteenth and early twentieth century. Here you see the first piece of land owned and farmed by a Swede, probably in South Dakota. There is the proud farmer in front of his small house on the prairie, the boasting Swedish-

American on the road, taking his tremendously big load to the market.

The modern Swedish-American is not present in these pages of a current history book, from which Swedish children today get their ideas about the world around us.

Nothing is said about how many Americans there are of Swedish descent, where or how they live, nothing about their social and religious life, nothing about their schools or organizations, and so on. There is no hint about the many Swedes who have made an "American" career and often reached high positions in modern American society.

In a way the modern Swedish-American does not exist for an ordinary Swede. He cannot be a reality for the Swedish school-boy or school-girl, in any case not if they get their knowledge from their textbooks.

There is no leading personage or idol among today's Swedish-Americans who is known to the common Swede; such knowledge could help to focus interest in Sweden on this part of their history.

The general impression in Sweden seems to be that the Swedish-American is always looking back and even longing back, that Sweden is very much on his mind, and that he of course sees this land in rosy colors, but also with critical eyes. His critical view of Sweden and Swedish opinions with regard to politics, sex, religion and so on, are often shared by many Swedes, but this is frequently overlooked. Sweden looks upon the Swedish-American strictly from a Swedish point of view, as an emigrant, and nowadays very much through the eyes of Vilhelm Moberg. The Swedish-American is never looked upon as a supporter in the conservative's fight against the radicals in Sweden.

To the radicals the Swedish-American is a doubtful figure, somewhat funny, and not a man really worth serious interest.

Thus, the present-day Swedish-American is not in the focus of public interest in Sweden, even if there is a great deal of sympathy and awareness in many quarters about Swedish-America and what it has meant for Swedish-American relations.

Thanks to the books and perhaps more the films of Vilhelm Moberg's books, Kristina and Karl Oskar are the most well known Swedish-Americans in Sweden today. It is perhaps of some significance that even the young generation shares some of these views because of their interest in pioneer and rural life. It could very well be that this interest also might create increased attention to their own family's relations with the United States, a concern for the relatives who once emigrated and their descendants.

And in order to get the common Swede interested in the real Swedish-American today one must perhaps start out from this interest in the emigrants and the immigrants.

These observations might seem harsh and too generalized. But from what I have said it is quite clear that the common Swede, the man in the street, has no idea at all of the Swedish-Americans as an ethnic group. And when one is not conscious of the present situation, one has no idea about the future.

The Scholar's Overview from Finland

REINO KERO: Earlier I reported on what the Finns of Finland have been thinking about their American cousins during the last twenty-five years. I can't say what the man in the street in Finland thinks about the future, so I must indicate only what I myself am thinking about the future in this respect.

I must say at first that I am much more pessimistic concerning the Finnish culture in the United States than many of my friends here. When we think about the present and the future of Finnish immigrant culture in America two facts must be remembered. First, the Finns like other Scandinavian ethnic groups emigrated to the United States more than fifty years ago, the Finns a little later than the other Scandinavians. Thus, most of the first generation of Finns have already died and those still living are quite old. Secondly, it must be remembered that the Finnish immigrant group has been quite small compared with some other immigrant groups. This means that there are quite a few second, third, and fourth generation Finns in America, if the number of Finns is compared with some other immigrant groups.

On the basis of these facts two things can be said. First, that the culture of the first-generation Finns will disappear totally in the near future; the Finnish newspapers here will certainly disappear. Secondly, the future of Finnish-American culture, if there is any, depends upon the activity of a quite small group of second, third, and fourth generation descendants of the immigrants. Although the old Finnish immigrant culture will disappear in the near future, I think, however, that in the years to come there will still be a group of people in America who are interested in knowing something about Finns and Finland, and that most of these people will be second, third, and fourth generation Finns. Because travel is becoming easier and easier, these groups will visit Finland more than will other Americans. The most active of them belong to the Finlandia Foundation and have something Finnish in their houses like Finnish steambaths, but I think that Finland, Finnish culture, and their Finnish origin will be for them something that might be called a general and traditional interest. I would hesitate calling this group an ethnic group that is different from other American third and fourth generations of people. Thus, we Finns of the mother country don't expect to find much Finnish in American society after twenty to thirty years. We have sent here about 10 percent of Finland's population at the beginning of the century to make Americans and America Finlandized and thus a civilized people! We can't say more, because we have not succeeded. We are now sending our people to Sweden. We have already sent an army of 300,000 Finns to Sweden and we will see if this might be more successful.

The Scholar's Overview from Norway

INGRID SEMMINGSEN: I would like to begin with an ethnic joke which might illustrate a trend and a possibility; even if I am violating the rules that there shouldn't be any ethnic jokes about other people. I remember a story I heard about a factory in Gothenburg, where there were many nationalities, Finns among them. The company organized a Swedish-language program to teach all these various nationalities Swedish, but to no avail. Whereas after a while all the different nationalities spoke Finnish!

I must stress that I recognize that America, from my point of view, is a pluralistic society and that I feel a certain difference when I meet a Norwegian-American, a Swedish-American, or other Scandinavian-Americans. In my opinion each has a different profile. I feel something like kinship toward them that is not so easy to feel toward many other Americans I meet. They are closer to us in some ways.

I agree with Lars Ljungmark that it is not easy to express the Norwegian image of the Norwegian-Americans. It is certainly not easy to summarize. But I do think we still have in our minds that old picture of the Norwegian-American coming back, showing his gold nuggets and perhaps bragging about America. That's true. But there is also another trend. Every year larger crowds of Americans of Norwegian descent are coming back to visit old friends and relations in Norway. Many of them go back to a valley or village to find out where their ancestors were born. They visit more and more often with their distant relatives in Norway. Some years ago I was invited to such a family reunion, because a second cousin or third cousin from California, whom I didn't know, was coming back to Norway. I met her for the first time in my life and found out that her grandfather was a brother of my grandfather. It was an altogether pleasant and revealing experience. I think there are many experiences of that kind. It may make us more familiar with each other in a new sense. This we can hope at least.

My second point is that we face another challenge from the university point of view where the emphasis is on *exchange*. We have to have exchanges of people and ideas. And I would hope for an exchange of students, of teachers, and of all kinds of people, to a much larger degree than has taken place so far.

Something is being done through the Norway-America Association. The International Summer School does quite a lot. I know it would be very difficult to start—but I still want to suggest it—some kind of Scandinavian American Field Service exchange program, to get young Americans of Scandinavian descent over to Norway and Sweden and Finland and Denmark and Iceland and to get our youngsters over to Scandinavian families in the United States. I think that would be a very rewarding idea. I know it is difficult, but still I wanted to bring this to your attention.

From the university point of view, I think we have to see our studies in a broader context. Let me mention emigration history. In all countries today I think there is a great interest in social history; social historians and historically oriented sociologists are devoting themselves to the study of small communities, the family, the neighborhood, their cohesions, their inner tensions, and so on. I think that a study of emigration and of immigration could be put into a broader context of the breaking up of a community in the emigration country and the adaptation, assimilation, or acculturation process in the receiving country. This has been done to a certain extent, and I think we should work along this line. It could certainly be done in many other university subjects too.

We should further examine this aspect and the exchange of persons and the exchange of ideas. We should also look at these problems at different levels. No one mentioned a series in Norway put out by a Norwegian publishing house. They are small inexpensive booklets on Norwegian heritage, Norwegian history, Norwegian mythology, and so on. I do not know if they are sold in the United States, but tourists buy them when they come to Norway. This has been a happy venture for this publishing house. I also think that other fields, *rosemaling* and folk dance and so on, are important and that we need informational material in the English language. I think there are possibilities for exchanges and impulses on many, many different levels. We must do our part, too.

The Official Attitudes

Chairman's Remarks

TORE TALLROTH: It should be pointed out that, at least for Sweden, a very substantial part of the overall information budget is directed toward the United States. In the Swedish budget for information close to 25 percent of all available funds are earmarked for the United States. It must be remembered that we haven't gone so far as to issue specialized programs or books for Swedish groups, or American groups of Swedish origin here. However, this general American approach might be the best one if we try to increase our activities in the exchange of persons and ideas with the United States.

Another point to be remembered is that we are in general responsible for information about Sweden abroad. The money is given for that particular purpose. Therefore we must consider how much money should be devoted to joint Scandinavian projects. I am very fond of Scandinavian cooperation, I love Scandinavia, whatever it might be, but it is much easier to work for a specific national purpose. It simplifies administration and programming. A serious question therefore is: is it right that we in the Scandinavian countries devote more money, policy, or effort to Scandinavian cooperation than to direct individual Swedish, Finnish, Norwegian, and Danish efforts? Is it useful for the different countries to have a more Scandinavian approach, etc.? These are some of the questions that arise in considering how to allocate our budget.

The Danish Official Attitude

ERIK HØGSBRO HOLM: The Danish official policy towards Danish emigrants is expressed once a year on New Year's eve when the monarch, over the radio and TV, sends his greetings to all Danes abroad, thanking them for being good Danes. As an example of the direct connection between Denmark and the United States, I want to point out that after the establishment of the first national park in the world in Denmark 101 years ago, it only took forty years before America had its first national park abroad, and the Rebild National Park is still the only American National Park outside the union.

From the Danish point of view I should like to make the following observations. The first and second generations of immigrants were not always happy about the developments in the mother country. They wanted, more or less, that Denmark should stay as it was on the day of their departure. Perhaps they wanted to have an excuse for leaving. But the mother country didn't stand still. It has certainly progressed, and in the last decade this progress has come at a faster rate than in the United States. I think that to a large extent Danish emigrants have come to look upon the mother country through the eyes of some of the Danish-Americans, and thereby have come to a better understanding of what has taken place.

The lack of an official policy towards immigrants in America does not mean that Denmark has no policy towards America; on the contrary. In the Scanpresence context I think it is true to say that Denmark hopes to have through the immigrants a helping hand in influencing the policy of the United States. And why such a wish to influence? Simply because America is the biggest and most resourceful country in the world and therefore a world leader.

What Denmark expects of her emigrants is one thing; quite another thing is what the emigrants expect of Denmark and

Scandinavia as a whole. I have a dream that this gathering of
scholars would go out to the many thousands of Scandinavian-
Americans and inspire them to the same kind of cooperation we
have seen between the Scandinavian mother countries. I have
a dream that such an approach might result in establishing a Nordic forum, a Nordic council in America for the benefit of America
and also for our benefit. Such a council could have many obvious tasks, such as the publication of a Scandinavian-American
magazine. There are thousands of ideas. But human touch and
human contacts should have the priority.

The Norwegian Official Attitude

ROLF BERGENDAHL: It is evident that Scandinavian immigrants in
North America have made distinct contributions to the building
of America and to the evolution of American life. We have been
told about the Scandinavian immigrant role in the economy, in
the sciences, and in the arts, as well as the influence of immigration on social life and as regards customs and habits. For instance, the consumption of lutefisk and Norwegian aquavit.

As an official of Norway, I think it is appropriate to express the
official view in Norway as seen from the Norwegian Ministry for
Foreign Affairs. I would like to emphasize that the Norwegian
Minister of Foreign Affairs is deeply interested in supporting all
measures for the preservation of the Norwegian presence in
America. For Norway this is of particular importance since our
emigration to America has been so extensive in proportion to our
population at home. We have been told that Scandinavian emigration to North America has virtually come to an end. In fact,
for Norway the emigration pattern has completely changed during the last decade. Today Norway receives more immigrants from
America than vice versa. According to the migration statistics
published by the Central Bureau of Statistics in Oslo, 12,304 Norwegians emigrated to America during the five-year period 1966–
1970. That is about 17 percent of the total immigration, giving

Norway a net immigration surplus of about 3,000. The net immigration probably represents a very high percentage of return migration from America. This is an interesting phenomenon, the explanation for which is probably to be found in the improved economic conditions in the mother country, as well as in a higher degree of cultural uniformity, better communications, and lower legal barriers at national boundaries.

The return migration from America to Norway, however, should not imply a weakening of the Scandinavian influence in America; on the contrary, it strengthens it, since bonds will be forged both ways. The passing of first-generation Scandinavians and the aging of the second generation make it even more essential for an official in Norway to take an active part in promoting the links between the mother country and the Norwegian ethnic group.

As an important measure in this work I would like to mention the activities of the Norwegian Ministry for Foreign Affairs in spreading information on modern Norway in America through publications, films, exhibitions, TV, radio, student exchanges, participation in Norwegian studies at American colleges and universities, donation of books to American libraries, and translations of Norwegian literature. The Norwegian government also gives financial support to the International Summer School at the University of Oslo which admits many Americans. Support is also given to the United States Educational Foundation in Norway that is, the Fulbright Program. The official Norwegian contribution to preserve the interest and links between the mother country and America is unfortunately not as extensive as is desired. Rather limited funds are appropriated in the Norwegian state budget for this purpose. We hope, however, for an improvement in the future.

I feel a strong urge to point out the importance of the excellent work done by the many different Norwegian-American and Scandinavian-American organizations and the cooperating organizations in the mother country as well as the American universities and colleges originally founded by Scandinavians. Their activities promote a greater interest in the mother country, which again reinforces ethnic feeling and awareness. We all realize that harmonious international relations are extremely important in the world of today. We have close links between Norway and the Norwegian-Americans and their institutions. We have the best possibilities for the promotion of a good relationship and for the preservation of a Norwegian Scandinavian presence in America.

A Student's Point of View

AUDUN TOVEN

I am a student representative and I'll just discuss a couple of viewpoints. I would like to call attention to the Norpresence, Norwegian Presence, here in America and indicate my real concern for the maintenance of a genuine Norwegian culture and tradition. The student's role in this is important. After emigration comes to a standstill, I think there is one group that will still come here, not in great numbers but quite a few, and that is students from the Scandinavian countries. There will still be students from Norway coming to different universities and institutions either on scholarships or otherwise, studying for longer or shorter periods. The University of Washington has had a number of them during the time that I've been connected with that institution. But I think it is true that few Norwegians have been involved at all in the ethnic groups in the area, sometimes by choice. They are here for a specific purpose. They don't care. They aren't interested. They don't have time. Others have had a genuine interest in trying to help out in ethnic organizations, but they are often turned down and turned away from those organizations and what they stand for and what they do. The Norwegians come to meetings of Sons of Norway or other ethnic groups and they have to go through all the rituals, and take part in drill teams and other activities in which they are not at all interested, so they turn away and they don't contribute at all. I think possibly that these organizations should change slightly. Maybe it is impossible, maybe they should just preserve the old ideas and do the old things. But if they do not change, I think they will lose this group of Norwegian students, and I'm afraid also the young people, the young Norwegian-Americans. I don't think that young people will go on forever just singing *"Kan du glemme gamle Norge"* (Will you ever forget old Norway?). They want to do something more than that, something contemporary. When students suggest changes and wish to talk about modern Norway, they are disappointed and frustrated at the kind of attitudes they meet in those organizations.

I guess I am wondering if it is possible for those organizations to change slightly, instead of only perpetuating a romantic idea of the old country. And I believe the leaders have a responsibility to try to introduce such change. They should take the initiative and do something about it.

Discussion

TORE TALLROTH: I think we are faced with an important problem; how to bring in new groups and new interests in the exchange between our countries and the United States. We have noticed changing patterns. The discussion going on in the United States, and many of the ideas in all areas of society—education, social planning, environmental policy, etc., are of strong interest to Denmark, Finland, Norway, and Sweden, and vice versa. It is not presumptuous to point to the fact that basically we all belong to the same system of society, an industrial society, where changes are always taking place and will be taking place at an even faster speed. That is the mark of the industrial society or perhaps post-industrial society. We all can learn from each other's experiences, achievements, and failures.

Perhaps this need for exchange of ideas and information could be channeled, both ways, through the better services of institutions, universities, organizations, etc.

A shift in concentration regarding the fields of study is also needed, a move to more modern times and to more modern problems without excluding the traditional fields of study. Anyhow, more attention should be given to the problems of modern society, problems which we all are or will be experiencing.

This would also be valuable in other respects. First it would help to give a more accurate picture of present-day Scandinavia to people in the United States, and help to familiarize the Scandinavian countries with present-day America. Young architects, doctors, social scientists, young politicians of Scandinavian descent should be encouraged to study or work in their particular fields in the various Scandinavian countries and thus, in a more genuine way, meet Danish or Swedish colleagues. This might help to change and enrich the picture in Sweden, Finland, Denmark, and Norway of the ideas and present ways of thinking among Americans of Scandinavian origin, and also bring closer the ideas and ambitions of young professionals in American society. I think there is great merit to this kind of contact: experts from the United States meeting their Scandinavian counterparts for an open discussion and exchange of views.

Young Americans of Scandinavian descent should be encouraged to go to the Scandinavian countries, not only because they are of Scandinavian origin, but because the Scandinavian countries might be able to offer them valuable experience in their own particular fields. This might also help to modernize the picture of the Swedish-American, the Norwegian-American, etc., in their countries of origin. I am sure there will be a meeting of minds among the young people, regardless of origin. All young people, maybe all of us, are faced with and grapple with the same problems, problems that do not have any strict borders. Maybe these efforts to encourage exchange on professional grounds rather than on sentimental grounds, as I indicated, might change all of our ideas and images. People, especially people interested in specific fields, should be encouraged to keep in touch with the Scandinavian countries because Sweden, Denmark, Finland, Norway can offer them new ideas and new experiences, and a Scandinavian origin may help to ease their entry into and contacts with colleagues and experts in their particular fields in these countries.

We must try to find a common ground of interest, not based on ethnic grounds, but on common professional grounds. And young Americans of Scandinavian descent might be more interested in studying and discussing their problems in the countries where they already have some sort of background and affiliation.

REINO KERO: Maybe I should qualify somewhat my statements about the Finnish newspapers in this country. I am a pessimist. But one must remember that I visited most of the editors of the Finnish-American newspapers in 1966 and then prophesied that in five years at least four of these newspapers would disappear. Well, seven years later all of these newspapers were still in existence. Perhaps my pessimism can inspire my Scandinavian friends here to prove that I am wrong. Nobody would be happier than I to find out after twenty years that I was again wrong in my pessimism.

TORE TALLROTH: We will find out about this if the University of Minnesota and the Scandinavian Airlines are kind enough to sponsor a new seminar as an anniversary in 1998. I might not be here then, but I will leave a mental note to my successor.

BJØRN JENSEN: I have in my office a very nice record of old Norwegian folk songs, which might be of interest to many. I think Professor Semmingsen had in mind the "Tokens of Norway" series of books. It deals with traditions and traditional subjects such as folk dancing and recipes. But the series also includes books about the history of Norway, music, the economy, and so forth. This series of books is available in the United States through Heritage Productions and through Sons of Norway and the Norwegian-American Museum which has sold at least 1,500 copies of the books.

TORE TALLROTH: I should like to call attention to an adminis-
trative factor to be remembered when we discuss books and
material about Scandinavia. The ideal thing for universities and
libraries would be to have a Scandinavian book, a book about
Scandinavian literature, art or architecture, about social policies
in the Scandinavian countries. But it is much more difficult to put
together such a Scandinavian book, covering the same field in all
the Scandinavian countries, than to have separate national books,
one about Danish art, one about Finnish art, and one about Norwegian art, and so on and so on. This is one of the reasons why
there are so few truly Scandinavian books. There are always
difficulties in getting the Scandinavians together in joint projects.
It takes time to get officials in these countries to work together,
and to get Scandinavian scholars to make a joint approach in the
fields of publications, the theater, the social sciences, etc. will be,
I guess, more difficult and time-consuming.

MAGNE SMEDVIG: There is some risk that we get an erroneous
impression from Mr. Toven's remarks regarding lodgery in Sons
of Norway, which I might help to clear up. Mr. Toven comes
from Seattle, an area where some of the older traditions, maybe
unfortunately, are maintained. I might use the American Lutheran
Church as an analogy and its problem of getting new churches
built in the suburbs, where its parishioners are moving, while you
already have an established church in an urban area. There is a
similar problem for Sons of Norway. We are organizing new
branches, perhaps one each month, which have an entirely different format and structure, really aimed at the twenty-first century. To be healthy and to be able to grow and blossom, a tree
needs to have its branches pruned once in a while. But don't
judge the whole tree by just one branch.

JOHN CHRISTIANSON: I wanted to comment briefly on the point
raised by Professor Semmingsen and the chairman, regarding the
value of exchange and travel in terms of bringing points of view

up to date and making people on both sides of the Atlantic aware of what's happening on the other side. Of course, this helps us to see a more accurate picture. But travel, I think, can also preserve set ideas and reinforce misconceptions rather than correcting them.

Many of the tours mean more today than the traditional tours that we have had in the arts and crafts fields. They have brought to Scandinavia people of a wide variety of interests, people with a strong involvement in American life. And very few of these have been Scandinavian-Americans.

At the same time we have noticed that in these programs and in other programs as well, even when Swedes and Danes of American descent are involved, we often have to work with Scandinavia as a whole. We have to deal with at least two countries, more usually three countries, and sometimes four countries. The concept of tourism as a group going from the United States or Canada just to one Scandinavian or European country is too limited. There has to be a broader base, and the younger people want to move around more and see more.

We are conscious of a greater youth traffic, which of course has been stimulated by the low youth fares. Now I notice that the Civil Aeronautics Board is beginning to take a jaundiced view toward this price policy.

We are also aware of a greater traffic of other specialized youth groups, hockey teams, choirs, etc. The interesting thing is that this is a sort of exchange, and we are getting young Scandinavians coming in. This is at the moment on a limited scale, but we think it will grow and be built up.

We also find that our tourist colleagues in Scandinavia, through some sort of package deals, are beginning to run "special interest" tours to the United States for Scandinavians. This is a very good thing, and it is also encouraging that for the first time we have Scandinavians coming to this country who want to go to places other than Bay Ridge in Brooklyn.

The other point I would like to make is that one often gets

a rather distressing feeling of a fragmentation of the limited resources of all the official agencies of the different Scandinavian
countries. We are naturally all for the preservation of the individual identity and of the differences between the Scandinavian
countries. This is a point of balance. The moment we Scandinavians stop being different from the Americans the impulse to go
to Scandinavia will virtually disappear.

But at the same time, none of the Scandinavian countries has
enough resources, and none of the Scandinavian-American communities here has one nationality with sufficient resources to do
all of the things which we would like or hope or want to do.
Somewhere there must be a middle ground in the pooling of resources in order to be able to make a greater impact and to en-
sure a high quality, higher than each of us may have as an
individual country. It is necessary to preserve the identity, but
also necessary to pool the resources. We have tried to do this
with regard to the tourist offices, especially with the distribution
of publicity material.

Håkan Berggren also suggested the publication of a coordinated film catalogue, listing all available Scandinavian films. This
would indicate where the gaps are and where the films are available. Money could be spent fruitfully.

There may be other areas and opportunities to be examined
with a view to practical cooperation. On a basis of commercial
experience, I find a good deal of attraction in the suggestion of
organizing some sort of Nordic council which could help to search
out these areas of cooperation. We can perhaps do certain things
together which individually we never will be able to do.

TORE TALLROTH: Instead of trying to summarize this discussion,
I just want to make a few points. One is the interrelation between
a person's image of the Scandinavian countries in the United
States and the image of the United States in the Scandinavian
countries. This should be kept in mind by all of us who work in
this country and in the field of Scandinavian-American relations.

I also think our discussion has brought out an increased awareness in our countries of the importance of close contact with Americans of Scandinavian descent.

One last thing to remember is to work for a closer community of ideas, where both the Scandinavian countries and the United States try to be partners in an international community of higher unity.

SUMMARY REPORT OF THE SEMINAR

EINAR HAUGEN: So much has already come out at this conference that there is very little indeed that I can add. The initiative
was admirable, and the resulting seminar has been a unique experience. It is the first time that so many persons and institutions
interested in the preservation of the Scandinavian heritage have
been brought together. The most striking part of it is not that the
five Nordic nationalities have been brought together; this has already been done on a cultural and academic level by The American-Scandinavian Foundation and the Society for Advancement
of Scandinavian Study. But here we have brought face to face
representatives of the academic and non-academic community.
Representatives of the churches and the secular societies have
sat down together with editors and authors, professors and diplomats. And there have been no explosions. Perhaps, as one speaker
put it, "we have been too nice to each other."

Haunting Issues

I should like to make this summarization a personal statement
of thoughts and reflections that have occurred to me during this
conference. In order to illuminate some angles of the problem
we are considering I would like to refer to my own experiences.
The conference has been exciting to me because it has brought
out into the open problems that I have had to face and issues
that have haunted me as far back as I can recall.

Spirit into Values

When I started to teach Scandinavian studies and especially the Norwegian language forty-two years ago, I thought of myself as a kind of final caretaker of Scandinavian ethnicity, one who would help to give it a decent burial while transmitting its spirit into values for my students. Most of my peers in and out of school showed absolutely no interest in their heritage. In an American town of mixed ethnic backgrounds like Sioux City, Iowa, I stood out as an oddball in my grammar school and in high school by taking an active interest in my parents' culture. Few if any of my peers spoke their native language at home or accompanied their parents to meetings where most of the members were two and three times as old as they. Ethnicity was dead or dying, something one did not even speak about, but tried in a shame-faced manner to forget. Perhaps I was unduly pessimistic in thinking that all ethnicity would disappear in America with the passing of my generation.

Ethnicity and Interest

Let me now turn to what has here been called the Scandinavian Presence. It seems to me that two quite different problems have been discussed under this term. They may really be only two faces of the same problem, and in that case they form a Janus which we may look at from two different sides. One face is that of Scandinavian *ethnicity,* the other that of Scandinavian *interest.*

Ethnicity is that which ties us together by blood or family, and by extended links through our friends, our neighborhood, or our church. We used to call this "nationality" or even "race," but these words have become impossible, and so "ethnicity" has taken their place. For the immigrants, and in many cases for their children as well, ethnicity creates a community in which they can find security, comfort, warmth. It is the American-Scandinavian or rather Scandinavian-American community, with its dual ties to America and Scandinavia, chiefly through one's kin. When a member of this community goes to visit his or her father's homeland, he discovers that he has become hyphenated: he is a "Norwegian-American" or a "Swedish-American," etc. There is even a slightly derogatory air about these terms, as if one were some kind of odd hybrid. Perhaps this was why I liked it better when a Norwegian friend described me as "an American with Norway as his profession" rather than merely calling me a "Norwegian-American."

Friends of Scandinavia

The other face of the Scandinavian Presence that we are considering here is the interest in Scandinavia on the part of Americans who are not necessarily influenced by ethnic ties. This is what publicity men would call the "image" of Scandinavia among Americans regardless of ethnic background—the kind of thing that attracts travelers, scholars, and readers to Scandinavia. It is this aspect of the Scandinavian Presence that primarily interests the diplomatic representatives of the Scandinavian countries among us and of course our hosts, Scandinavian Airlines. There are many Americans who have lost their hearts to one or more of the Scandinavian countries, and who have done yeoman work in promoting their interests. Such people are called *Norgesvenn* or *Sverigesvän,* a "friend of Scandinavia," a term of great honor in these countries. Our problem here is the process of turning the "Scandinavian-Americans" into "Friends of Scandinavia," which should in principle be easier than doing the same for other Americans. It is my own ambition some day to be called a *Norgesvenn* rather than a *Norsk-Amerikaner,* and thereby to convert a tie that has been established by my parents into one that I have knit for myself.

How can ethnicity be converted into interest? We cannot continue to depend for this interest on ethnic ties that dissolve with the passage of time and the homogenization of American society. As one participant reminded us, where are the Swedes on the Delaware? Even Marcus Lee Hansen's thesis concerning the growth of interest in ethnicity in the third generation is only a half-truth. When one considers the size of the third generation, those whose ethnicity has persisted or has been aroused are a pitiful percentage of the whole number. Even so, their potential interest has to be nurtured and encouraged.

Phases of Ethnicity

So far we have treated ethnicity as if it were a unit. It is far too complex to be left as such. Let me distinguish for you what I have called "primary" ethnicity from "secondary" ethnicity. There are not many in this room who have genuinely experienced primary ethnicity, unless they grew up in a small rural Scandinavian community in the old country. I have myself an extremely vivid memory of two years of my boyhood, ages eight and ten, that I spent living in a closed Norwegian valley that was essentially pre-industrial. While I lived there I learned to speak the local dialect and to share the completely unselfconscious feeling of belonging in such a community. These people did not think of themselves as peculiar in any way; they did not think about ethnicity, they just simply were ethnics. When I get back there today, I see that modern communication has made its inroads, and the old ethnicity is on the way out in a community where supermarkets, cars, radios, and television are almost as available as they are here. Primary ethnicity is fading out there, too, and has to be kept alive by deliberate planning and thinking, through local historical and folkloristic societies, and the encouragement of local crafts and costumes.

But something of that old ethnicity has survived among many immigrants, although the process of "de-ethnicization" began on the day they arrived in America. I would describe the process rather as one of a gradual replacement of the old ethnicity with a new, American ethnicity, making the immigrant the master of a dual ethnicity. I have observed this in the development of my parents, some of whose primary ethnicity survived even while they were becoming loyal and devoted Americans. In our family we lived in two worlds: on the one hand we were Norwegians in exile, voluntarily segregated from our immediate neighbors and choosing our friends among other Norwegians wherever they might be living in our city. They were the people who came to the parties at our house and to whose houses we were invited. They were the people with whom we went to church, and in due time to the *bygdelag* or home-valley society to which my parents belonged. On the other hand we also lived in an American world, which determined the social and economic position of my parents and eventually my own future.

New and Old Adam

Although I lived in the Norwegian immigrant world of my parents, I also had to play the role of being an American boy. The split was fairly complete: I went through the whole system from kindergarten to the Ph.D. without ever hearing a word about my Scandinavian heritage except when I chose in college and graduate school to make it my major subject. This dual ethnicity has been part of the experience of most people in this room. But dual ethnicity is an uncomfortable thing, though it can be highly rewarding. Rölvaag once wrote an article in a newspaper in Norway trying to explain this to his countrymen at home. He called it "The New and the Old Adam," with an allusion to the Bible: the Old Adam was the Norwegian character, which gradually had to yield to the New Adam of American character. The new ethnicity gets the upper hand over the old ethnicity.

What then emerges is something I would like to call "secondary ethnicity." This is not the same as the "new ethnicity" of which

Fishman spoke, which may turn out to be a passing fad. Second-ary ethnicity is a *conscious* ethnicity, and it is less dominant in a person's life than the primary ethnicity we spoke of before. In teaching Scandinavian languages and culture I was conveying secondary ethnicity, for the culture I taught students was often different from the local and primary ethnicity that their forefathers had brought to America. They may have come with a dialect, but I had to teach them a standard language, the official language of writing and literature.

Family and Church

In the family secondary ethnicity often expresses itself as a genealogical interest, which, as the secretary of *Nordmanns-For-bundet* tells us, is of growing importance to many Scandinavian Americans. In the Middle West especially there are still strong ethnic neighborhoods that offer potential support for activities that teach Scandinavian culture. The churches have a great po-tential here, though we have to accept the fact that their primary purpose is not the fostering of ethnicity. Different churches, even among the Scandinavians, have played different roles in this re-spect; generally, the smaller and less socially ambitious churches have preserved the culture best. If we compare with other groups, we find for example that the Catholic church has nearly every-where discouraged local ethnicity in favor of a more universal view. The church helped to kill Gaelic in Ireland in the nineteenth century, while in Wales the Methodist church helped to keep Welsh alive because it was in opposition to the high-church Anglicans who used English. The American Lutheran churches used the Scandinavian (and German) languages just as long as these lan-guages were useful to their mission, but abandoned them when they seemed to be a hindrance. Only those small groups like the Mennonites, who insist on keeping themselves apart from the rest of the world, can also preserve a language of their own. Even so the Lutheran churches of Scandinavian origin, and the colleges they founded, are large potential reservoirs of individuals who are or can be interested in their heritage.

Another and most important factor in maintaining ethnicity is travel. Travel keeps personal ties alive across national boundaries and of course within the country. All of us are clearly aware of the significant interrelationship between the development of cheap air travel and the maintenance of personal relationships with our Scandinavian kinsmen.

Finally, there is reading and academic study. We hear that people don't read any more. If so, it is deeply deplorable, for books and newspapers are rich storehouses of all that is valuable, whether old or new, in the world around us. Reading is crucial to gaining insight into ourselves and our own past and therefore an essential part in the maintenance of secondary ethnicity. Colleges are the epitome of reading, places where young people are given the fantastic opportunity of spending free time learning rather than doing.

Ethnic Organizations

I have had experience all my life with ethnic organizations, and it is my feeling that many of them are built on shallow soil. It is good to hear that they are making moves to improve their offerings, for they have generally failed to offer anything of real quality to their members. I recognize the problem in organizations where few if any have adequate preparation for giving guidance on programs of Scandinavian culture. There should be more cooperation here between the organizations and the departments of Scandinavian languages at colleges and universities. The organizations should recognize their obligations, not merely by calling on these departments for an occasional program, but by employing as program consultants students who have graduated from their courses. In acting as consultant for various private societies I have found that only a small percentage of the members have any background that would enable them to prepare an interesting program on a Scandinavian topic. I recommend the method of the Ygdrasil Society in Madison, Wisconsin, where every member has to prepare a research paper of his own for presentation to the group. Without study, most people do not know what is interesting or important. And who is available as a speaker from the outside? It was a bright idea to bring some of the young men and women who are studying Scandinavian into this conference—like Lars Johnson, Laurence Berge, Michael Karni, Audun Toven, Solveig Zempel—our future lies with them.

The Immigrant Press

Another problem area is that of the Scandinavian-language press. I grant that these papers are invaluable sources for historical study, as Kenneth Bjork pointed out, but the very letters from the readers and the local news that make them interesting for the historians give them a limited and parochial scope. They reveal a lack of vision or of high cultural goals that keeps them out of the mainstream of American life. Any change in this situation will require more and better-trained staffs, which I know is difficult if not impossible under present conditions. There have been such men as Kristian Prestgard on *Decorah-Posten* in its heyday or the still active Carl Søyland on *Nordisk Tidende* to this day. Only if we can look to more men like these will the press fulfill a function in the future; and we cannot overlook the possibility of an English-speaking press for Scandinavian groups.

Underlying all these arguments is the necessity of converting ethnicity into interest, of exploiting the former to maintain the latter. It is natural that Scandinavians should form the core of people interested in American contacts with Scandinavia, but it is far from necessary or the only possibility.

Unfortunately, it is a fundamental fact that to most Americans Scandinavia is culturally marginal. Even with modern means of communication ignorance about the Northern countries is massive, as anyone can find out by asking a few questions of his fellow Americans. My predecessor at Wisconsin, Professor Julius E. Olson, told me that McGuffey's Reader, which he used in his boyhood, had only one piece of information about Scandinavians: a smudged picture of a man wrestling a bear on its hind legs—and you could not quite tell which was which! It's a little discouraging to spend your life teaching Scandinavian studies and find that people still think that Scandinavians are fighting bears!

What we are fighting is the monolithic American school system. Let's make no mistake: the school system was designed to make Yankees of us all, and it has largely succeeded. The great idea of universal education which we owe to the eighteenth century has also proved to be an instrument of social control. In the American school, history is taught as a straight line of descent from the Near East to the United States. As I was taught it, the public school regards culture as having spread from Mesopotamia over Greece to Rome, France, England, and then America as the climax of it all. Anything that is not on this grand line is in limbo. Where is Scandinavia? Nowhere at all, or rather on a sidetrack that branches off from Rome and France via Germany into the far North. Many great Scandinavians have had to go via Germany and France to become known in England and America, for example, Ibsen, Strindberg, and Edvard Munch. Channels leading directly from Scandinavia to America have been few.

Even so the gap has not been unbridgeable, and Scandinavian immigrants have, with the help of interested Americans, played a role in building bridges here. One such bridge has been the Leif Ericson story, which gives us a role in the very discovery of the New World. Scandinavian artists like Jenny Lind, Ole Bull, Kirsten Flagstad, and Birgit Nilsson have made their marks. Writers, from Hans Christian Andersen and Kierkegaard to Ibsen, Strindberg, Hamsun, and Undset, have been read and admired.

From the thirties on, social experimentation and advances have appealed to Americans seeking the middle way between capitalism and communism. Scandinavian films have made an impact, above all through the work of Ingmar Bergman. Sports stars from Sonja Henie on have become headliners. And we cannot overlook the impact of Scandinavian sex—sin in Sweden, pornography in Denmark—like it or not, these are real parts of the Scandinavian image today.

Intimacy/Relevance/Quality

This is the kind of material we have to work with in Scandinavian departments and organizations, in newspapers and book publications, if we wish Scandinavia to be an interesting and exciting experience for Americans. The realistic basis for future developments is the ease of travel, the opportunity to get over to Scandinavia and for Scandinavians to come here. Within this framework, we need to combine and offer to our fellow Americans three significant qualities:

1. *Intimacy,* by which I mean a vital personal touch that is often missing in our increasingly depersonalized and dehumanized America. This is one of the benefits ethnicity brings with it. It may not have high prestige, but at least it is deeply and humanly significant and satisfying to all of us.

2. *Relevance,* by which I mean contemporaneity of interest. This is difficult, because it builds on the shifting sands of popular taste and opinion. In the late 60s the "counter-culture" was the big thing, but it looks as if the 70s may be quite different.

3. *Quality,* by which I mean work that can command respect and prestige outside our group. Most of what our ethnicity has produced is second- and third-rate stuff, and if we are to appeal to Americans, we have to have good things to show. There have been bad translations, poor textbooks, the promotion of fantastic ideas. Some of these may have satisfied the level of intimacy,

but were inadequate on the level of relevance, and impossible on the level of quality.

Some Recommendations

Finally, I would like to make some recommendations, not as resolutions, but as ideas that occur to me at the end of a wonderful, candid, and significant conference.

1. Means should be made available to stimulate more and better cultural products in the organizations and the newspapers, helping to keep them alive by giving them things to work with and raising their quality. Here I think academic departments have not only a genuine responsibility, but a challenge as well. While I have always felt that scholarly research was crucial in an academic life, I have not shared the distaste that some of my colleagues feel for participation in non-academic organizations. I did not teach at Wisconsin for thirty-three years without absorbing something of its spirit: "The borders of the campus are the borders of the state." I believe that the borders of Scandinavian Studies are the borders of the Scandinavian community in the first instance, but beyond that also the American community and the world.

2. Ethnicity should be recognized as a secondary interest with a legitimate place among other serious cultural interests. Its pursuit should be encouraged, even when we recognize that leisure-minded Americans cannot be expected to make it their only, or even main pursuit. As the ethnic tie weakens by the natural passing of the generations, we might hope that it will be transformed into a continuing interest on the part of Americans, with or without ethnic ties.

3. Academic work in Scandinavian studies should be strengthened by liberal financial support from Americans of Scandinavian background as well as by institutions in Scandinavia—wherever possible, without making us "agents of a foreign power." Aca-

demic studies are the most promising, most important, and, we hope, the most enduring field of Scandinavian study in America. But we need books, scholarships, professorships. We should have Scandinavian cultural centers, comparable to the German Cultural Center of Boston, from which I receive propaganda every week. Even though Germany has a financial strength that may outrun that of all the Scandinavian countries together, that is no excuse for passivity on the part of the latter.

In the end what we are talking about is value; not merely cold scholarship or objective opinions on what has happened or is happening. We have to believe that we do have values to offer that will mean something to Americans of today and tomorrow.

Appendix: Seminar Participants

The following is an alphabetical list of the participants in the Scanpresence Seminar with their titles and appointments at the time of the session. For simplicity, references in the record are by name only.

Those whose names have been marked with an asterisk (*) were members of the core group which, at a meeting at Bergen, Norway, in June, 1972, recommended that the Seminar be held and outlined its agenda. Others who attended that meeting were Mr. Preben Hansen, then Press Chief of the Danish Ministry of Foreign Affairs; Mr. B. John Heistein, Vice President and General Manager of SAS in North America; and Messrs. Søren Bertelsen, Odd Medbøe, Olle Nyman and Henning Ostergaard of SAS in Scandinavia.

The core group put the details planning for the Seminar into the hands of the committee on arrangements, made up of Professor Nelson as General Chairman, with Professors Hasselmo and Vecoli and Messrs. Cohen and Engen.

* HARRY BACKELIN
Eastern Area Manager
Scandinavian Airlines System
North American Division
Jamaica, New York

NORMAN BANSEN
Professor
Department of Danish and
    English
Dana College
Blair, Nebraska

LAURENCE BERGE
Teaching Assistant
Department of Scandinavian
  Studies
University of Wisconsin
Madison, Wisconsin

ROLF L. BERGENDAHL
Chief of Division
The Royal Norwegian Ministry
  for Foreign Affairs
Oslo 1, Norway

CONRAD BERGENDOFF
President Emeritus
Augustana College
Rock Island, Illinois

HÅKAN BERGGREN
Director
Swedish Information Service
New York, New York

HARALDUR BESSASON
Professor
Department of Icelandic
The University of Manitoba
Winnipeg, Canada

KENNETH O. BJORK
Professor
Department of History
St. Olaf College
Northfield, Minnesota

K. VALDIMAR BJORNSON
Treasurer
State of Minnesota
Minneapolis, Minnesota

CARLO CHRISTENSEN
Cultural Counselor
Embassy of Denmark
Washington, D.C.

JOHN CHRISTIANSON
Professor and Chairman
History Department
Luther College
Decorah, Iowa

* S. RALPH COHEN
Director of Public Relations
Scandinavian Airlines System
North American Division
New York, New York

SIGURD DAASVAND
Editor
Nordisk Tidende
Brooklyn, New York

CLAES DAHLGREN
Director
Swedish Broadcasting Corporation
American Office
New York, New York

HOLMFRIDUR DANIELSON
President
Manitoba Drama League
Winnipeg, Manitoba, Canada

B. R. EGGAN
Teacher of Norwegian
Minneapolis, Minnesota

WALFRID ENGDAHL
President Emeritus
Swedish Cultural Society
  of America

Minneapolis Chapter
Minneapolis, Minnesota

* ASBJØRN ENGEN
Vice President and
  Director of Public Relations
Scandinavian Airlines System
  Consortium
Stockholm, Sweden

DONALD EVERSOLL
Director of Fraternal Affairs
The Danish Brotherhood in
  America
National Headquarters
Omaha, Nebraska

JOSHUA A. FISHMAN
Director and Visiting Professor
Language Behavioral Section
The Hebrew University of
  Jerusalem
Jerusalem, Israel

ERIK J. FRIIS
Director of Publications
The American-Scandinavian
  Foundation
New York, New York

GENE G. GAGE
Secretary
The American-Scandinavian
  Foundation
New York, New York

TOPI HALONEN
Editor
Amerikan Uutiset
New York Mills, Minnesota

* JOHAN HAMBRO
Secretary General
Nordmanns-Forbundet
Oslo 1, Norway

A. JOHN HARRISON
Manager–Special Interest Travel
Scandinavian Airlines System
North American Division
Jamaica, New York

NILS HASSELMO
Professor and Chairman
Center for Northwest European
  Language and Area Studies and
  Department of Scandinavian
University of Minnesota
Minneapolis, Minnesota

EINAR HAUGEN
Professor
Program in Scandinavian,
  Germanic Languages and
  Literatures
Harvard University
Cambridge, Massachusetts

ERIK HØGSBRO HOLM
Press Attaché
Danish Information Office
New York, New York

VAINO A. HOOVER
President
Finlandia Foundation
Santa Monica, California

LLOYD HUSTVEDT
Professor
St. Olaf College

Secretary, Norwegian-American
Historical Association
Northfield, Minnesota

RALPH J. JALKANEN
President
Suomi College
Hancock, Michigan

BJØRN JENSEN
Director
Norwegian Information Service
New York, New York

LARS JOHNSON
Teaching Associate
Department of Scandinavian
Studies
University of Wisconsin
Madison, Wisconsin

WALTER JOHNSON
Professor and Chairman
Department of Scandinavian
Languages and Literature
University of Washington
Seattle, Washington

MICHAEL G. KARNI
Teaching Associate
Program in American Studies
University of Minnesota
Minneapolis, Minnesota

ERICK KENDALL
Special Assignments Editor
Midland Cooperatives,
Incorporated
Minneapolis, Minnesota

REINO KERO
Professor

Institute of General History
University of Turku
Turku, Finland

DUANE LINDBERG
Program in American Studies
University of Minnesota
Pastor, Zion Lutheran Church
West Union, Iowa

LARS LJUNGMARK
Professor
Historiska Institutionen
Göteborgs Universitet
Göteborg, Sweden

ODD LOVOLL
Department of History
University of Minnesota
Assistant Professor
Department of Norwegian
St. Olaf College
Northfield, Minnesota

ENOK MORTENSEN
President, Danish Interest
Conference
Lutheran Church in America
Frederic, Wisconsin

ERIK MORTENSEN
Academic Director
Scandinavian Seminar
New York, New York

PETER A. MUNCH
Professor
Southern Illinois University at
Carbondale
Carbondale, Illinois

HARALD S. NAESS
Professor
Department of Scandinavian
   Studies
University of Wisconsin
Madison, Wisconsin

MARION J. NELSON
Professor
Department of Art History
University of Minnesota
Minneapolis, Minnesota
Director, Norwegian-American
   Museum
Decorah, Iowa

PAUL NYHOLM
Professor Emeritus
Wartburg Theological Seminary
Blair, Nebraska

DOUGLAS J. OLLILA, JR.
Professor
Department of Religion
Augsburg College
Minneapolis, Minnesota

* NILS WILLIAM OLSSON
Director
American Swedish Institute
Minneapolis, Minnesota

DAVID W. PREUS
Acting President
The American Lutheran Church
Minneapolis, Minnesota

CARLTON C. QUALEY
Professor Emeritus
Carlton College
Research Fellow

Minnesota Historical Society
St. Paul, Minnesota

GERHARD T. ROOTH
Editor
Nordstjernan-Svea
New York, New York

FRANKLIN D. SCOTT
Curator
Nordic Collections
The Honnold Library
Claremont Colleges
Claremont, California

INGRID SEMMINGSEN
Professor
Historisk Institutt
Universitetet i Oslo
Blindern, Oslo, Norway

* MAGNE SMEDVIG
General Manager
Sons of Norway International
   Headquarters
Minneapolis, Minnesota

C. PETER STRONG
President
The American-Scandinavian
   Foundation
New York, New York

* TORE TALLROTH
Director
Swedish Council for Information
   Abroad
Ministry for Foreign Affairs
Stockholm, Sweden

AUDUN TOVEN
Department of Scandinavian

University of Washington
Assistant Professor
Pacific Lutheran University
Tacoma, Washington

TATU TUOHIKORPI
Cultural Attaché
Consulate General of Finland
New York, New York

BENT VANBERG
Editor and
    Public Relations Director
Sons of Norway
International Headquarters
Minneapolis, Minnesota

RUDOLPH VECOLI
Professor
Department of History
University of Minnesota
Minneapolis, Minnesota

RICHARD B. VOWLES
Professor
Department of Scandinavian

Studies and Comparative
Literature
University of Wisconsin
Madison, Wisconsin

DAVID A. WARD
Professor
Department of Sociology
University of Minnesota
Minneapolis, Minnesota

WESLEY WESTERBERG
Chancellor
Kendall College
Evanston, Illinois

BERTIL G. WINSTROM
Grand Master
Vasa Order of America
    Grand Lodge
Mequon, Wisconsin

SOLVEIG ZEMPEL
Teaching Associate
Department of Scandinavian
University of Minnesota
Minneapolis, Minnesota

Mr. Paul Rusten of Heritage Productions, Minneapolis, was in charge of recording the proceedings and Mr. Martin Solberg of SAS was responsible for physical arrangements. They were assisted by Richard Auld and Rudi Jensen, students at the University of Minnesota.

Index